Best-Sellers and Their Film
Adaptations in Postwar America

Modern American Literature
New Approaches

Yoshinobu Hakutani
General Editor

Vol. 28

PETER LANG
New York • Washington, D.C./Baltimore • Bern
Frankfurt am Main • Berlin • Brussels • Vienna • Oxford

Jane Hendler

Best-Sellers and Their Film Adaptations in Postwar America

From Here to Eternity, Sayonara, Giant, Auntie Mame, Peyton Place

PETER LANG
New York • Washington, D.C./Baltimore • Bern
Frankfurt am Main • Berlin • Brussels • Vienna • Oxford

Library of Congress Cataloging-in-Publication Data

Hendler, Jane.
Best-sellers and their film adaptations in postwar America: From here to eternity, Sayonara,
Giant, Auntie Mame, Peyton Place / Jane Hendler.
p. cm. — (Modern American literature; vol. 28)
Includes bibliographical references and index.
1. American fiction—Film and video adaptations. 2. American fiction—
20th century—History and criticism. I. Title.
PN1997.85 .H46   791.43'6   00-062967
ISBN 0-8204-5210-6
ISSN 1078-0521

Die Deutsche Bibliothek-CIP-Einheitsaufnahme

Hendler, Jane:
Best-sellers and their film adaptations in postwar America: From here to eternity, Sayonara,
Giant, Auntie Mame, Peyton Place / Jane Hendler.
−New York; Washington, D.C./Baltimore; Bern;
Frankfurt am Main; Berlin; Brussels; Vienna; Oxford: Lang.
(Modern American literature; Vol. 28)
ISBN 0-8204-5210-6

Cover design by Dutton and Sherman Design

For Scott

Contents

Acknowledgments

Throughout each stage of writing this book, I was fortunate to have had many people who continued to support this project in a variety of ways and to believe in its value. I owe much to Susan Edmunds and Harvey Teres for their generous assistance and for providing critical insights and asking tough questions, which were invaluable to me in thinking through my ideas. Susan also has played a special part in my scholarly pursuits as a mentor and friend, and so it is with affection and gratitude that I acknowledge her participation and her many words of encouragement. I am grateful to Lester Friedman and Margaret Himley for giving careful, productive readings of the book in its earlier stage. I would especially like to mention with the fullest appreciation the innumerable hours, unflagging support, and energy that Steven Cohan has devoted to my work. I am deeply indebted to Steve for his insightful comments, his rigorous questions, his breadth of knowledge and wonderful enthusiasm for films and popular culture of the 1950s—which helped to inspire my own, his constant urging me to develop my abilities further, and his advocacy on my behalf in every aspect. Steve's contributions to my development as a scholar and to this work have been invaluable.

I gratefully acknowledge the Department of English and the Writing Program at Syracuse University as well as Illinois State University's Department of English Studies for providing supportive intellectual climates in which to work during the various stages of researching and writing. Senior Editor Heidi Burns at Peter Lang Publishing, Inc., has been a godsend in helping me prepare the final drafts of this book and for giving me helpful feedback and many kind words of encouragement.

I have good friends and colleagues to thank for spurring me on with their advice, inspiration, and love: Carey Cummings, Kate Dole, Patricia Dunn, Patricia Featherstone, Ken Lindblom, Jill Swiencicki, and Roxanne Wheeler—they all have contributed to this book in ways they may not realize. (Thanks for being my second family, Ken and Patty). Finally, I want to thank my family, John and Elizabeth Wilson, Audrey Wilson Carson, and my sisters, Joan DiMaria and Janet Huck, and their families for their unflagging faith in my abilities. To my husband Scott who has been with me through every stage of this book, I cannot say enough. Scott has shared in all the ups and downs of this project, listening to endless hours of "book talk," helping me keep perspective at frustrating points, and, as always, sustaining me with his friendship, humor, and love.

1

The Fifties Best-Seller: Texts, Contexts, and Gender Identity in the Postwar Era

"The fifties," writes Jean Baudrillard, "were the real high spot for the US ('when things were going on') and you can still feel the nostalgia for those years, for the ecstasy of power, when power held power. In the seventies power was still there, but the spell was broken" (107). Indeed in the wake of racial violence, student revolts, the Women's Movement, Vietnam, and Watergate, power and authority have become increasingly demystified. For those who had gained dividends, economically, politically, or otherwise, from the postwar heyday of Anglo-American hegemony, a turn to political conservatism in the seventies and beyond constituted an attempt to "right" the balance. Within this climate of disruption and confusion, the 1950s emerged as the historical benchmark of cultural cohesion, progress under capitalism, and simpler, happier times. Conservatives constructed a mythic version of the decade that was filtered through sentiment and nostalgia for the family togetherness and cultural cohesion, as evidenced in such popular entertainment as *Happy Days*, *Laverne and Shirley*, *Grease*, and *Back to the Future*. More recently, as James Bowman argues in *The American Spectator*, the fifties revival in mid-nineties films, such as *Forrest Gump*, *Blue Sky*, *Quiz Show*, and *Corrina, Corrina*, tends to cast the decade as "the age of innocence"; ultimately, Bowman contends, this tendency is a reflection of our culture's self-indulgent nostalgia rather than any accurate representation of the fifties. Whether in popular culture or political discourses, the fifties continue to be interpreted through an impressionistic haze as a time when America was safe, stable, even bland, and when the interests of power and the people appeared synchronous. After all, had not everyone back then worked optimistically toward the same things—prosperity, material comforts, upward mobility, and a gradual, but steady resolution to racial and social injustice?

Perhaps because the 1950s were America's "real high spot," at least in terms of economic growth and affluence, they continue to hold representational sway in our present-day accounts of national identity or to serve some particular ideological purpose. Constructing the fifties as America's Golden Years is an imaginative gesture that had little to do with the decade's "reality," however. If, in fact, "power held power," not all people experienced its ecstasy or benefited from its effects. Moreover, as numerous recent scholarly accounts of the fifties demonstrate, the postwar glory days were, on closer inspection, much more dynamic, turbulent, and troubled than some of our current retrospective images would suggest. One needs only to look at some of the decade's cultural trends and phenomena to discover the contradictions, the growing discontent with middle-class conformity, and the efforts to resist oppressive structures and practices—all of which signal the decade's heterogeneity.

The evidence is both wide-ranging and informative: The fifties appeared to be full of happy, flourishing families in modern suburban homes, yet the threat of world annihilation was considered real enough by many to induce them to construct well-equipped bomb shelters in their backyards. Others, like the families in John Cheever's *Wapshot* novels, quietly fell apart under the strain of suburban anonymity and trying to keep up with the Joneses. Motherhood and domesticity were glorified and stay-at-home moms were regarded as the stabilizing force that could prevent a variety of social ills; in reality, however, "women accounted for thirty-four percent of the labor force in 1950" and "thirty-eight percent by the start of the next decade" (Crispell 38). Present-day conservatives point to the postwar years as a time when men were "men" and women were "women," but they ignore that by 1958 nearly 500,000 pounds of tranquilizers were being mass-marketed mostly to women—clearly an indication that female discontent with rigid sex roles was treated (by a male-dominated medical community) as a psychological dysfunction rather than as a social problem. Strikingly disparate images of masculinity were held up as "heroic" models: The man-in-the-gray-flannel-suit shared representational space with Mickey Spillane's commie-hating, woman-hating, crime buster Mike Hammer, and the anguished, alienated teen idol James Dean. Homosexuals were publicly demonized during the Cold War, but few people remember that the Mattachine Foundation, established in 1952, and its publication, *One*, were the "unofficial" beginnings of a homosexual civil rights movement. In light of the racial strife of the sixties, we tend to forget that Chicano communities were forming consciousness-raising groups and that Little Rock, organized sit-ins, and the growth of Black Muslim membership in the mid-to-late fifties all signaled a public insurgence against white supremacy. Furthermore, in the midst of a significant expansion of corporate capitalism, McCarthyism, and the Red Scare, intellectuals, such as C. Wright Mills, Erich Fromm, and Herbert Marcuse, continued to present cogent leftist critiques of capitalism.

One of the indices—and the focus of this book—through which we can identify this disjuncture between mainstream and alternative expressions of social "reality" is the popular novel, particularly best-sellers, which, because of their enormous popularity, were clearly characteristic of the decade itself. Although they insistently signify middlebrow or mainstream culture, fifties best-sellers are a valuable source for locating the social tensions and fissures of the decade, precisely because their narratives are solidly rooted in social and historical circumstances. Serious literary critics berated middlebrow culture for its mediocrity and its function as escapist reading; even so, the best-seller, as a form of popular culture that engages everyday experiences of "ordinary" people, had the capacity to represent the cultural diversity as well as the contestation between mainstream and marginalized values and attitudes. For example, Nelson Algren's best-selling *Man with the Golden Arm* (1949) ushered in this decade of economic and social optimism with its portrayal of the horror confronting a returning war veteran in Chicago's seamy underworld. Likewise, J.D. Salinger's *Catcher in the Rye* (1951) and Evan Hunter's *The Blackboard Jungle* (1954) shocked middle-class parents, whose lives seemed secured by the postwar economic boom, with revelations of teen discontent and juvenile delinquency. Millions of readers were attracted to religious themes, as evidenced by the dominance of mid-fifties nonfiction best-sellers, such as Norman Vincent Peale's *The Power of Positive Thinking* (1952), Catherine Marshall's *A Man Called Peter* (1952), and Billy Graham's *The Secret of Happiness* (1955). However, in only a few years Jack Kerouac's *On the Road* (1957), William Burroughs's *Naked Lunch* (1959), and Allen Ginsberg's *Howl* (1956) became cult classics for a growing number of disaffected young people who rejected established norms and traditions. Furthermore, while Pat Boone's conservative advice to teens in his top-selling *'Twixt Twelve and Twenty* (1958) was eagerly ingested by hundreds of thousands of young readers, Grace Metalious's racy *Peyton Place* (1956) was hidden until teens could read it out of parents' sight. Readers began to demand "adult" themes in their books, and the publishing world complied: James Jones's *From Here to Eternity* (1951), John O'Hara's *Ten North Frederick* (1955), and Norman Mailer's *The Deer Park* (1955), to name a few, offered stories that pivoted around moral compromise or decline, adultery, divorce, vulgar language, and sexually explicit scenes, including homosexuality. *Lolita* (1958) and the unexpurgated version of *Lady Chatterley's Lover* (1932) made the best-sellers list in 1958 and 1959, respectively. Political and social conflict was the subject of best-sellers like Jerome Wiedman's *The Enemy Camp* (1958), which focused on anti-Semitism, and *The Ugly American* (1959), a fictionalized account of U.S. diplomatic failures in Southeast Asia.

Even so, the diversity of social life represented in popular literature is offset by the image of postwar America as quiescent, conservative, and homogeneous within the decade itself. That is, this image has not only pervaded post-1960s representations, but informed social and political thought during the 1950s as well. According to historian Jackson Lears, this perception grew out of the emergence of a cultural consensus that arose within a new corporate order at the end of World War II. Lears points out that "a hegemonic historical bloc was formed by the groups often characterized as a 'new class' of salaried managers, administrators, academics, technicians, and journalists" (50). Members of this bloc endorsed "pragmatic interest-group politics and an expanded 'mixed economy' undergirded by business-government cooperation"; they feared "extremist crusades at home and an implacable Soviet threat abroad," which explains much of their nearsightedness towards demands made by women, blacks, and other marginalized groups (Lears 51). Because this consensus was "based on the spread of affluence and the promise of upward mobility," the mood of the 1950s was decidedly optimistic, which inclined many postwar contemporaries to "dismiss intractable problems ... and accentuate hopeful signs" (Lears 38). For some, consumer capitalism and free enterprise were hailed as vehicles for social change, a means of eventually eradicating poverty.[1] However, one of the consequences of this cultural accord, which assumed a powerful hegemonic force in mid-century America, was to "propagate monolithic values rooted in the promise of classless consumption" (L. May 7). In the political arena, open dissent and conflict from either the left or the right was discouraged. Rather, as Arthur Schlesinger describes in *The Vital Center* (1949), an emphasis on pluralistic debate and compromise within the established system of rules and parties gave the 1950s its distinctive centrist cast.

The onset of the Cold War had a direct bearing on this cultural consensus as well. A fear of international Soviet expansion and the perceived threat of internal communist infiltration generated a climate of anxiety and hysteria. In a 1950 Gallup poll, 70 percent of the respondents believed Russia was trying to rule the world, and 41 percent felt the U.S. would be in another war within five years (Oakley 6). Senator Joseph McCarthy, along with the House Un-American Activities Committee (HUAC), served to deepen suspicions and heighten paranoia with their investigations of internal subversive activities. In the face of the Red Scare, dominant groups sought to restore a sense of equanimity, national security, and strength by representing national identity and social reality under capitalism as coherent and unified. However, this conservative insistence on representing "America" as a homogeneous nation of white, Anglo, middle-class, nuclear families simultaneously restricted or repressed demands by such disenfranchised groups as women, blacks, homosexuals, and lower classes, demands that might deflect energy and interest from the central national purpose of containing communism. Both corporate consensus and Cold War politics, then, functioned concurrently to mute social conflict and to represent American culture as a monolithic entity. Alternative expressions of social "reality," however, continued to exist at the margins of this representational domain.

This is not to suggest that Cold War consensus was greeted with enthusiasm from all intellectual corners. In fact, many intellectuals working in a variety of fields and disciplines, such as William Whyte, David Riesman, Talcott Parsons, and Dwight MacDonald, worried that America had become a mass culture, erasing individuality and innovation through standardization, conformist thinking, and political stagnation. However, as Lears points out, by situating their cultural critique in a dichotomy of mass culture/individual autonomy, these writers fostered the perception that the decade was indeed homogeneous, and they failed to target or address the centers of power and hegemonic groups that gave shape to the social order. Scholars like C. Wright Mills and Eric Fromm who did attempt more overtly political critiques of power and culture were misunderstood or marginalized within their fields (Lears 42–43). More pertinent to the purposes of this book, though, is the point that particular historical circumstances of the Cold War and postwar corporate restructuring gave distinct shape to the ideological terms by which dominant groups, who were invested in sustaining this consensus, projected a unified image of America that obscured the historical reality of cultural fragmentation, diversity, and discontent.

Gender and National Identity

One of the most effective means of consolidating an image of America as homogeneous was to link symbolically representations of national identity and masculinity, a union that appeared in all kinds of cultural artifacts, including comic books, novels, popular magazines, television, and film. As both Steven Cohan in *Masked Men* and Robert J. Corber in *In the Name of National Security* point out in their research on cinematic representations of postwar masculinity, the culture's preoccupation with national security and definitions of nationhood became ideologically bound up with the dominant discourses concerning "manhood" and "manliness." The paradigmatic masculine figure of the white, middle-class husband, father, and family breadwinner was central to the process of signifying a strong, cohesive nation, a process that necessarily subordinated or repressed alternative brands of masculinity. Even so, Cold War politics, according to Cohan, produced contradictory representations of the ideal male identity, "requiring a 'hard' masculinity as the standard when defending the nation's boundaries, yet insisting upon a 'soft' masculinity as the foundation of an orderly, responsible home life" (*Masked* xii). Thus, the emphasis on foregrounding the relationship between nation and male gender identity brought pressure to bear on the category of masculinity itself, resulting in a "crisis" over what constituted the proper male role. As Cohan succinctly states elsewhere in his analysis of Hitchcock's *North by Northwest* (1959), "The pressing need to see gender and nationalism reinforcing each other made masculinity a ready site of ideological crisis because neither ever rested on a singular or stable platform; the national interest shifted, depending on the perspective from which it was viewed, and so did expectations about what constituted proper gender identities and behavior" ("The Spy" 46). Moreover, because femininity was inevitably the referent in determining what constituted masculinity—that is, it functioned as masculinity's "Other," its negative marker of difference—gender itself became imbricated in larger ideological issues of the Cold War era, indeed emerging as one of the primary signifiers of nationhood.

It is not surprising, then, that masculinity and femininity, as well as the related topic of sex, became the subject of public discourse and scrutiny at the height of Cold War anti-communist hysteria. In fact, gender roles and sexuality were not only the subjects of inquiry for social scientists and the medical community. The findings of these types of research were then represented in popular magazines such as *Look*, *Good Housekeeping*, or *Reader's Digest*. Best-sellers and films also were preoccupied with questions of what constituted proper gender roles. In addition, popular texts became saturated with more explicit descriptions of sex than Americans had previously seen. What emerged within this discursive milieu as the hegemonic response to the "crisis" of masculinity and national security was a regulatory effort to maintain a rigid gender hierarchy and to define "normative" sexual practices as heterosexual and monogamous. As Elaine Tyler May points out in her comprehensive study of Cold War ideology and family life, this rationale of stabilizing and fixing gender roles was bolstered by the notion that America needed "strong, manly men to stand up against communist threats" and maintain a thriving, virile, capitalist economy (93–

94). Therefore, it became incumbent upon women to refrain from interfering with or undermining traditional values or gender roles. Their contribution in fighting the Cold War amounted to providing a stable and nurturing home and family life. Not surprisingly, the words "family togetherness" became a familiar catchphrase of the 1950s.

The postwar celebration of home and family did not begin with the Cold War, however. It originated as part of a highly successful campaign to entice women to quit their wartime jobs and make room in the workforce for returning veterans. Notably, only one-third of the women who participated in a 1946 survey thought a job was more interesting than housework (Filene 166). Furthermore, with the escalation of anti-communist anxiety and Senator McCarthy's assertions of rampant internal subversion, the American home and family took on heightened significance, gaining tremendous status as a refuge in an insecure world. In short, as Elaine Tyler May tells us, the family became reified as a sign of the American Way of Life (14). As such, the official policy of communist containment came to bear on private issues of gender and sexuality. Policing and marginalizing "subversive" activity within the nation's geographical boundaries became discursively linked to what May calls "domestic containment," which functioned by maintaining a distinct gender hierarchy that excluded large numbers of women from the workforce and regulated female sexual behavior (20–25).

Domestic containment also depended on making manifest the symbolic link between sexuality and national security. Sexuality considered to be out-of-control, depraved, or perverse—that is, sexuality not contained within heterosexual, monogamous marriage—signaled moral decay, lack of will or maturity, and civic irresponsibility. Such practices were not only inconsistent with the image of a strong, vigilant nation, but they became politicized as potential grounds for subversive activity and breaches in national security (E. May 93–97). Regulating female sexuality, then, amounted to glorifying and sanctioning motherhood and homemaking, which were touted as both professional activities and civic virtues (E. May 102). Uncontained female sexuality, in particular, whether represented by the promiscuous woman, the lesbian, or the sexually predatory woman, was yoked to the kind of general moral degeneracy that would lead to weakened national defenses and the decline of family life.

Even mom did not escape scrutiny. Women who were supposedly over involved with or controlling of their children were likely to be accused of "momism," a pejorative label coined by Philip Wylie in his 1942 best-seller, *Generation of Vipers*. "Moms" were particularly perilous to sons who were smothered with large amounts of maternal anxiety or encouraged to have an overly sentimental attachment to mom. They were in danger of growing up to be passive weaklings, lacking in vitality and virility (E. May 74–75). "Mom" became a familiar image in popular culture in the early fifties, particularly in anti-communist films. Michael Rogin's study of such films shows that strong, overbearing mothers, along with "errant" female sexuality, were consistently made responsible, either directly or indirectly, for internal subversive activities.[2] The less explicit message in these films was that mothers were responsible for raising principled, virtuous sons, who would not succumb to sexual "perversion" or moral degeneracy, for this was the slippery slope leading to passivity in the face of communist spread, blackmail by communist infiltrators, or worse yet, conversion to Marxist ideology. Women who did work outside the home raised the terrifying specter of engendering hordes of nihilistic, rebellious youths, sneering at the American Way of Life. The most effective method of preserving a "free" society, then, was to reproduce the model home of the fifties, which, as Elaine Tyler May notes, consisted of a "male breadwinner and a full-time female homemaker, adorned with a wide array of consumer goods," in other words, "an abundant family life" (16–17).

In addition to regulating female gender roles and sexuality, ruling groups also scrutinized and denounced homosexuals for presumably weakening national security and promoting "un-American" values. In the climate of Red Scare witchhunting, it became unwise to engage in free or "aberrant" sexual practices since these activities left one vulnerable to charges of subversion. According to an article in *Time*, "Deputy Under-Secretary John Peurifoy ... told Congress that [the State Department] had gotten rid of 91 employees for homosexuality" in February 1950. Shortly thereafter, a Senate investigating committee spent approximately seven months looking into the "problem" of homosexuals serving in government positions. To their horror, "they found a record of homosexuality or other sexual perversions among workers in 36 of 53 branches of Government as well as in the armed forces." The committee, reported *Time*, was highly disturbed by the possibility that spies could extort state secrets from homosexual employees by threatening them with the disclosure of their sexual practices ("Object Lesson" 10). Within Cold War discourses, then, the homosexual became the repository of all that was considered not masculine, therefore a deviant of natural "maleness," and consequently a risk to the nation's security.

One of the effects of the policy of domestic containment and policing "aberrant" sexual practices, was, in Michael Rogin's words, "to depoliticize politics by blaming subversion on personal influence" or psychological disturbance, so that the "political consciousness" became subordinated to "sexual unconsciousness" (245). Therefore, communist activity could be conceived as originating not in social injustice, but in a breakdown of traditional values and in the inversion of gender roles; these "problems" could then be addressed more easily through professional intervention in private lives in order to maintain intact, well functioning homes and marriages. Elaine Tyler May makes the point that the dramatic rise of professionals, such as psychologists, psychiatrists, and others who rendered advice and solutions for everyday living problems, reinforced the policy of domestic containment in that their "expertise" detracted from political solutions to problems and larger social issues in general (14). Questions of material conditions and gender oppression were more readily reconfigured in the language of the personal and private, which effectively displaced any serious claims to social justice and activism. A further consequence of this displacement was to sustain postwar consensus by projecting a more coherent, unified vision of America's national and cultural identity, a vision that undoubtedly eased the Cold War atmosphere of paranoia and anxiety.

Therefore, one of the primary mechanisms for regulating or suppressing alternative representations of "reality" within Cold War consensus was to limit the available meanings attached to gender identity. In examining the regulatory function of gender, however, we cannot overlook the fact that gender is not monologic but intersects with other social coordinates, such as sexuality, race, ethnicity, and class. This dynamic produces a regulatory effect on these categories as well. In mainstream America of the 1950s, these coordinates became represented in discourse and practice so as to endorse middle-class, Anglo-American, heterosexist, androcentric values and attitudes. In effect, social "reality" and national identity became signified, both in the 1950s and in the decades following, in homogenous terms through gender.

Best-Sellers and the Fifties Culture Wars

Postwar best-sellers are rich sites in which to investigate the convergence of masculinity, femininity, and nationhood since popular novels both reflected, and reflected upon, the culture's preoccupation with delineating "appropriate" gender roles. Considering that best-sellers were marketed to a mainstream reading audience, they tended, as one might expect, to stabilize and privilege those images of masculinity and femininity that were compatible with dominant representations of "America," in effect, contributing to the process of universalizing national identity. However, while best-sellers potentially reinscribed the culture's dominant gender ideologies, they functioned more complexly in the 1950s than otherwise supposed. Their representational practices also had the capacity to reintroduce into mainstream America representations of the gender diversity and conflict that Cold War ideology sought to obscure, along with the culture's heterogeneity and fragmentation. As in all forms of popular culture, it is possible to find both hegemonic and counterhegemonic discourses in best-sellers. As Andrew Ross puts it: "[Popular culture] contains elements of disrespect, and even opposition to structures of authority, but it also contains 'explanations' ... for the maintenance of respect for those structures of authority" (3).

Fifties best-sellers offer an abundance of opportunities to locate the tensions between the conservative, resistant, and suppressed "voices" in representation. For example, Edna Ferber's *Giant* (1952), the saga of a wealthy Texan cattle baron, brings to the fore the conflict between the dominant and silenced "voices" of American history by recovering the suppressed history of white male exploitation and its silencing of racialized and/or feminine Others. Jones's best-selling *From Here to Eternity* also features the contestation inherent in the formation of masculinity. An army novel, *Eternity* portrays the lower ranks or the ill-educated "dogface" soldiers (synonymous with the lower class) in a sympathetic light; nonetheless, it attempts to naturalize a certain brand of middle-class, heterosexual masculinity as hegemonic. At the same time, however, the novel problematizes this representation of ideal masculinity as "natural" by demonstrating that gender is constituted within a social context; that is, gendered subjects are formed within particular historical circumstances and within a network of power relations, thus disrupting the notion of a stable, coherent, normative male identity.

Best-sellers were not a new literary phenomenon, of course, but due to the heightened interest in reading and the promotional efforts by publishing companies, they acquired a special significance in postwar culture. Publishers and book sellers documented notable increases overall both in the production and sales of books, and as best-seller historian Alice Payne Hackett notes, "during and just after World War II more books could have been sold than were available" (2). Postwar prosperity and increased leisure time afforded more people the opportunity to purchase and read books, but publishers had primed reading audiences during World War II by distributing to military personnel millions of paperback printed as special

Armed Services editions. As a result, many veterans returned home after the war with an appetite for reading (Hackett 3). Kenneth Davis reports in *Two-Bit Culture* that between 1943 and 1947 an astonishing "total of 122,951,031 volumes were delivered to the army and navy" (72). Overseas troops could read anything from Melville's *Moby-Dick*, Steinbeck's *The Grapes of Wrath*, Betty Smith's *A Tree Grows in Brooklyn* to James Thurber's *My World and Welcome to It* (Davis 75). Moreover, when the paperback revolution took off in the early 1950s, young adults who had been "brought up on paperbacks" were ready and waiting for more easily available, inexpensive books (Hackett 3).

Book clubs added further impetus to the enthusiasm for reading by delivering a new release each month directly to subscribers' homes. Readers apparently relished this service of receiving all the new and "important" books, for once wartime restrictions on paper and other materials needed by the publishing industry were lifted, the book clubs experienced a boom (Hackett 2). "The major clubs had been in existence for a number of years but it was not until the postwar period that all their monthly selections sold into the hundreds of thousands"; by 1954, combined sales of all book clubs were 50 million copies, up from 2 million in 1929 (Hackett 2–3, 5). Book club sales increased the likelihood of a novel becoming a best-seller, since being a book-of-the-month both enhanced its sales in retail stores and increased its exposure in other literary outlets.[3] Moreover, because book clubs promised that qualified literary critics chose the "best" books from all the new releases, they authorized these selections as worthwhile for non-club members as well.

Best-seller lists shared with book clubs this function of endorsing particular novels for readers. Although consumer demand for reading material ultimately created these weekly lists, readers seemed to welcome informed advice about purchasing books. In fact, they had been accustomed to literary critics serving as mediators of culture since the 1920s and 1930s when book reviews appeared regularly in newspapers and "book talk" programs flooded the airwaves.[4] Unlike the 1930s, however, a new social ethic emerged in the early 1950s, identified by sociologist William Whyte as the "organization ethic," which promoted the idea that personal adjustment to the demands of the corporate organization and other forms of group life was the appropriate choice over an insistence on isolated, rugged individualism. The social pressure that necessitated belonging to "The Group"[5] augmented the reliance on best-seller lists and the sale of books, which, in effect, created new best-sellers and maintained sales of those already on the list. It was smart to be "well read" in the fifties, to give the impression of being "in the know." In the newly emerging class of white collar workers and professionals, it made good business and social sense to be conversant about the top-selling books. Imagine attending the ubiquitous fifties cocktail party or backyard barbecue and being excluded from the latest buzz about James Michener's current release, the hilarious Auntie Mame, or when Marjorie Morningstar would lose her virginity!

However, it was not just an increased appetite for reading or group pressure to be familiar with the latest books that made best-sellers characteristic of the 1950s. They were frequently transposed into other textual forms, such as condensed books, paperbacks, and films, all of which recirculated a version of the original text. Because the film industry experienced a sharp reduction in profits due to a decline in theater attendance in the early half of the decade, producers depended upon scripts based on best-sellers in order to capitalize on prior advertising used to promote the novels and therefore to be guaranteed an eager and waiting film audience. According to Davis, because paperback publishers relied on volume sales in order to profit from selling inexpensive editions, they, too, depended on best-sellers to reduce their risk factor, and, like film producers, they benefited from previous promotional campaigns. In turn, selling the film and subsidiary rights to a novel became lucrative for hardcover publishers. This reciprocal relationship also had an effect on which books were published. Davis notes, "if a manuscript promised to garner further profits from its transpositions, then it was more likely to be signed on for publication" (146). The intertextual play between these various incarnations not only sustained the high level exposure of the original text, but amplified and reconstructed the meanings of the narrative as well.

While producers and distributors of popular culture were profiting handsomely from the various incarnations of best-sellers and while reading and film audiences were avidly consuming these narratives, the observers and preservers of high culture and "art" were less than enthusiastic over this trend. Popular culture became the target of a coterie of postwar intellectuals who felt compelled to warn the populace of the detrimental effects of "lower" forms of culture and to govern the consumption of culture by designating "taste" as the primary index of the nation's cultural health. The critique of popular culture in the 1940s and 1950s—often referred to as mass culture—was strongly informed by the work of the Frankfurt School in the 1930s and 1940s, which had employed Marxist inquiry and psychoanalysis to probe questions of aesthetics, mass culture, and entertainment.[6] According to such influential members of the School as

Max Horkheimer, Theodor Adorno, and Herbert Marcuse, the culture industries under capitalism produced a mass culture that was homogeneous, standardized, and predictable. The effect of consuming such products was to dull the mind and manipulate workers during their leisure time into accepting their present-day social and material conditions as adequate and fulfilling. In this scheme, mass culture was situated in opposition to high culture—"authentic" or "affirmative" culture—which purportedly embodied ideals denied by capitalism and presented, in Marcuse's words, a "subversive negativity," so that its consumers would realize the contradiction between social reality (the oppressive conditions under capitalism) and the oppositional, transcendent elements of high culture (58). Seeing this contradiction would supposedly induce people to desire a better future. Mass culture, in contrast, presented a mere illusion of relaxation and escape; workers, their senses stunted, passed their leisure time similarly to work hours—in resignation to the present and in psychological adjustment to the status quo.

While the explicit Marxist critique of the Frankfurt School was downplayed in the 1950s, their work continued to influence postwar intellectuals' views of high versus mass culture. While the specific effects on consumers and the relative value of popular cultural products continued to be the subject of debate throughout the 1950s, middlebrow—the realm of the best-seller—was the main target of attack by Dwight MacDonald, Clement Greenberg, and Irving Howe. The initial attacks on middlebrow culture were launched in the late 1940s by critics who targeted both its producers—"The Lords of Kitsch," in MacDonald's words—and its consumers ("Theory of Mass Culture" 60). This offensive prompted *Harper's* editor, Russell Lynes, to write a tongue-in-cheek essay in 1948 in which he hoped "all middlebrows ... would have their televisions taken away, and be suspended from society until they had agreed to give up their subscriptions to the Book-of-the-Month-Club" (qtd. in Shelley xiv). Nonetheless, by the 1950s the assault was fully engaged. The problem with middlebrow was that it most assuredly contaminated high culture by deceptively packaging itself like high culture, without adhering to either its complexity or its adversarial relation to society (clearly an echo of the Frankfurt School).[7] These ideas were put forth in MacDonald's well-known essay, "Masscult and Midcult":

> The danger to High Culture is not so much from Masscult as from a peculiar hybrid bred from the latter's unnatural intercourse with the former. A whole middle culture has come into existence and it threatens to absorb both its parents.

This intermediate form—let us call it Midcult—has the essential qualities of Masscult—the formula, the built-in reaction, the lack of any standard except popularity—but it decently covers them with a cultural figleaf. In Masscult the trick is plain—to please the crowd by any means. But Midcult has it both ways: it pretends to respect the standards of High Culture while in fact it waters them down and vulgarizes them. (MacDonald *Against* 37)

MacDonald did not see the divisions between high, middle, and low culture as arbitrarily imposed, but as organic and readily discernible categories. Moreover, as did many of his contemporaries, he refused to see that what signified as high culture was also a commodity and subject to fluctuations in market value. Implicit in these delineations is a correlation between the three "brows" and social class, a correlation that MacDonald claimed did not exist in the "classless" society of postwar America, despite his preference that it should. "If there were a clearly defined cultural *elite*," MacDonald insisted, "then the masses could have their *kitsch* and the *elite* could have its High Culture, with everybody happy" (*Against* 34). Even so, cultural critics like MacDonald were to remain unhappy because middlebrow appeared to be obliterating the difference between art and kitsch and between the elite and the masses.

Middlebrow culture, however, was not always condemned for its supposed lapses in meaning, style, and other literary qualities. Joan Rubin Shelley points out that the designation or "middlebrow" emerged in the 1920s and 1930s with an increased effort to make various forms of high culture available to a wider audience.[8] This democratizing effort ranged from the formation of book clubs, night schools, and extension courses, to radio programs offering book reviews, to a thriving lecture circuit and the birth of magazines, such as *The Saturday Review of Literature*, which promoted and reviewed new publications (xi–xii). Middlebrow culture began to flourish due to advances in technology that allowed for less costly means of producing magazines, books, music, and films. The increase in demand for cultural artifacts, in turn, encouraged businesses to invest in the culture industries.

By the 1950s, the mass-marketing trends of the previous decades designed to reach an ever-expanding middle class were thoroughly entrenched in the culture industries and were augmented by a dramatic increase in publishing houses specializing in inexpensive paperbacks, condensed books, and book clubs. Each of these means of consuming culture, however, heightened the pejorative connotations of middlebrow. Intellectuals decried the assault on Taste and Art by a culture that could be compacted or made into "portable" commodities. Fifties critic, David Cort, denounced the advent of *Reader's Digest Condensed Books* in 1950, claiming that reading a condensed novel was comparable to watching an autopsy: "Two pages of effective writing come out as one paragraph of pasted-up bits" (135–36). Book clubs, if not performing an autopsy, were accused at the very least of lobotomizing the American mind. Charles Lee pointed out in his 1958 chronicle of the Book-of-the-Month-Club that the preservers of high culture worried that the market demand for volume sales precluded the book clubs' selection committees from choosing new releases that were rich and nourishing; moreover, if readers continually deferred to others in selecting their books, their powers of discrimination and appreciation for "better" books would undoubtedly become dulled (117). Paperback books, however, were considered the most menacing element of literary production because they had the potential to reach a mass audience through their very public presence and ready availability in drug stores and five-and-dime stores, which made their "objectionable" material more easily available to adults, teens, and minors alike. Paperbacks caused such consternation that Congress formed the Gathings Committee in 1952 to investigate this new "pox" on the nation.[9]

No doubt the anxiety of highbrows critics and intellectuals was exacerbated by their perception that, in general, aesthetic standards were declining or stagnating. Harold Strauss, editor-in-chief of Alfred Knopf, Inc., during the 1950s, placed the blame for declining standards on the "illiterate American writer," who lacked moral and artistic courage in favor of economic security and less demanding projects (8–9). Strauss also faulted current novels for their "dreary topicality" in lieu of serious substance (9). John Aldridge echoed some of Strauss's concerns in his influential *After the Lost Generation* (1951), claiming that postwar writers offered no new literary developments or techniques, nor had they fully sought and exploited new subject matter relevant to the decade, hence their work lacked a sense of uniqueness and value. Aldridge was somewhat sympathetic to postwar writers, though, noting they had to write in the shadow of Hemingway and Fitzgerald's generation, which had had a "sense of loss and negation, a new world to discover, and a single perspective for protest" on which to base a literature of value; in contrast, post-World War II writers were left with no new discoveries to make; they could merely work within those previously established traditions (242–43). Aldridge also cited the prevailing sense of moral relativism following World War II and the magnitude of its unspeakable atrocities—the Holocaust and the atomic bomb—as factors in stagnating literary standards and output.

Clement Greenberg and Malcolm Cowley concurred with Aldridge's view that postwar "literary" novels (as opposed to popular novels) lacked the adversarial function of the prewar avant-garde. Greenberg, troubled that contemporary writers no longer possessed the confidence to experiment freely with formal concerns and abstraction, in short, to function as an oppositional force, claimed: "The avant-garde itself … is becoming more and more timid every day that passes. Academicism and commercialism are appearing in the strangest places. This can mean only one thing: that the avant-garde is becoming unsure of the audience it depends on—the rich and the cultivated" (101). Implicitly, the blame here is on the lure of middlebrow. Because writers were increasingly under the pressure of the market to sell their works to an ever-shrinking elite audience, their output was invariably thought to be contaminated by popular culture and its eager audiences. Thus, what asserted itself on the awaiting public was "rear-garde" kitsch, "the debased and academicized simulacra of genuine culture" (Greenberg 102). Cowley, focusing more on the social context in which postwar writers worked, claimed in *The Literary Situation* that the challenge for serious writers was to respond to the failure of the enlightenment, of a belief in progress, and of man's ability to use moral judgment, self-control, and kindness. Failing to meet this challenge, Cowley concluded, postwar fiction retreated from addressing social and political problems in favor of dealing with moral and personal issues for which resolutions could be found. However, most problematic in Cowley's assessment was that the serious postwar novels "express a new sympathy for the middle-class virtues," which could be articulated as an affinity for order, resolution, and the simple virtues (58).

As Greenberg and MacDonald implied, middlebrow was even more threatening to the aesthetic standards of "good" literature than lowbrow "trash" because middlebrow permitted the convection of ideas, images, and conventions to circulate back and forth between the two poles of culture. Low culture might offend the cultural elites' sensibilities, but they felt assured of retaining a smug and safe distance from such "crass" and "mindless" productions. Indisputably formulaic pulp fiction—"several stages beneath the utterly worthless," said Cowley (106)—presented no real threat to "serious" literature. However, with middlebrow serving as a conductor between high and low, the likes of Spillane's Mike Hammer seemed less distant from Shakespeare's Iago. Even the physical proximity of *Madame Bovary* sardined next to *Peyton Place* on a drugstore bookrack would give pause to the cultural watchdogs. Middlebrow was to be discouraged, to be sure, but it also held a strategic position in structuring taste by creating a retaining wall between "art" and "trash." In the 1950s, however, the wall had apparently sprung a leak that the intellectuals' proverbial fingers could not stop up. Again, in "A Theory of Mass Culture" MacDonald lamented, "there is slowly emerging a tepid, flaccid Middlebrow Culture that threatens to engulf everything in its spreading ooze" (63–64).

In certain cases, book reviews of popular novels were instrumental in destabilizing the arbitrary boundaries between the levels of culture. Many best-sellers appeared to have literary pretensions or were reviewed favorably in terms of their literary qualities. After the release of *From Here to Eternity*, for instance, author James Jones was hailed as the next Thomas Wolfe and compared to the youthful F. Scott Fitzgerald (along with other critics' assertions that Jones was an unschooled "primitive"). When distinguished Hemingway scholar, Carlos Baker, reviewed Grace Metalious's scandalous *Peyton Place* in *The New York Times Book Review*, he called her "a pretty fair writer for a first novelist," finding her novel in keeping with the tradition of the small-town chronicles of Sherwood Anderson, Edmund Wilson, and John O'Hara. No doubt reviewing the "literariness" of a potboiler like *Peyton Place*, a novel that had become synonymous with sex, contributed to a sense of indignation and anxiety in those who feared the decline of a refined, elite western literary tradition.

Furthermore, because "literary" and "popular" tended to be mutually exclusive categories for serious critics, the very popularity of middlebrow artifacts made them suspect. Thus, Chandler Brossard's review of *From Here to Eternity* began on a condescending and cautionary note: "So many people shouted its praises that I decided it couldn't be really good if so many people liked it" (117). Brossard shared common assumptions that popularity signaled a lack of real aesthetic worth and that most consumers could be deceived into thinking they were reading something of great value because so many others were reading or had read it. (Incidentally, Brossard decided he did not like Jones's novel). Then, of course, Metalious's novel, which sold a staggering six and a half million copies within a year and a half of its publication, received few shouts of praise from critics, aside from Baker's qualified appreciation. Nevertheless, readers, unconcerned with aesthetic value, contributed to *Peyton Place*'s popularity precisely because it was so *good*—that is to say, packed with sexual intrigue, juicy love scenes, and melodramatic flair.

The adult themes, vulgar language, and explicit sex scenes in popular novels like *Peyton Place* or *From Here to Eternity* presented an even more profound threat to cultural health than middlebrow's presumed unoriginal and nonadversarial quality. Barbara Klinger notes that postwar cultural production experienced a general industry trend toward more 'adult' entertainment and was becoming increasingly oriented toward a kind of sexual sensationalism and display in representation (51–57). Literary texts (and increasingly films) began to be identified with such narrative events as rape, incest, adultery, other sexual activity, and salty language, which were often regarded by reviewers as merely obscene rather than achieving a kind of realism. Explicit descriptions of sexual acts and the language of sex, in general, came to be a defining feature of best-selling novels in this decade. In retrospect, this should come as no surprise; competing discourses of sexuality along with many undercurrents of social change in the 1950s would eventually lead up to the sexual revolution of the sixties. However, the guardians of culture read this as an omen of the collapse of decorum and taste. Popular culture in this view was seen not so much as a form of domination as the Frankfurt School had posited, but as the road to social anarchy and disrespect for traditions and authority.

Critic Anthony Harrigan sounded an early warning signal about sex in the "new realism," which appeared soon after the end of the war: "Americans are in the hands of a cultural ruling class which … is conducting us to ruin" (108). Targeting such writers as John Steinbeck, John O'Hara, Tennessee Williams, and Gore Vidal for ushering in a "new orthodoxy of immorality," Harrigan argued that they were "determined to force the acceptance of pornography as medical science, filth as artistic realism, and abnormality as a mere difference of opinion" (106, 108). *Saturday Review* editor, Harrison Smith, concurred, declaring "this phase of contemporary erotic literature … is a dismal trail, leading nowhere, and the sooner it gets there the better." Smith optimistically predicted "this minor phase of the prevalent exhibitions of the disillusionment and despair of our creative writers [will] soon pass and leave few regrets behind" (26). Both Harrigan and Smith engaged in a strategy present-day cultural critic James Twitchell describes as characteristic of self-appointed cultural gatekeepers: By isolating and naming what was "trash," they hoped mainstream audiences would then pass it by (9). In a less partisan approach, psychologist Albert Ellis, who undertook a study in the 1950s on the attitudes and treatment of sex topics in popular culture, concluded that "the American public will not take a work of fiction to its heart if the story does not simultaneously imply that unconventional sex behavior is the nastiest—and tastiest—business imaginable" (19). Taken together, however, all three of these views point to a persistent rupture or gap between what reading audiences either desired or accepted in their books—candid language and adult themes—and what the guardians of cultural health viewed as an assault on literary standards and civilization itself.

The real horror of best-sellers for fifties critics, however, was the overt and unabashed representation of the "unspeakable": homosexuality. Writing in the *American Mercury*, Alfred Towne expressed a deep repugnance at what he imagined was a pervasive homosexuality in American culture, specifically in books, films, and magazines. This "new taste dominates the cultural scene," wrote Towne, to the point where a "shower room fellowship" was ever-present, or at the very least, homosexual overtones in the prose, "already verging on the emotional lush, will become tropical, over-ripe, with exotics of all types flitting through it" (4–5). His near-hysterical, Chicken Little-panic not only fueled the attack on popular texts, but coincided with the intense anxiety promulgated by Cold War discourses that homosexuals were security risks. Towne was not alone in his indictment. One year later, the Gathings Committee alleged in its prehearing statement that "some books expiate upon homosexuality .... Other books extol by their approbatory language accounts of homosexuality, lesbianism, and other sexual aberrations. Books which deal with various phases of these subjects, introduced into the record as evidence include ... *The Tormented, Women's Barracks, Spring Fire, Unmoral, Forbidden, Artists' Models*, and *The Wayward Bus*" (Davis 235). Concurring with Towne, but situating his criticism of homosexuality within the Freudian discourses of the medical community, *Harper's* editor, Bernard DeVoto, set out to psychologize postwar male authors who were themselves known to be homosexual or who included homosexual themes in their works. Asserting that homosexuals were not fully adult since their sexual development had been arrested at an infantile stage, DeVoto determined that "biologically the homosexual has failed absolutely" (69). Homosexual literature, then, could only be a "fiction of infantilism," incapable of "deal[ing] maturely with adult experience" (69–70). This rendering of homosexuality served to reinforce the prevailing notion in the 1950s that homosexuals were neither fully masculine nor completely mature, as opposed to the "adult" male who willingly took up the roles of husband and family breadwinner.

As these examples demonstrate, postwar intellectuals limited the discourses upon which they could draw to analyze how popular culture functioned for readers by fixing these texts in a system of differences, which defined high culture as genuine, serious, adversarial, resistant to commodification; low culture as formulaic, frivolous, mind-numbing commodified trash; and middle culture as some insatiable creature from a mediocre lagoon. Legitimating certain forms of culture as valuable and managing other forms by situating them as high culture's "Other" restricted critics thinking to questions of aesthetic standards, thus allowing them a limited, albeit powerful role to play: that is, acting in the capacity of cultural police or, in Andrew Ross's words, "inspectors of the nation's cultural health" (51).[10] Their insistence on legitimizing what was "good" and "bad" taste had a reciprocal effect on augmenting their own positions of authority. However, this elite group seemed to ignore or was naively unaware that its pronouncements constituted an ideological act of creating class and social distinctions in that people were stratified according to the level of culture they consumed or participated in. Concomitantly, by flatly dismissing and denying the fact that millions of people were partaking of all kinds of popular culture, fifties intellectuals failed to see that popular texts were indeed the dominant "voices" within the culture. By reading their popularity as an omen of collapsing decorum and taste, these cultural watchdogs failed to give serious consideration to what so intrigued audiences about popular texts.

The entrenchment of New Criticism in the academy after World War II aided the cultural gatekeepers of the literary world by institutionalizing a methodology for ascertaining what constituted the "genuine" aesthetic object. By privileging formalist qualities of a text—its internal unity and coherence—New Critics could "objectively" determine if it was good or bad art. Best-sellers failed this test every time. They were simply too formally "messy" and, worse, they were stubbornly enmeshed in the social and historical roots of the culture. The New Critical preoccupation with formal and aesthetic qualities effectively curtailed inquiry into the social and historical permutations, authorial influences, or reader reception of a literary text. Novels like *From Here to Eternity*, whose formal "gaffes"—its multiple story lines, linguistic diversity, and inclusion of numerous incidental scenes—were not in the service of either some purely aesthetic or avant-garde ideal, were ignored by serious critics. Neither would the problems of young love in *Marjorie Morningstar* (1955) or *A Summer Place* (1958) qualify as timeless and universal or intellectually rich and nourishing; nor would the dilemmas of the white collar professionals in *The Man in the Gray Flannel Suit* (1955) or *Ten North Frederick* (1955), who must decide not whether, but how to accommodate themselves to the system, have withstood the litmus test of modernist experimentation. Granted a formalist investigation of the irony, formal complexity, or ambiguity within a popular novel perhaps would not be a particularly compelling activity. However, because they told stories about everyday life and offered resolutions to the social problems and contradictions portrayed in them (for better or for worse, ideologically speaking), best-sellers were speaking to audiences in varied and important ways. Moreover, they reveal something about the anxieties, values, and discourses of that particular historical moment, and thus they draw us, as they drew postwar readers, into larger social formations through their links to other cultural forms and discourses.

I am mindful that, as realistic texts, popular novels tend to be ideologically conservative rather than transgressive. According to Catherine Belsey, realistic texts tend to foreclose on counterhegemonic representations because of their investment in illusionism, narrative closure, and discursive hierarchies. Audiences are courted to accept the illusion that certain meanings and subjectivities are "truth" because these representations have been previously made self-evident or natural within dominant discourses. Furthermore, realistic texts move toward inevitable closure, a recognizable and familiar order, so that "the conventional cultural and signifying systems" of the society are reestablished. Finally, the narratives tend to sustain a hierarchy of discourses, "placed for the reader by a privileged, historic narration which is the source of coherence of the story as a whole"; all other discourses are subordinated to this dominant one, again, with the possibility that readers will construct a single interpretation of the text and constrain the choices they make as to its meaning (70). However, Belsey claims, while it may be the case that the realistic text is "determinate ... in its attempt to create a coherent and internally consistent fictive world, the text, in spite of itself, exposes incoherences, omissions, absences, and transgressions which in turn reveal the inability of the language of ideology to create coherence" (107). The readings of the best-selling novels in this book are especially attentive to these textual inconsistencies, which give evidence of their efforts to censor, deny, or recuperate transgressive discourses and images.

Heteroglossia in the Best-Seller and Its Film Adaptation

While the Frankfurt School claimed that the culture industries simply reproduced the status quo and while serious literary critics decried the contamination of art and taste by middle and low culture, neither of these viewpoints accounts for the popular novel's discursive multivalence. This linguistic plurality—what New Critics would denigrate as a novel's "messiness" or its formal shortcomings—is what I associate with Mikhail Bakhtin's notion of heteroglossia, which is precisely what makes the best-seller significant. Heteroglossia, or the plurality of "social voices" contained within the novel's language utterances, accounts for the disorder and disunity of discourses in a given culture and a literary work (Bakhtin 263). Novels, according to Bakhtin, contain both "centripetal" and "centrifugal" linguistic forces, the centripetal forces being those that work towards verbal and ideological centralization and unification. However, because of their linguistic plurality, novels also act as centrifugal forces by displaying and redistributing the diversity and the stratification of voices— heteroglossia—inherent within all discursive constructions. The centrifugal forces, then, constitute a means of offsetting the hierarchy of discourses created by authoritative groups in a culture (271–72). Bakhtin argues persuasively in *The Dialogic Imagination* that the variety of languages and individual voices within a novel does not render the novel unartistic or quasi-artistic; rather, stylistic and linguistic multiplicities are the very features that distinguish the novel from other literary genres (263). Heteroglossia makes the novel, including the popular novel, an active, interesting site for investigating the ideological conflicts and the stratification of "voices" within the text and for studying the relationship between the text and its cultural contexts. Acknowledging the heteroglossia within the popular novel opens it up in ways that offer another means of reading against the restrictive New Critical methods of interpretations, the Frankfurt School's view that the 'popular' was a politically static category, and the conventions of realism, which, as noted earlier, move the narrative toward the ordering and hierarchizing of its discourses.

Because best-sellers of the 1950s were frequently adapted for the screen, the film version offers another means of locating the plurality of social voices or the heteroglossia of a novel. Film adaptations are not simply reproductions of the novel because they inevitably rely on a different set of artistic conventions and visual images in transforming novel to film.[11] Even so, the postwar film adaptation not only recirculated a version of the original text to a wider audience but often became the means by which the novel was remembered. For example, while readers boosted *From Here to Eternity* to the number one spot on the best-seller list in 1951, many people opted to watch the enormously popular 1953 film version in lieu of reading the hefty 861-page novel. Screenwriter Daniel Taradash condensed the narrative to feature the story of three soldiers' quest for manhood, as opposed to the novel's interlocking stories of multiple male characters. However, the plurality within the novel was not entirely erased, as I will argue in the following chapters, but reintroduced through the film's visual dimension and the star texts of Montgomery Clift, Burt Lancaster, and Frank Sinatra, which added further layers to the representations of gender and sexuality of Jones's characters.

Film versions also heightened interest in the novel. Hackett reports that *From Here to Eternity* returned to the best-seller list in 1953 after the film was released; audiences purchased over a million copies of the seventy-five cent paperback edition, plus 68,500 copies of a special hardcover edition (at a lower cost than the original) of the film narrative (193). Certain best-sellers, such as Patrick Dennis's *Auntie Mame* (1956), were recirculated as both film and stage productions. In *Auntie Mame*'s case, Rosalind Russell starred as Mame on Broadway and in the Hollywood film, so that novel, stage, and film characters became inflected by, if not conflated with, Russell's star persona. The result here was the construction of multiple "Mames," all of whom took critical aim at traditional female sex roles.

Often the process of condensing a film for a two-hour running time necessitated deleting certain storylines and characters, which inevitably produced ideological shifts from novel to film. Furthermore, during the fifties, Hollywood movies were still subject to censorship by the Hayes Production Code. Therefore, large parts of a novel's sexually explicit themes, images, and gender "transgressions" were expunged before releasing its film version to the public.[12] In addition, the Catholic Church's Legion of Decency brought pressure to bear on the film industry and its consumers by continuing to advise its congregants about which films were acceptable to attend. In the film industry's process of condensing and sanitizing a film, some of the variety and diversity with regard to gender identity and sexuality was abridged. However, producers and directors could avail themselves of another means to redefine representations of gender and sexuality: stardom or star images. According to Richard Dyer, star images are produced through a combination of a star's former film roles and the images and impressions presented in a wide variety of media texts that detail a star's lifestyle, personality, and important events affecting his or her life. Moreover, Dyer claims that "love, marriage and sex are constants of the image" (*Stars* 39). Because star image is one largely produced by how a star is gendered and created as a sexual being (which always intersects with race, class, and ethnicity), stardom is one of the most productive areas to investigate regarding gender identity in film and the intertextual play with its literary form. While the film had to condense or eliminate a novel's explicit sex passages or particular adult themes, a movie star often reintroduced these elements visually or extratextually, through what audiences "knew" about a star's personal life or public image. That is to say, a film character often is defined less by specific parameters from the narrative and more by the glossy 8 X 10s of the production company's advertising office and the latest articles in the fan magazines. Stars like Lana

Turner—the "Sweater Girl"—and Montgomery Clift—an "intense" young man—brought to their roles powerful images of sexuality and gender. Turner, frequently the subject of media gossip and scandal about her private love life, brought a certain sexual undercurrent to her role as the repressed mother in *Peyton Place*, while Clift's image and former screen roles of sensitive, lonely, intense males conditioned viewers to expect a similar performance of masculinity in *From Here to Eternity's* Private Prewitt.

In addition, the condensations and alterations of a narrative often revolve around stardom; that is, directors will feature stars and certain star qualities, in effect, subordinating story lines and character construction within the original text. For example, Hollywood screenwriters added a daughter to the Benedict family in *Giant,* in order to create a love interest between the hot, new starlet, Carroll Baker, and the national teen obsession, James Dean. Casting choices and star images also introduced extratextual meanings into Edna Ferber's literary constructions of gender and national identity. Fifties heart throb, Rock Hudson, the gorgeous Elizabeth Taylor, and James Dean all imparted particular resonances to their characters, heightening their glamour and generating more sympathy or appeal for them. In Dean's case, by the time of *Giant's* release, he had been dead for a year and had achieved a wildly popular cult status; this and his riveting screen presence muted the novel's portrayal of Jett Rink, a millionaire oil man, but an abysmal failure as a human being. Instead of soliciting the novel's moral reproach of the drunken, arrogant Rink, James Dean created a potential allure for this character, rather like the simultaneous fascination and aversion one has for Milton's Satan or Shakespeare's Richard III. Such differences, as well as the similarities, between the best-seller and the film, have significance for speculating on how popular texts may have shaped notions of identity for postwar audiences. Interpreting a novel in light of its film version projects more distinctly how one narrative represents particular constructions of culture and identity, which may be mutually reinforcing or more or less progressive than its counterpart.

Films often reinforced the ideological workings of the novels; but just as often, by condensing, altering, or sanitizing the original for the screen, the film throws into relief both the multivalence of the novel and the shifts in historical and social circumstances that occurred between the release of the novel and the film. Because the film better illuminates the reception of the novel, by drawing out or complicating viewers' perceptions of the narrative, this investigation pairs each best-seller with its cinematic reproduction in order to explore their intertextual significations and the ideological formation and contestation between hegemonic, resistant, and suppressed discourses and representations.

The popular novels and films adaptations I will discuss in the following chapters include James Jones's *From Here to Eternity* (1951), Edna Ferber's *Giant* (1952), James Michener's *Sayonara* (1954), Patrick Dennis's *Auntie Mame* (1955), and Grace Metalious's *Peyton Place* (1956). Each novel achieved best-seller status and became a blockbuster film, indications that the narrative reached hundreds of thousands of readers and viewers. Two of the best-sellers were written by authors with established reputations: Pulitzer Prize winner, James Michener, was not only a household word by the early 1950s, but, based on his work before *Sayonara*, he was known for bringing "Asia" into the living rooms of American homes. Edna Ferber, a writer since the 1920s, was already well known for her regional and historical novels and her short stories about a successful businesswoman, Emma McChesney. Although Jones, Dennis, and Metalious were literary newcomers, their first novels were all runaway best-sellers, unique in the treatment of their subject matter. Although any number of popular novels would prove interesting and useful for a historical investigation of this kind, I have selected these particular texts not only because they achieved widespread exposure and popularity, but because together they offer a cross-section of historical and cultural issues pertinent to gender and national identity.

All five narratives share a preoccupation with constructing male and female subjectivities, which worked to constitute particular notions of "Americanness" for fifties audiences. My approach to analyzing the relationship between gender and national identity involves making connections between the textual constructs of gender and its intersections with race, class, and sexuality, and their contextual representations and discourses within postwar America. Each of the narratives, being rooted in specific social environments and historical conditions, foregrounds a different set of social, political, and culture issues, including communist containment, race relations, American global hegemony, family life, the rise of corporate culture and Group Life—all of which are linked symbolically to gender and images of nation. This study entails a close examination of the discursive strategies and narrative practices of these selected texts in order to paint a clearer picture of their ideological workings. Historicizing these discourses and representational practices is a significant component of this book because this approach offers a way to speculate on the conditions that make possible particular readings and interpretations of alternative expressions of social "reality." In this case, Janet Staiger's and Barbara Klinger's historicist approach in their work on interpreting film provides an important model for this study. Staiger and Klinger stress the importance of looking at a variety of discursive formations and social networks that actively contribute to the meanings of a text. As Klinger points out, investigating the historical dimensions of textual production and reception helps scholars avoid monolithic interpretations of either particular texts or the historical circumstances in which the text was produced (xiii). In short, textual studies should be what Staiger calls "context-activated" (95).

In order to link best-sellers and films to other cultural discourses, the following investigation relies on a variety of contextual materials of the 1950s, including popular magazines, medical and scientific findings, film and book reviews, and other forms of popular culture. The study also draws on recent social and political histories of the 1950s, film studies, and the theoretical perspectives of Cultural Studies to frame the analysis of identity and culture. As a methodological tool by which to examine Cold War gender ideologies, I use current feminist and gender studies to denaturalize the dominant fictional ideals of masculinity and femininity of postwar America. In addition to theoretical work by Chris Holmlund, Wendy Hollway, and Eve Sedgwick on gender masquerade and social constructions of sexuality, Judith Butler's theory of gender performativity and Robert Connell's work on hegemonic masculinity are especially useful for illustrating how gender, as it was represented in the 1950s, is neither a natural nor a fixed category of identity, but, in fact, a fluid and multiple construct formed within a network of discursive histories.

Using the regulatory impact of gender as a focal point, my aim is to show how best-sellers and their cinematic (re)presentations became forums for exhibiting, in Judith Butler's words, the "gender trouble" that hegemonic groups in society felt compelled to control—specifically the "trouble" generated by errant females, homosexuals, and those coded as feminine. The dominant ideologies of gender and sexuality in this decade were constituted by the discourse of Freudian psychoanalysis, which understood sex as both an innate biological drive "expressed" in accordance with a fixed binary of "male" and "female" and a key determinant of personality. Put simply, biological sex ("male," "female") certified gender ("masculinity," "femininity"); gender, in turn, determined how (hetero)sexuality was expressed. In this paradigm, which established the parameters of "normal" adult sexuality, Freud postulated that the sexual aims are very different in the sexes. Femininity and female sexuality is subordinate and passive compared to masculinity and an active male sexuality, which is straightforward in that it aims for a "discharge of sexual products" (Freud 73). Women need to put aside their "childish masculinity" at puberty by transmitting their sexual excitation from the clitoris to the vagina; thus the "essence of femininity" derives from women's repression of sexuality at puberty in making a transference to vaginal sexuality (Freud 87). Widespread cultural recognition of this postwar conceptualization of sex and gender is evidenced in this passage from "Modern Marriage," published in a 1956 issue of *Life:*

> Men are designed by nature to sire children and women to bear them, and from these elementary facts, psychiatrists say, come their differences in emotional needs. For women, the sexual act itself implies receptiveness and a certain passivity, while the long period of human gestation and the extraordinarily long period of a child's development implies a need for protection and support for the mother. These primary feminine qualities—receptivity, passivity and the desire to nurture—color a woman's entire emotional life. For the male, the sexual role requires aggressiveness and a certain degree of dominance, even of exploitiveness .... These male characteristics are carried over into everyday living in many ways. (Coughlin 109)

The texts included in this book, then, do not radically displace this conceptualization of sexual difference; rather, they problematize the stability of its binary structure and thus its presumption of universality.

In arguing that these five narratives presented alternative discourses pertaining to gender and sexuality, I do not wish to make claims about how readers and filmgoers actually interpreted them. Obviously, it is impossible to know precisely how audiences made sense and meaning of the images and representations presented in these texts, or whether indeed they understood alternative expressions of "reality" as resistant or subversive. However, in theorizing how these popular texts functioned for postwar reading and viewing audiences, I propose that diversity exists not only within the texts themselves, but within and among readers and viewers as well. Film historian Robert Sklar argues that scholars need to go beyond an Althusserian conception of the culture industries, which views them as state apparatuses that merely reproduce and then interpellate audiences into dominant ideologies. Cultural production is not simply a process of "one-way hegemonic domination," whereby audiences are passive recipients of images, ideas, and values. Instead, Sklar maintains, popular texts contain within them ideological struggle and contradictions. Therefore, there is more than one way audiences may construct meanings in a text (31). Furthermore, as problem solving genres that emphasize personal or relational aspects of everyday life, novels and films can offer audiences a variety of ways in which to reflect upon their experiences, including allowing them to articulate their own feelings of dispossession and alienation.

This book creates a picture of how particular social and historical conditions during this decade may have shaped people's thinking about themselves and their nation. In other words, an awareness of the prevailing ideologies and historical events of a given culture provides us with some access, however limited, to the possible interactions between audiences, texts, and contexts. Revealing the multiplicity, discontent, and contradictions within texts enables us to see their potential for opening up spaces that allowed audiences to identify with dominant as well as nondominant positions and alternative viewpoints. Furthermore, we can begin to see the dynamism of this historical moment. Clearly, the turbulence of the 1960s was not incidental, nor did its discontent and rebellion burst forth spontaneously. It had been bubbling beneath the surface hold that hegemonic groups had on cultural representations within the 1950s.

What will begin to emerge from this book is not only a more accurate representation of the heterogeneity within postwar culture, but a way of considering the value of popular culture—particularly the best-seller—both in the lives of its immediate consumers and in scholarly investigations. Recontextualizing the best-seller in its historical and social roots gives us a way to think beyond the views of postwar intellectuals, who could only berate the flood of popular texts for fostering social anarchy and disrespect, or for breeding an intellectually stagnate populace who seemed blissfully ignorant of its role in cultivating the collapse of western civilization. This book aims to reassess the discursive possibilities of "middlebrow" culture in fostering multivariate, even counterhegemonic readings. These forms of popular culture give evidence of the struggle over definitions of "men" and "women" and what is or is not acceptable in terms of male and female roles. The wider implications of this project include constructing a clearer picture of the ideological uses to which gender can be put as a means of preserving the repressive structures and institutions—for both men and women—which create and sustain the status quo. In keeping with recent feminist accounts of gender and sexuality, this project endeavors to build on their contributions to a feminist cultural politics in conceptualizing social and political transformation.

2

Masculinity and Male Power in James Jones's *From Here to Eternity*

In 1951, the same year that *Betty Crocker's Picture Cook Book, Better Homes and Gardens Garden Book,* and *Better Homes and Gardens Handyman's Book* ranked second, fourth, and fifth on the annual nonfiction best-sellers list, James Jones's *From Here to Eternity,* regarded both then and now as one of the great war novels of that period, topped the list for fiction. According to best-seller chronicler Alice Payne Hackett, "Jones's first novel outsold every other fiction title in the bookstores, reaching a total of 240,000." Two years later 68,500 copies were sold in a special movie edition, making it the fifth-ranking best-seller of 1953. However, Hackett notes, "if outlets other than bookstores had been considered for these annual lists, *From Here to Eternity* would have outdistanced by far any other novel, for 2,000,000 copies of its paperbound 75-cent edition, brought out to coincide with the appearance of the movie, were sold" (193). Matching the novel's financial success, the 1953 film version was a top money-maker for Columbia Pictures, second only to *The Robe,* and swept the Academy Awards, receiving eight Oscars out of an impressive thirteen nominations.[1] Clearly, while middle-class Americans were perfecting a meatloaf, pruning, and tinkering with do-it-yourself projects, part of their attention was drawn to the literary and visual recreations of the recent war and, particularly, to Jones's portrayal of military life at Schofield Barracks, Hawaii, just before the attack on Pearl Harbor.

Considering that books about gardening, home improvement, and *From Here to Eternity* were marketed primarily to the same audience of white, male, middle-class consumers, there appears to be a rather striking contrast between the images of masculinity, symbolized by the gardener and do-it-yourselfer in the culture and the rough-and-tough foot soldiers within the novel. Publications, such as the *Garden Book* and *Handyman's Book,* fostered the domestication of demobilized war veterans, now asked to relinquish the aggressive, antisocial behaviors they were permitted to display as soldiers, as well as to forgo the camaraderie of living within all-male groups. The Organization Man—the white, middle-class, upwardly mobile businessman, who was the breadwinner and mortgage holder on a modern suburban home—represented the collective ideal of male identity, which had emerged from the new corporate order at the end of the war.[2] His weekends and leisure time were spent at home, presumably reading up on lawn fertilizers or engrossed in some woodworking project in his basement.[3] In contrast, *From Here to Eternity* recreates a version of prewar army life that is brutish, hostile, and often violent. Its male figures are representative of the "marginal" men of the Depression: young, rootless, uneducated males—men on-the-bum, ex-Wobblies, and escapees from middle-class domesticity—who in the years before World War II left home to ease the financial burden on their families. Severed from kinship ties and the socioeconomic mainstream, the men in Jones's novel opt to master precision drill in order to call G (George) Company home and soldiering their "profession," therefore appearing to be oddly out of step with the postwar cadences of commuter trains carrying gray flannel suited men to and from their company.

How, then, did Jones's quintessentially male narrative appeal to audiences in their present-day cultural milieu, in which the domesticated, organization man signified manliness? What discourses of masculinity in the 1950s help us understand *From Here to Eternity* as a product of its time? One explanation may lie with the conflict rooted in the culture's conception of masculinity. Despite the restructuring of gender roles after World War II, which restored control of the workplace to men and reinstated them as heads of the household, various cultural representations of the American male repeatedly portrayed this figure as symbolically castrated by the multiple demands imposed on him by his boss, coworkers, wife, and family. Home and office were the very places in which men were supposed to be the "boss," yet they also were places where men felt increasingly impotent.

Perhaps *From Here to Eternity* functioned as a compensatory narrative by reinvigorating masculinity perceived to be under pressure and by recovering the integrity and coherence of the white, heterosexual, male self through the nostalgic recreation of a world in which males coexisted outside of the confines of domesticity. Furthermore, the novel is primarily concerned with the issue of power and powerlessness, an issue central to masculine identity and authority. Considering *From Here to Eternity*'s tremendous popularity, the struggle for personal power in a world that negates it clearly resonated with the postwar "crisis" of masculinity. Although the novel condemns overt aggression and brutality in keeping with the demobilization of war veterans, it does not question patriarchy *per se*, but asks readers to consider what kind of male should have rightful authority over others. The main thrust of the novel, then, performs the function of regulating and standardizing masculinity—representing "real" men—in the image of Sergeant Milton Warden and, to a certain extent, Private Robert E. Lee Prewitt, both of whom possess a certain toughness, inviolability, and moral authority.

The following investigation of male gender formation in *From Here to Eternity* draws on Robert Connell and his colleagues', Tim Carrigan and Robert Lee, work on hegemonic masculinity. Their theories demonstrate how gender is relational and thus allow for an analysis based on the differences of power not only between men and women, but also between groups of men. As Connell argues, it is the "interplay between different forms of masculinity [that] is an important part of how a patriarchal social order works" (*Gender* 183). In this conceptualization, masculinity is socially constructed through hierarchical relations between men. Furthermore, it interacts with a range of other social coordinates, such as class, race, ethnicity, sexuality, and age, therefore, requiring an analysis that goes beyond gender in order to understand gender (Connell *Masculinities* 76). Hegemonic males, then, inhabit their positions of power and authority by virtue of their ability to "legitimate and reproduce the social relationships that generate their dominance" (Carrigan, Connell, and Lee 179). In short, dominance rests on the production and containment of male "others," particularly the homosexual "other."

Focusing primarily on the interrelationships between four male characters and their different embodiments of masculinity, this chapter investigates the social fields of masculinity in *From Here to Eternity* that produce and maintain a range of positions of power and powerlessness. The novel clearly endorses G Company's Sergeant Warden as a hegemonic model for the dozen or so subordinate males in his troop and certainly as a fantasy figure for postwar audiences. Three nonhegemonic males, Privates Prewitt and Maggio and Corporal Isaac Bloom, function as contrastive figures that serve as gauges by which to measure "manliness." As signifiers of class, ethnic, and/or sexual differences, these rear rank soldiers authorize Warden's hegemony and his brand of masculinity. However, they also play a central role in destabilizing the coordinates—Anglo-American, middle-class, heterosexual—that codify hegemonic masculinity. That is to say, the novel's own representational practices ultimately break down, calling into question the self-evident, "natural" position of hegemonic masculinity. The nonhegemonic males' refusal to be contained within these established parameters of gender identity exposes the origins of hegemonic masculinity as constructed in a social milieu in which relations of power and exclusionary practices structure men's relations to men. The "naturalness" of hegemony ultimately unravels when the dominant masculine ideal is shown to be symbolic rather than "real." The latter part of the chapter presents a particularly revealing example of how masculinity is socially produced: The novel, despite its attempt to run a "straight" course in the gendering of power relations between men, runs aground when hegemonic masculinity's most troubling and feared specter—uncontained homosexuality—disturbs the homosocial grounds on which it is premised.

The 1953 film version is an important component of this analysis because, although the film recirculates the novel's endorsement of hegemonic masculinity in the figure of Sergeant Warden (Burt Lancaster), it offers both reductive and productive readings of the novel. By condensing Jones's narrative, the film discards the novel's inclusion of multiple masculinities, which are key in introducing the novel's disruptive elements.[4] In other words, the film appears to "repair" the novel's deconstructive impulses. Like the novel, the film does foreground the overarching question about what constitutes manhood but simplifies this question by situating it along two complementary axes: one being a democratic/undemocratic continuum, the other axis forging ideal male identity in a contest between self and society. However, as much as Hollywood's version tends to clarify and distill the novel's gender complexity, making the cinematic text seem more ideologically seamless, the star text of Montgomery Clift (Private Prewitt), in particular, appears to reintroduce this complexity. While Burt Lancaster's star image and performance in *Eternity* function to reinforce Warden's hegemonic masculinity and while Frank Sinatra (Private Maggio) largely served as a contrastive figure to both Warden and Prewitt, Clift not only reinserts a subversive homoeroticism into the film, but potentially disrupts the untrammeled notion of a coherent, self-evident masculinity with his popular rebel image. Therefore, the novel's references to homosexuality and the homoerotic dimensions of homosociality that Hollywood expunged may have been reintroduced on screen through Clift's star persona.

"Changed Radically and Dangerously": The Postwar Crisis of Masculinity

Scientists who study human behavior fear that the American male is now dominated by the American female. These scientists worry that in the years since the end of World War II, he has changed radically and dangerously, that he is no longer the masculine, strong-minded man who pioneered the continent and built America's greatness. (Moskin 77)

What does dear mother do when sonny comes home from college all full of revolt and dis-satisfaction with the way the world has always been run? They find him a sweet young thing thats around handy to relieve himself on and they finagle till they got him married to her, and then sonny quiets down to his duty and lets his revolt run off and accepts the status quo. (Sgt. Warden, From Here to Eternity*)*

According to Carrigan, Connell, and Lee, "the essential feminist insight that the overall relationship between men and women is one involving domination or oppression ... is a fact that is steadily evaded, and sometimes flatly denied, in much of the literature about masculinity written by men" (140). This insight is particularly applicable to postwar America, if we consider the above statements as representing the persistent strain of male discontent and castration anxiety within public discourses of the 1950s. Both the scientists cited in *Look* and Jones's Sergeant Warden assume that patriarchy is the natural order of things, whereas gender role inversion is unnatural, even dangerous. More to the point, judging by these excerpts, as well as by numerous other magazine articles and scientific studies of the decade, men were invariably cited as the oppressed group in society. And their victimizers? Overbearing moms, demanding wives, and, ironically, the very structure that upheld the hegemonic status of men: corporate organization.

Corporate organization, symbolized by the Army in *From Here to Eternity*, demands group loyalty and team playing. In the 1950s, however, these modes of behavior began to be coded in terms of male discontent and oppression. The inability to assert individualistic impulses and exercise personal autonomy or decision making within corporate structures robbed the outer-directed, organization man of his "rightful" exercise of masculine power and authority. As Barbara Ehrenreich documents in *The Hearts of Men*, conformity and Group Life, both on the job and within his look-alike tract home, were equated with a loss of manhood. Much of the period literature on male discontent, states Ehrenreich, indicated that "conformity destroys not only men's souls, but their very manhood" (31). The stakes in this matter were purportedly high for reasons beyond the emasculation of individual males. Note in the quote from *Look*, it is the "masculine, strong-minded man" who is the nation builder. As the United States squared off with the Soviet Union igniting the Cold War, this link between manhood and nationhood was profoundly reinforced in the public imagination. In the ensuing Red Scare, primary importance was given to maintaining traditional sexual and social binaries as a viable means of securing the nation from communist subversion. Men in aprons and women in trousers signified more than an ominous gender inversion at the level of the family. In the discourses of the Cold War, this forecast the kind of social chaos that made America vulnerable to communist infiltrators. Within this milieu, then, *From Here to Eternity* may have performed the function of reinvigorating hegemonic masculinity within the context of "corporate" life through Warden's status as the virile and tough, but fully committed "organization man."

Postwar gender anxiety was perhaps exacerbated by the rapid transformation of American society after World War II. As historian Eric Goldman puts it, "nothing seemed unchanging except change" for mainstream Americans. Free enterprise coexisted with a post-New Deal welfare state and welfare capitalism; the control of communities by "white, Protestant, old-stock families" was challenged; "Negroes, Catholics, Jews, and the sons of recent immigrants jostled the one-time elite for jobs and status" (Goldman 119). Such economic and political contestations, which involved questions of national identity, directly challenged the hegemony of ruling groups. The growing visibility of America's heterogeneity, along with the emergence of the organization ethos and anticommunist hysteria, all contributed to the perception that masculinity—universalized in the image of a white, middle-class, Euro-American—was indeed in crisis.

What were the stakes, though, in circulating the notion that American manhood was "changed radically and dangerously"? In part, because hegemonic masculinity must continually procure consent to, or compliance with, its authority, the ascendancy of one variety of masculinity over others is never stable nor static. The assertions by subordinated groups, who seek to legitimize their own values and interests, must be carefully balanced; when challenges or resistance to the power and authority of dominant groups persist or threaten to overwhelm, masculinity is said to be in "crisis." In a sense, however, hegemonic masculinity is always in "crisis," for, in order to sustain its image as coherent, universal, and deserving of its status, it must always be forming and reforming itself through the manipulation of cultural discourses, images, and practices. A rather striking example of this strategy in the 1950s is the demonizing of homosexuals and women during the Red Scare. By making national security, freedom, and democracy incumbent upon maintaining traditional social and sexual binaries, hegemonic males could more readily "persuade" all members of society to uphold the status quo, particularly if traditional ways of organizing society were presented as evidently the best way to preserve national ideals. Those rejecting the status quo were discursively marked as potential public enemies who fostered the destruction of the American Way of Life.

However, a "crisis" of hegemonic rule concomitantly allows subordinate groups to air their grievances or enhance their political or social position by forcing the dominant group to accommodate their needs or recognize their legitimacy in return for continued consent to rule. The public nature of such a crisis creates the very moments in which subordinate groups can refute, redefine, or expose their oppressors' manipulation of representations that negates their own identities. This analysis of *From Here to Eternity* pays close attention to these dynamics, specifically in terms of how mechanisms for reproducing hegemony contain their own seeds of disruption.

Authority and Position Make the Man

Filmgoers who crowded the theaters to see *From Here to Eternity* in 1953 remembered or "read" the novel through a visual recreation that focused almost exclusively on Sergeant Warden and Private Prewitt. By streamlining the novel, the film foregrounded a binarized relationship between these two men as hegemonic/nonhegemonic, which, in contrast to the novel, pitched the film narrative toward a narrower reading of gender. The film, however, does replicate fairly closely the novel's rendering of the Prewitt-Warden story: Prewitt, a loner and arch-individualist, transfers into G Company after having quit the Bugle Corp because another man is made first bugler, even though Prewitt is the best bugler on the post. He immediately runs into trouble in his new unit by refusing on moral grounds to join the boxing team, because months earlier he accidentally blinded his sparring partner. However, Commanding Officer Dana Holmes (Philip Ober) is seeking the regimental boxing championship, so he sets out to break Prewitt's will by ordering the boxing team to give him the "Treatment," a kind of hazing that consists of verbal harassment, sabotage of his field performance, and assignment to the most exhausting, disgusting tasks of straight duty. Sustained by his stubborn conviction that "if a man don't go his own way he's nothin'," Prewitt manages to endure torment and loneliness of the Treatment with the help of his girlfriend Lorene (Donna Reed), a "hostess" at the New Congress Club, and his buddy Angelo Maggio.

First Sergeant Milton Warden is strong, powerful, and, like Prewitt, a man of conviction, but rather than being a staunch individualist, Warden's loyalty is to the Company. As such, he concentrates on running the most efficient outfit in the army, a task made difficult not only by Captain Holmes's arbitrary, inept treatment of his subordinates, but by the discord Prewitt's presence generates in the Company. Warden further complicates his life when he begins a risky, torrid affair with Holmes's wife, Karen (Deborah Kerr), who pressures Warden to become an officer so they can eventually marry. This solution is untenable for Warden, however, because he despises the corruption, elitism, and ineptitude of the officer class.

The film, unlike the novel, uses a familiar organizing structure in movies of the 1940s and 1950s, which Ina Rae Hark has identified as a democratic/undemocratic dichotomy in which male-male conflict fuels the action. In this case, Prewitt's refusal to box generates conflict between boxers and straight-duty soldiers. As Hark points out, narratives of this period, such as Westerns, war movies, epics, and science fiction, which are primarily concerned with masculine power and authority, are driven forward when "the rightful exercise of masculine power has been perverted by unmanly tyrants ... From Robin Hood to Rambo, captive or outlawed men revolt because the powerful subject positions within their societies have been usurped by male oppressors who don't qualify for them .... Thus the usurpers often display characteristics not marked as signifiers of masculinity in codes of male film performance at the time" (152). Part of the film's cultural work is precisely this kind of regulation of male identities through the production of good/democratic and bad/undemocratic males, effectively limiting the terms by which masculinity is conceptualized. In other words, the film version of *Eternity* asks audiences to think about manhood in terms of ethics and moral authority, aligning masculinity with American ideals of fairness and justice. The novel, however, foregrounds gender more explicitly—which, as we will see, is a more potentially disruptive category—as a regulatory mechanism that organizes other social coordinates (ethnicity, race, class, sexual preference) in its formulation of a male ideal.

In the film, the brutes and tyrants eventually are overthrown: Holmes resigns from the Army after his endorsement of the Treatment is discovered, and boxing-bully Sergeant Ike Galovitch (John Dennis) is busted to private for picking a fight with Prewitt, a fight earning him respect even from the other boxers. The sadistic Sergeant "Fatso" Judson (Ernest Borgnine), who beats Maggio to death in the Stockade, is killed by Prewitt to avenge his buddy's death.[5] This advancement of justice is absent in the novel, again, underscoring the film's abridged thematic concerns. Jones's novel treats the question of "good" and "bad" masculinities with much more ambivalence: Holmes is *promoted* by the Army, rather than booted out. Galovitch draws a knife on Prewitt, which lands Prewitt in the Stockade while Galovitch remains unpunished. Although Prewitt kills Fatso, Fatso's superior officer, the unflinching, cold-blooded Major Thompson, still oversees the savagery that rules the Stockade. Overall the novel's outlook is cynical and bitter, indicating the struggle for empowerment and justice within such a rigid hierarchy is much more problematic than simply restoring power to a few "good" men.

However, by foregrounding the issue of "good" and "bad" masculinities, the film indirectly spoke to fifties anxieties about emasculation. By situating male-male conflict in the context of oppression and moral ineptitude, the restoration of patriarchal authority to more democratic, "deserving" males is seen as necessary and just, which, in turn, naturalizes the idea that such powerful subject positions are indeed the exclusive domain of men. Granted one could argue that a democratic social order allows for the expression of opposition to dominant structures and discourses, which then creates the potential for social transformation. The film, however, implies that reinstalling the "democratic" males to power is a sufficient response to social inequalities (signified in the army by differences in rank). Moreover, by displacing questions of gender onto questions of democracy, gender hierarchies are seen to function quite naturally within a democratic order.

In addition to its emphasis on (un)democratic males, the film's focus on Prewitt and Warden further reduces the novel's complexity by situating their differences in the context of the perennial self/society struggle. Both men experience powerlessness because they are committed to an organization that restricts personal freedom and turns individuals to objects. Verifying manhood, then, becomes defined in terms of maintaining autonomy and personal integrity in an organization that effaces these traditional signifiers of manliness and is ruled by brutes and tyrants. Warden emerges from this conflict relatively unscathed, but Prewitt is finally crushed by the very organization he considers his home. Forced to go AWOL after being wounded in the process of killing Fatso, Prewitt eventually tries to return to his Company, but he is shot by patrolling MPs, who, overly anxious about Japanese saboteurs in the chaos following Pearl Harbor, mistake him for the enemy. Warden survives these initial encounters with the Japanese primarily because he has the ability, as Graham McCann states, to make "his accommodation with the system .... There is little doubt that [Warden] will survive the war, just as he survived the local army strife: his kind always wins; his tight fists and bright teeth and cool nerve will always see him through .... Prewitt seems supremely isolated in such an environment" (65).

What, though, might fifties audiences have found heroic about a man who makes "his accommodation with the system," given postwar anxiety about conformity and its association with symbolic castration? Peter Biskind's reading of the film poses a possible answer: While emphasis on conformity, outer-directedness, and group life raised the specter of emasculation, the values of cooperation still outweighed dissent, and teamwork prevailed over Prewitt's lone-wolf approach to life. "Individualism, as a professed value," states Biskind, "had been on the skids for some time, but it was in the fifties that it got its final shove downhill" (52). Thus, Prewitt—"a wormy apple"—must die because his "individualism had gotten out of control" (82). Warden may have posed an acceptable compromise between America's mythic ideal of individualism and the commitment and responsibility to the community, which had become so imperative to Cold Warriors, because he knows when to follow orders and when to disregard them and take matters into his own hands if he sees the organization faltering (Biskind 84). Moreover, the film's self/society and democratic/undemocratic axes intersect in the figure of Warden, which had clear implications for affirming the ruling interests in postwar America. That is to say, hegemony is defined in terms of an organization man whose ability to compromise is defined as the judicious exercise of male power rather than the display of emasculation. Furthermore, organization life, and by extension corporate America, is symbolically linked to democracy through Warden's hatred of tyrants and bullies. The film, then, produces a chain of signifiers that realigns corporate interests with toughness, virility, *and* democratic ideals, which together could allay the decade's most imminent Cold War anxieties.

Biskind's reading of Sergeant Warden in Hollywood's *Eternity* is a useful point of entry into the novel as well because the novel also privileges Warden's hegemony as the company man who is invested with phallic mastery and superiority, attributes encoded by various physical, sexual, and social signifiers. Jones's Warden is physically fit, his "bulging muscles ... ripple tautly" when he moves (46).[6] Brawling enlisted men look shame-faced and drop their weapons at his command—his mere presence likened to a fearless "avenging genii of Discipline and all Authority" (234). His (hetero)sexual prowess confirms his virility and, in turn, his manliness. When Sergeant Leva invites Warden to accompany him to the New Congress Club, Warden sneers, "When I have to pay for it I'll quit" (47). Refusing to participate in activities like communal trips to a brothel, which foster homosocial bonding within the troop, reinforces Warden's hegemonic status by maintaining the social distance between himself and the males in his charge. In effect, this distancing reproduces the kind of hierarchical structure of corporate America, one that prescribes when, where, and how one male may interact with another. As a company man, Warden also gains dividends from patriarchy. He has authority over other males in his capacity as director of the mundane affairs of G Company and as referee over the querulous, sometimes violent, males in his charge. "I'm the guy that runs this compny [sic]," he warns Prewitt (64). In this respect, he functions as a stabilizing, regulatory figure, playing a key role in containing other masculinities—precisely the activity on which hegemonic masculinity rests.

Although Warden is cynically aware that he, too, is a subordinate male—his roommate Pete calls him "a stooge for Holmes"—he resists such authority by subtly manipulating his lazy, inattentive Captain, who "would strangle on his own spit if he didn't have [Warden] around ... to swab his throat out for him" (65). Getting Prewitt a weekend pass is simple because Holmes signs anything Warden puts in front of him. Usurping Holmes's phallus, as it were, is also played out sexually in Warden's seduction of his commander's wife, Karen. The narrative continually attempts to naturalize Warden's status by juxtaposing his own self-aggrandizing appraisal, that "he had never met a man who was amazingly adept at anything he put his hand to as was Milton Anthony Warden" (36), with the explicit fakery accorded to Holmes's command. "Holmes," sneers Warden, "is a dumb bastard that signs papers an [sic] rides horses an wears spurs an gets stinking drunk at the stinking Officers' Club" (64). While Holmes's masculinity ostensibly is erected on a series of (empty) signs—spurs, riding horses, signing papers—Warden's is presumably the result of his "natural" abilities to outdo and lead other men. The codes by which his manliness is constructed attempt to disavow its dependence on the social trappings and tropes of authority and position. However, behind this representation of the "natural" versus the "fake" lurks the question: If one kind of masculinity is masqueraded or manufactured, then are not all masculinities based on particular kinds of performances rather than arising from natural properties?

The film visually reinforces the novel's association of Warden with phallic superiority through Burt Lancaster's star text and performance style. Lancaster's physicality and gestures delineated a kind of hard masculinity: set jaw, ramrod posture, and a commanding stare. He frequently placed his hands on his hips, creating the impression of a large, impervious figure, ready for action or confrontation. Even in rare moments of repose, he appears to contain an inner energy and brute strength. Undoubtedly, Lancaster's star persona inflected characterization at this level, authenticating Warden's manliness. In his prior roles—always the star—Lancaster appeared in a variety of film genres, first playing all-brawn-and-no-brain types in *The Killers* (1946) and *Brute Force* (1947), then moving on to roles that included a secret service agent in *Mister 880* (1950), Jim Thorpe in *Jim Thorpe—All-American* (1951), a western hero in *Vengeance Valley* (1951), swashbuckling adventurers in *The Flame and the Arrow* (1950), *The Crimson Pirate* (1952), and *His Majesty O'Keefe* (1953), and a washed-out alcoholic husband in *Come Back, Little Sheba* (1952). His versatility notwithstanding, Lancaster became pegged as a tough guy known for his athleticism and animal magnetism. A 1953 *Look* article, whose very title—"The Story of a Hard Man"—configures him at once in terms of sexuality, physicality, and temperament, stated that his "virile good looks" were a considerable force in making him a major box office draw. Underscoring the link between virility and size, the article reported that "he is six-feet-two and weighs 180 pounds, with a 42-inch chest and a 31-inch waist. Rigorously self-disciplined, he is all bone and muscle, and looks 29 instead of his actual 39," and he "stubbornly refuses to have anyone do his stunts for the screen" (93). By foregrounding Lancaster as the phallic body with unquestioned virility, *Look* worked to fix the "truth" behind his image, one that informed his portrayal of the tough Army sergeant.

Fifties' publicity accounts of Lancaster's rise to stardom also forged his image out of the classic American myth of success: the self-made man. The narrative typically begins with young Burt growing up in humble surroundings, an East Harlem street kid who took odd jobs to supplement his parents' income; it continues with his ten-year career as a circus acrobat and ends with his success as a Hollywood actor/producer. (His Norma-Hecht Productions was one of the first successful ventures by a studio actor who moved into film production). Thus, Lancaster could be credited with more than just good looks and muscles. *Look*, in fact, summed him up as having "brawn and brains and an acid tongue" (93). Put another way, the *New York Times Magazine* called Lancaster a "paradoxical mixture of grown-up Dead-End Kid and conscious intellectual" (Jamison 20). His star image appeared to embody the contradictory qualities of "ordinariness" and "specialness," a contradiction Richard Dyer claims the star system readily reconciled in the myth of success (*Stars* 48).

While both the film and novel are fairly relentless, then, in authorizing Warden as the consummate male, the film momentarily disrupts the seamless quality of this representation in the famous "sexy" beach scene (considered shocking for its time) in which Karen and Warden passionately consummate their affair. Clad only in tight-fitting swim trunks, Lancaster/Warden's bulging muscles and well-defined physique—pure beefcake—were openly displayed and functioned equally with Deborah Kerr's body to captivate the audience's gaze and interest. Not only is Lancaster/Warden objectified for both female and male spectators, therefore inviting the potential for scopic homoeroticism, he virtually dominates the series of beach shots, foregrounding the visual interest of the camera and viewers in his body. In "Don't Look Now," Richard Dyer reminds us that when the male body is situated as sexual spectacle, it creates instability in the ruling ideology that constructs sexual difference through an active/male versus passive/female nexus of looking. The eroticized male spectacle can connote powerlessness and passivity through objectification in relation to dominant ideologies of masculinity in the same way that the female body traditionally has functioned.

Because the kind of objectification to which Lancaster/Warden's body becomes subjected disrupts the relations of power inscribed within the gendered codes of looking and being, the film compensates for this violation by emphasizing Lancaster's muscles and other signifiers of his power.[7] In the beach scene, his dominance is maintained in several ways. First, low-angled, straight-on shots highlight his muscles and size, filling almost the entire frame with his body and encouraging (male) viewers to identify with him as a powerful ego ideal; full-length shots, positioning Lancaster in front of high cliffs and the sky, equate his "natural" muscularity with the naturalness of the landscape. He physically dominates Karen by standing or lying over her and at one point displays his will to control by wrestling Karen to her knees when she tries to leave. Furthermore, phallic lack is dispelled by Lancaster/Warden's ability to bring out Karen's sexuality—"nobody ever kissed me the way you do," she murmurs—and later by his aggressive interrogation of her past sexual "transgressions" at Fort Bliss.[8] However, implicating the hegemonic male in the homoerotic by staging Warden/Lancaster as the specular object of desire—for *both* men and women—momentarily jeopardizes his masculinity. As a result, the film carefully manages these homoerotic elements in the beach scene through disavowal. (This brief cinematic disturbance of traditional gender binaries on which the dominant fictional ideal of manhood depends becomes inescapable in the novel, as the latter half of this chapter will show).

Notably, while Lancaster's beach image oscillates between the passive object of spectatorial looking and the active subject, elsewhere he is repeatedly hostile to the gaze, bellowing contentiously at other men, "Whatta' you lookin' at?" Warden's reassertion of spectatorial power brings to the fore the issue of who can do the "lookin" and what can be looked at within this patriarchal order. Warden (and Lancaster) invites a gaze that attempts to reproduce what Laura Mulvey calls "the ego ideal of the identification process" for the male viewer (20). Staging public scenes of empowerment and producing a variety of oppositional or alternative representations of masculinity—to be looked at—is also a requisite activity of hegemonic masculinity, because it exists only in relation to other subordinate males. In the film, the Treatment is the most prominently featured display of power and authority, which is played out on Prewitt's body through physical exhaustion, injury, or beatings. His subjected body, then, functions to authorize another's right to control it. While I am not suggesting Warden is responsible for the Treatment, he is rewarded for his compliance with the system that institutes it. More to the point, Warden's seemingly indestructible masculinity, signified by an unbruised, unbattered body, is the result of a system of rewards and punishments that, at times, becomes manifest in public spectacles of power.

Biskind's conception of the film as an affirmation of corporate interests over arch-individualism, symbolized by the man who negotiates the system rather than fights it, appears to have merit. Furthermore, it is tempting to read the novel in a similar manner. Undeniably, in the novel, Jones's Warden and his obstinate rear-rank soldier Prewitt encounter one another in "cold inherent antagonism" (63). To Warden, Prewitt is a "goddam hardhead" who "fouls up [his] outfit" by refusing to box. Prewitt, in turn, disregards Warden's zeal for efficiency and order, asserting, "I know where I stand" (65). Warden, at first, supports the Treatment, declaring "[Prewitt's] gotta be taught a lesson." When Prewitt is twice marched twenty miles to Kolekole Pass for sassing Galovitch, Warden "did not feel sorry for him," since "he asked for everything he got" (329). Prewitt just cannot "play it smart" or relinquish his lonely crusade for individualism. However, Biskind's binarized conception of Warden and Prewitt is finally an inadequate explanation not only of the novel but of the film as well, for Prewitt functions not simply as a marker of negative difference. He is, it seems, more than just "a wormy apple" to be gotten rid of.

However much Warden's masculinity in the novel is authorized by Prewitt's and other subordinate masculinities, Prewitt presents a competing site of masculinity, which undermines the kind of homosociality in the company that creates and sustains hierarchy. If Warden's relation to the men in G Company is hegemonic, which effectively maintains social distance and differences between males, Prewitt's relation to the troop is nonauthoritative and nonhierarchical. While he is a pivotal figure around which the antagonisms between boxers and straight duty soldiers circulate, he is, particularly in the novel, a central figure within a small, cohesive group of enlisted men who together play craps, cards, and blues guitar and exchange comic books and life stories. Among his buddies he is admired and respected for his all-around abilities as a soldier, bugler, fighter, athlete, poolshooter, and grassroots philosopher. He invokes a populist appeal as "champion of all underdogs," but it is his moral resolve against boxing that earns him admiration and, eventually, even the respect of Warden and the boxers. Prewitt achieves an almost mythic status by facing the Treatment with passive aggression—the safest form of resistance to his punishment. After Prewitt's grueling march to Kolekole Pass, Maggio congratulates him: "Man, I'm proud of you. I ony [sic] wish I had of been there to see it" (329).

In both novel and film, even Warden eventually softens toward Prewitt. While disparaging him as a "bolshevik," Warden also gets Prewitt weekend passes or "forgets" to write him up in the Punishment Book. When Prewitt goes AWOL after killing Fatso, Warden carries him "present" on the Company Roster for two weeks. While these gestures of clemency signify Warden's authority over Prewitt, just as later on his final act of mourning over Prewitt's dead body signals Warden's discursive jurisdiction over his memory, they also demonstrate Warden's increasing respect and attraction for his alternative style of masculinity.

Postwar readers and filmgoers alike, caught up in the other-directedness of America's new corporate culture, may have been as attracted on some level to Prewitt's lone-wolf approach as Warden found himself becoming. While a CEO might not favor "a wormy apple" like Prewitt in his organization, his refusal to conform fully to group expectations had a strong nostalgic resonance with one of America's mythic forms of white male heroism—what Louis Lyndon in a mid-fifties issue of *Woman's Home Companion* called "the reckless outlaw and rebel, the lonely individualist, the man who won't conform, who won't go along with the crowd" (42). Addressing the suburban housewife, Lyndon asserted that her husband's gray flannel suit had "become a straight jacket" and that this modern-day "captive male" was no longer able to find a suitable outlet for his "inborn attraction to violence and obscenity and polygamy ... and [his] inborn need to be different from others and rebel against them." "To be a truly masculine independent individual is the deepest of psychic needs," Lyndon maintained. However, for the company man, there is "precious little chance" of ever achieving the "heroic" status of radical individualist or nonconformist (107). Identification with such fantasy figures like Prewitt may have provided psychic recourse for the fifties male, who felt his "heroic" potential was constantly frustrated by both boss and wife. If the company man could not bring himself to "slam the door on the boss," as Lyndon put it (43), he may have experienced cathartic pleasure from Prewitt's rebuttal to Holmes after he demands that Prewitt apologize to Galovitch: "I have never liked being pissed on, Sir ... if apologies are in order, I think they are owed to me" (320–21).

In addition to presenting an appealing, if not nostalgic, alternative to hegemonic masculinity, Prewitt also registers a protest against the brutality and violence that are not part of hegemonic masculinity by definition, as Connell explains, yet are not incompatible with it either (*Gender* 184). As the novel tells us, Prewitt's strategy for enduring the Treatment is "to hate and be a good soldier." While hating shields him emotionally from his tormentors, being a good soldier is a performance that presents itself as institutional support but contains within it a critique of both its ritualistic abuse and the institution itself. Although Prewitt chooses to be a good soldier, after he is sentenced unjustly to the Stockade (an event omitted from the film), he joins a small "elite" group of recalcitrant prisoners in Barrack Two—"the toughest of the tough"—who are unwilling to conform to group life (read mainstream society). In their effort to resist authority, this close-knit clan was as supportive and cooperative toward one another as they were closed and resistant toward the sadistic guards. If being a "good" soldier could effect some limited resistance, being a "bad" one could be put to use against the system as well. By appropriating the normative discourses constructing them as "criminal" and "unredeemable losers," the prisoners could then subvert their institutional meanings by making "losing" and "loser" signify pride and status: "They were the cream. They wore their barrack number like a medal of honor and guarded its bestowal as jealously as any Masonic Lodge ... ever guarded theirs. They could not fight back and win, so they were very strict with their great pride in losing, and they were so meticulous that when they did take a man in it was an occasion and they went all the way" (648). Prewitt lives by an alternative code among society's "misfits," but being taken in by the men in Number Two does not involve a violent rite of passage, as one might expect; instead, they greet a new arrival by making his bed and quietly stopping by his bunk to say hello.

Biskind's view of the film also neglects to account for how the star text of the immensely popular Montgomery Clift inflects his character. Clift, by presenting an entirely new style of masculinity in postwar films, rivaled, perhaps even surpassed, the appeal of Burt Lancaster for certain viewers. Sexy, photogenic, handsome, Clift was at a high point in his acting career in 1953, sought after to the point where he was able to exercise considerable control over studio deals and to insist on final decisions about scripts, a power that few actors and actresses possessed at that time. Along with Marlon Brando and James Dean, Clift represented a new kind of Hollywood hero in the early fifties—the youthful rebel male. Like Private Prewitt, Clift's rebellion was not associated directly with political or social causes, but was articulated in personal terms of nonconformity and a loathing for pretension and hypocrisy. Style of dress, personal habits, and lifestyle constituted the visible signs of the rebel. The "bum uniform"—a torn tee-shirt, blue jeans, and an otherwise grubby appearance—became the trademarks of this new young screen hero, signaling disregard for a middle-class preoccupation with sartorial codes of "success" and social propriety. Accordingly, in 1949, the *Saturday Evening Post* labeled Clift "the sloppiest dresser in America" (Frank 108). Despite his upper-class upbringing and classical education, Clift's "bum" look reinforced the media's portrait of him as just an ordinary guy with an independent streak and an intense sincerity about his acting. This "ordinariness," intensity, and stubborn insistence on retaining his professional integrity produced a close fit to *Eternity*'s Prewitt, making star persona and film character mutually reinforcing representations. Seeing this compatibility, James Jones actively lobbied for Clift to be cast as Prewitt in place of Columbia's first choice, John Derek (LaGuardia 103).

Not a product of the Hollywood studio system or its acting coaches, Clift got his start on Broadway in the 1940s and was a rising star of the New York theater before heading to Hollywood. This, and his association with the Actors Studio and Method acting, distinguished him as a "serious actor" when he arrived at MGM in 1946 to film *Red River* (1948)—"serious," of course, being opposed to "movie star," which, in New York theater circles, meant glamour, popularity, and selling out one's talent in order to remain gainfully employed. Seeing acting as an art form, which required deep perceptiveness and a commitment on the actor's part to give the most "authentic" performance possible, Clift brought an unusual intensity to his acting. Because the Method actor supposedly drew from personal experiences as the raw material for performances and sought the "truth" of the role from within, this style of acting signaled the interiority of both actor and character. Method techniques include the use of hesitations and meaningful pauses in speech, silences, intense stares or avoiding eye contact, low-key gestures, awkward but subtle movements, and the improvisational use of objects that do not directly follow the narrative. These physical behaviors supposedly signal an inner psychological state or the interiority of both actor and character, which often suggested confusion, stress, or neurosis. Clift's use of the Method, along with his earnestness and dedication, paid off for him in film reviews and fan magazines, which invariably applauded his performances as intense and, ironically, as "natural."

Clift's unwillingness to embrace the "successful" Hollywood lifestyle was a significant component of his unconventional behavior and his public appeal. Despite his financial windfall after his first released film, *The Search* (1948), he rejected the fancy cars and expensive homes and, whenever possible, avoided the lavish parties and publicity circuit that went along with being a movie star. "The one thing I don't like is living in Hollywood," he claimed. "There's such an aura of adulation that you lose all contact with ordinary people. You even forget they exist" (Frank 108). Having to rely on film studios for the opportunity to do what he was most passionate about—saying something important through acting—and, at the same time, condemning Hollywood's phony, tinsel town atmosphere clearly placed Clift in a contradictory position. However, his aloofness from the studios and his attempts to control his public image and protect his privacy merely served to heighten his appeal and demand. Ironically, studio publicists were quick to exploit Clift's contempt for Hollywood by forging his image out of his nonconformist attitude and behavior, then promoting him as one of the new rebels of the big screen (LaGuardia 71).

An integral part of Clift's new look and appeal was his strikingly different presentation of masculinity both on screen and off. He projected an extreme sensitivity, inner turmoil, and introspection, all signifiers of his rebel image. In his film roles, Clift injected a kind of psychological complexity into an array of somewhat unconventional characters, which invariably found themselves in adverse circumstances or alienated from mainstream society. While this new male hero did at times display characteristics associated with traditional representations of masculinity—decisiveness, self-assuredness, and individualism, Clift frequently exhibited vulnerability, alienation, and even a kind of melancholy or pensiveness. His style came to influence both Hollywood moviemakers and a whole generation of young actors who followed Clift, as evidenced by the increasing presentation of inner angst and uncertainty as acceptable male behaviors for film characters.

In effect, Clift's image added complexity to male identity by mixing it with feminine characteristics, thus radically altering the look of maleness emanating from the movie screen in the late 1940s and early 1950s, which before that time had been represented by tough guy heroes, such as Humphrey Bogart, John Wayne, and Gary Cooper. In *Red River*, for instance, Clift's Matthew Garth is able to stand up to his reckless, aggressive, stepfather, Tom Dunson (John Wayne) because he is both tough and morally resolute; however, he is sensitive and flexible, as well, which allows him to empathize with the anxiety and fatigue experienced by the other cowboys on the cattle drive. Clift/Garth offered audiences a way of thinking about "manliness" as neither aggressive nor domineering, yet still "masculine." Clift's next role as an Army engineer in *The Search* (released in 1948, before *Red River*) again combined masculine and feminine cues. In caring for a young German orphan who is trying to locate his mother during the chaotic aftermath of World War II, Clift projected a tender, maternal side right along with the "ordinariness" associated with young GIs stationed overseas. Clift's portrayal of Prewitt in *From Here to Eternity* presented another sensitive, anguished, vulnerable male, who also displayed qualities associated with orthodox masculinity. Indeed, his most memorable moments in *Eternity* come at the point in which he cradles the dying Maggio in his arms and afterward plays taps for him, tears streaming down his face. However, Clift's Prewitt is "fully masculine," thick skinned, and tough in the face of adversity without displaying overt physical aggressiveness. Clift had the ability to express toughness and resilience without using physical force in *Eternity*. He used his eyes, minute gestures, and facial muscles to communicate an intensity and conviction necessary to withstand the brutality of G Company's boxers.

It is difficult to pinpoint precisely how Clift appealed so strongly to such a broad range of filmgoers. In light of the cultural transformation occurring in postwar America, which privileged a new ethos of other-directedness and group conformity, Clift's brand of masculinity appeared to contain contradictory qualities. His role in *Red River*, for instance, was in some ways in keeping with the need to read social cues and be willing to cooperate rather than compete with others. The Clift persona seemed to reflect the decade's movement away from an emphasis on hyper-individualism and hard-nosed entrepreneurship toward a more relaxed, "softer" masculinity. However, his "rebellion" against middle-class values no doubt appealed to those who either chaffed against them or who saw themselves situated at the margins of dominant discourses, which promoted male breadwinning and monogamous marriage as acceptable roles for men. Richard Lippe sees the association of Clift with marginal screen figures as expressing a complex, "positive masculinity," which significantly excluded aggressive, dominating forms of behavior (37). One could argue, though, that in *From Here to Eternity* Clift/Prewitt seems to invite punishment, masochistically, and is killed pointlessly by fellow soldiers, which, Lippe claims, are two things that appear to disqualify him as a hero. However, Clift's tremendous appeal to both men and women suggests filmgoers were indeed responding to alternative configurations of gender, which contested the film narrative's affirmation of traditional masculinity in the form of Lancaster's Warden.

Representing the Ethnic Other

In the opening scene of Hollywood's *Eternity*, Frank Sinatra squats over a pail, combing the ground for cigarette butts. This first glimpse of Angelo Maggio reveals his status within the troop, coded nonverbally by his rank (a cue to social class), his performance of a menial task, and his ethnicity, signified by Sinatra's "Italianness." Following this scene, Maggio's snide remarks to Prewitt about G Company are juxtaposed to the brisk, imposing figure of Warden barking orders to his clerk. Maggio functions symbolically here to reinforce Warden's Anglo-American, middle-class hegemony. For filmgoers, Maggio also condenses the novel's entire array of ethnic diversity, which gets muted or voided altogether in the film. His figure, then, is fairly representative of how the novel's variety of ethnic "others" both underwrites and contests hegemonic constructions.[9]

In both novel and film, Maggio authorizes Warden's hegemonic status and acts as a kind of double to Prewitt: "another fuck-up like me," he proclaims (51). Both lower class, the two buddies share a keen sense of alienation from American society and bitterness over military corruption. The two are inevitably paired together in both punishment and fun, which consists of drinking, gambling, and "whoring" at the New Congress Club. However, this doubling also emphasizes their differences: Both Maggio and Prewitt authorize Warden's masculinity, but Maggio underwrites Prewitt's, as well, providing an ethnic counterpoint to his Anglo heritage. Maggio is constructed through a series of signs that connote his "Italianness"— diminutive but tough, hotheaded, gregarious, streetwise, Brooklyn-born, the son of immigrants, loyal to family. Impulsive and emotional, he offsets Prewitt's self-control and introspection and Warden's cool nerve, differences that become directly linked with gender. In the novel, for example, when Maggio engages Corporal Bloom in a potentially deadly fight, Warden—the "real" man—intervenes, disgustedly calling them "a couple of unweaned punks," "baby Maggio," and "little boy" Bloom (235). Because the film eliminates Bloom's character, this fight takes place between Maggio and Fatso; again Warden dramatically breaks it up, delivering the emasculating put down: "I'd trade the both of you for a good pair of Campfire Girls." The ethnic figure here is yet a boy, the feminized "other" of the masculine "self." Moreover, Maggio's mercurial temperament in the film seems to justify Warden's authority over him. Rather than drawing attention to Maggio's political and economic disenfran-chisement, then, the film focuses on his personal shortcomings.

Frank Sinatra also reinforced the association of Maggio with ethnicity. Although Sinatra's star image was organized around elements that often related inconsistently to one another, one of the key aspects of this image was his own Italian background, which was often exaggerated or falsified by his publicity agents. Although his mother was a shrewd businesswoman and local politician who maintained a comfortable income for the Sinatras (including his father), Sinatra was invariably reported to be a lower-class, runty kid from Hoboken, New Jersey, who had to learn at an early age to defend himself against street corner toughs. Young Frank's early successes were represented as a second-generation rags-to-riches story, but this sanguine image of America as a melting pot was somewhat tarnished later on by Sinatra's presumed association with the Mafia. In the aftermath of a lawsuit brought by Hearst columnist Lee Mortimer, who had been on the receiving end of Sinatra's fist after calling him a "Dago son of a bitch," Mortimer vindictively published an article in 1951 for *The American Mercury* claiming that "gangster wire-pulling behind the scenes" was partly responsible for Sinatra's rise to popularity and that the singer had been "adopted by underworld big shots for the specific purpose of making his sponsors seem respectable, shots for the specific purpose of making his sponsors seem respectable, thereby furthering their business enterprise." As proof, Mortimer cited instances in which Sinatra had been photographed with mobsters in Havana, one being the infamous "Lucky" Luciano (31–32).[10] The link between "Italian" and "Mafia" raised fears that Italians harbored divided loyalties between America and its "legitimate" government and a secret underworld that operated on a massive, parasitic level. The possibility exists, then, that this illicit, even sinister, aspect of Sinatra's star persona heightened the audience's sense of Maggio as "foreign," or not fully American.

Maggio's physical appearance contributed to his otherness, as well. In the novel, Prewitt's body is never scrutinized with the same intensity as Maggio's. Given only the briefest description of Prewitt's appearance, readers learn that he is a "very neat and deceptively slim young man"; he walks "catlike on the balls of his feet the way a fighter treads, hat tilted, clean, immaculate, decisive, the picture of a soldier" (24). This image of restraint and military bearing contrasts with the following catalogue of phrases sprinkled throughout the novel describing Maggio: "a gnarled disillusioned gnome cheated of his Valhalla" (53), "his gnomelike body" (61), "the little Wop" (92), "the dwarfed, narrow shouldered, warp-boned heir to a race of city dwellers" (174) "tiny narrow-chested bonyshouldered undernourished frame of him with the thin legs and pipestem arms" (625). Such emphasis on Maggio's body functions to define the limits of male physicality. If traditional masculinity requires the illusion of impenetrability and inviolability of the male body, Maggio's fragile, pathetic physique seems to predestine him to punishment and abuse by more powerful males. Prewitt, of course, also is subject to beatings, but he endures them stoically without experiencing the psychic dissolution and bitterness that affect Maggio.

Sinatra's star image is also consistent with Jones's imaginative rendering of Maggio as physically and psychologically vulnerable. In his nightclub and concert appearances, which aging bobby-soxers would have recalled, Sinatra had perfected a particular performance of masculinity that included, among other things, a certain defenselessness and exposure of inner feeling, signified by his "quivering smile." A British reviewer writing for *Time* pegged this quality after seeing Sinatra open in his first London concert in 1950: "Here is an artist, who hailing from the most amiably, rowdy and self-confident community the world has ever known, has elected to express the timidity that can never be wholly driven out of the boastful heart. To a people whose ideal of manhood is husky, full-blooded, and self-reliant, he has chosen to suggest that, under the ... crashing self-assertion, man is still only a child, frightened and whimpering in the dark" ("Whimpering" 47). Sinatra's screen tests for the film role also managed to convince skeptics that he was indeed the luckless Maggio, despite that his career was languishing to the point where he was considered unmarketable. Columbia chief Harry Cohn's first choice for the part had been Eli Wallach, but after viewing both his and Sinatra's screen tests, Cohn's wife Joan said of Wallach: "he's not skinny and he's not pathetic, and he's not Italian. Frank is just Maggio to me" (Kelley 211). Screenwriter Daniel Taradash agreed: "Frank ... looked so thin and woeful and so pitifully small that the audience would cry when they saw this poor little guy get beaten up" (Kelley 211-12).[11] These statements appear to confirm that one of the ideological aims of the film was to produce contrast and conflict between the "undemocratic" and "democratic" males. Director Fred Zinnemann captured Maggio/Sinatra's "pipestem arms" and "undernourished frame" in the opening scene by shooting him in a sleeveless undershirt, which both displayed his scrawny physique and suggested his contempt for the uniform, a foreshadowing of his rebelliousness. Clearly, the emphasis, then, that both Jones and Hollywood placed on Maggio's body contrasts with both Prewitt's "deceptively slim" durability and Warden's muscular, rock-hard body.

However, within this representation of the ethnic Other as less-than-fully-masculine lies a critique of hegemony's marginalizing practices and the aggression, dominance, and control exercised against subordinate males. In Jones's novel, despite Maggio's fierce pride in his ethnic heritage, he knows to most Americans he is really just a "Wop," destined to be a shipping clerk in Gimbel's basement or a straight duty private. The promise of advancement is specious: "You punch a timeclock all your life and kiss the boss's ass for a job you never liked," he gripes. "Gimme a right to work at a job I hate?" (660–61). Social equality is just as illusory for Maggio: "They shouldn't teach their immigrants' kids all about democracy unless they mean to let them have a little of it, it ony (sic) makes for trouble. Me and the United States is disassociating our alliance as of right now, until the United States can find time to read its own textbooks a little" (661). In the novel, his repeated vow to get out of the Army and go to Mexico to be a cowboy is an ironic twist on the American Dream, which invokes the mythic ideals of male freedom and autonomy. Realizing this dream is no longer possible in America, he eventually makes good on his promise, feigning madness to get a Section 8. The novel uses Maggio as an important register of protest, therefore allowing a brief, but radical, challenge to the systemic and institutional basis of social "reality."

The film places a slightly different emphasis on Maggio's protest against social injustice. Hollywood uses his character more or less as a helpless pawn in the conflict between the "brutes and tyrants" and "democratic" masculinities. In effect, the film engages with the issue of ethnic and class oppression by projecting this problem onto a few "bad" males, one of whom finally beats Maggio to death. Maggio's intoxicated "can't a man get drunk, can't a man do nothin'" speech stands as the single strongest expression of his frustration and rage against the harsh realities of American capitalism and its exclusionary Anglo culture. America is, in fact, a prison for Maggio, a place where lower-class, ethnic males have limited chances of escaping poverty and discrimination. Maggio can only move from "cell" to "cell." Fittingly, as he is marched into Stockade in the film, Maggio declares, "Gimbel's basement couldn't keep me and neither can this place."

However, before dismissing too quickly the film's inability to register the same degree of social protest as the novel, I refer again to Sinatra's star persona and his own personal politics, which may have served to offset the film's containment of Maggio's protest. Sinatra's stance against racism was well publicized, and he had made a number of public appearances on the subject. Even his damaging altercation with Lee Mortimer, which thanks to Hearst newspapers threatened to discredit Sinatra further by implicating him in both left-wing and Mob activities and rehashing his 4-F status during the war, produced an alternative reading. Another paper claimed that Sinatra's aggressive response to being called a "dago" "must have warmed the hearts of millions" by purportedly striking a blow against "race prejudice" ("Words and Music" 44). Perhaps the social protest associated with Jones's Maggio, which Hollywood omitted from the screenplay, may have been reintroduced by filmgoers through this particular knowledge of the star.

In some respects, the novel also truncates Maggio's protest. After his Section 8, three-fourths into the narrative, he is never heard from again. In this case, the novel also seems to silence his limited protest, making the Other disappear from the text without a trace. Maggio is unable to love either the U.S.A. or the Army, which contrasts with

Prewitt's ability to reconcile a wide range of institutional incongruities and justify this reconciliation by believing that the thing you love does not have to love you back. Unlike Prewitt, Maggio is unable to participate in troop life, but his absence does not entirely cancel his presence as voice of the oppressed. Indeed, as Prewitt says, "he left a very large hole" (707).

"Queer Hunting": Masculinity and Sexuality

The physical violence and economic exclusion that Maggio experiences, which insures the ascendancy of more powerful males over him and others like him, is not incompatible with the production of hegemonic masculinity. However, hegemony secures itself most effectively, as Antonio Gramsci maintains, when it contains differences through persuasion and "voluntary consent" and when it promotes masculine values and attitudes as beneficial to all men. In G Company the practice of male bonding, which involves both the exclusion and the sexual exchange of women, is the primary mechanism through which the troop is homogenized and unified. According to Eve Sedgwick, the sexual exchange of women between men symbolically serves "the primary purpose of cementing the bonds of men with men" on the basis of their sexual power over women and their mutual investment in patriarchy (26). The prostitutes at the New Congress Hotel function as the conduit through which male potency is affirmed in the rank and file, as does Karen Holmes for the noncommissioned officers. It is rumored that Karen had "laid half the [enlisted men] on the Post at Fort Bliss" before Holmes's transfer to Schofield. However, rather than creating disrespect for Holmes, who is unaware of this rumor, having had sex with Karen seems to solidify his subordinates' loyalties to him, since many of Holmes's men followed him to Schofield, gaining their sergeant's stripes in the process.

Excluding women from "masculine" activities also homogenizes G Company. In the novel, rigorous, exhausting training maneuvers display male power and virility and, at the same time, unite the soldiers in collective suffering. This kind of unity forged through pain and suffering resembles what Klaus Theweleit in *Male Fantasies* describes as a part of the process that molded young men into Germany's *Freikorps*, the ruthless core of Hitler's storm troopers.[12] Subjecting the body to punishment and pain gradually becomes translated into a form of pleasure, which disguises physical vulnerability so that "what is nice is what hurt." Experiencing bodily pain and, more importantly, accepting it as "experiences of satisfaction" not only produced a totality formation—the troop as a totality machine, but also the only acceptable means of communicating affection within the *Freikorps* (Theweleit 150). Such is the case with Jones's fictional soldiers as well.

In addition, the Japanese attack on Pearl Harbor generates an *esprit de corps* and nationalistic fervor, ostensibly reconciling male differences and antagonisms within the troop. Significantly, the onset of the war brings closure to the romance plots, thus resecuring Warden's and Prewitt's full commitment to this exclusive world of males. After languishing at Lorene's apartment, Prewitt, AWOL for weeks, renounces her in order to rejoin his company after the attack, realizing "one good thing about the Army. It kept you separated from your women so much they never had the chance to get sick of you. And vice versa" (867). In the film, viewers heard in more succinct terms why Warden does not marry Karen; in their parting scene she tells him flatly, "I know why. You're already married ... to the Army." Brandon French points out that for postwar males, *From Here to Eternity* supplied "a perfect fantasy retreat to the good old days of World War II, a celebration of the event which provided them with an honorable escape from domestic life." G Company is "where men are men and the women have all been evacuated" (59).

From Here to Eternity attempts to assure us that this male bonding is premised on a fundamental belief in masculinity as both "hard" and heterosexual. Particularly in the novel, however, this belief is shown to be illusory, since the homoerotic leaks, which such all-male communities must work so hard to stop up, continually disrupt and threaten the "purity" of its male bonds. As in any rigidly heterosexual society, the men of G Company constantly monitor one another to prevent displays of behavior unbefitting a "real" man. Barracks talk, in which homosexuality is associated with the nonmasculine, is the most common form of policing. The Treatment constitutes another site of surveillance and punishment because Prewitt's refusal to box could be interpreted as unmanly, even cowardly, behavior. Moreover, it is likely that Prewitt gets the Treatment because he has transferred from the Bugle Corps, a "queer troop," thus tainting G Company with his presence. (It is commonly known that Chief Bugler Houston promoted his "young angelina" to first bugler over Prewitt.)

Furthermore, boxing itself constitutes an ambiguous sign of masculinity. Considered the "most manly sport" in G Company (24), it is a spectacle of phallic power and an outward show of mastery over pain and vulnerability. However, while boxing purportedly confers the status of "real manhood," it also functions as a powerful symbol of male desire; that is, the spectacle of mostly naked, muscular bodies contains an element of eroticism, generated through audience identification and voyeurism.

Significantly, Jones's Prewitt voices the strongest condemnation of homosexuality in the novel. When Maggio tries to convince Prewitt to go "queer chasing" with him, he says, "I never did like queers. Every time I get around them I want to punch them in the head" (413). "They make me feel ashamed of something ... I don't know what of" (416). "Queer chasing" is a frequent practice among the enlisted men, who, invariably broke at the end of payday, try to con gay civilians into buying them drinks and dinner. As Maggio puts it, we're all "queer fodder" on payday. Although many of the soldiers engage in cruising, the novel stresses the distinction between the homosexuals they cruise and their own sexual orientation. Maggio assures Prewitt that it is a con game: "You got to play them like fish, see?" (415). This way, straight soldiers could distance themselves from gay males and continue to believe their own sexuality was uncompromised, as long as free drinks and dinner were part of the exchange. The business transaction reassures the straight males that they are in charge of the deal. According to Allan Bérubé in *Coming Out Under Fire*, which documents gay and lesbian participation in World War II, it was not uncommon for heterosexual males to initiate and engage in sex with other men, yet convince themselves that they were not queer. "Heterosexual recruits," claims Bérubé, "who had had the most sexual experience with women or who felt strong sex drives could initiate sex without being afraid that they were queer, especially if their partner was gay and played the 'passive' sexual role" (41). Playing the dominant role, then, allowed the straight partner to "retain [his] self-image as masculine and heterosexual" (42).

The very acts of surveillance between and within the soldiers, which work to maintain rigid boundaries of gender and sexuality, alert us to the fact that these boundaries are themselves not natural, but arbitrary, and, because they are arbitrary, these boundaries are not inviolable, but penetrable and fluid. Despite Maggio's insistence that the soldiers are not compromised by cruising the gay section of

Honolulu, this activity reveals a disparity between the conceptions of "masculinity" and "real men" in the troop. When Maggio tells Prewitt that "half the Compny hang out there at the Tavern [a well-known gay bar]" (416), we are inclined to question the overt contempt for homosexuality in the troop. When the naive, impressionable Friday Clarke, the Forest Gump of the outfit, is urged to cruise with two other soldiers, Prewitt paternalistically intervenes: "Listen, dont you let Bloom talk *you* into goin' queer huntin with him, hear me?" Friday, who worships Prewitt, replies, "Not me ... I dont like queers. They make me feel funny, they make me scared" (172). Apparently he is not scared enough, for later on Friday is hauled downtown along with most of G Company in a civilian-initiated dragnet of Honolulu's gay quarter. Overt contempt seems to mask unspoken desire.

As one of the authoritative voices in the narrative, Prewitt's aversion to gay males carries considerable ideological weight, yet his rejection of this form of masculinity reminds us, in Vito Russo's words, "that men who despise homosexuals ... find that their truest and most noble feelings are for each other" (70). Indeed the novel valorizes the buddy relationship, which suggests that the primary mode of desire is homoerotic. Bérubé reports that buddy relationships in the armed services often "easily slipped into romantic and even sexual intimacies between men that they themselves often did not perceive to be 'queer' .... Even heterosexual men could find themselves abandoning the norms of civilian life as they had to rely on each other for companionship and affection" (188–89). *From Here to Eternity* deflects attention from any romantic or sexual elements of its buddy relationships primarily through the Warden/Karen and the Prewitt/Lorene romance stories. Visiting prostitutes also camouflages bonds of affection between men. However, it is telling that when Prewitt, Maggio, and Stark go to the New Congress Hotel, it is not simply to have sex, but to participate in a ritual male outing, wherein the real pleasure is each other's company. Engaging in sex with the prostitutes is essential on these outings, for, in Susan Gubar's words, "as the imagined object of male desire and as the body that links men to men—they ratify men as male" (254). Just the same, though, there is a curious absence of heterosexual eroticism in Jones's novel despite its insistent heterosexual economy, perhaps, as Brandon French con-cludes, because a "seemingly ineradicable perception of women as the Enemy is a mainstay of Jones's plot" (57).

In keeping with the impulse to keep male bonds fully "masculine," the soldiers must disavow tenderness and affection: They banter, posture, quarrel, and tease, but rarely can they express serious emotions without embarrassment. Prewitt's soulful playing of taps one night draws the men to the porches to listen. They feel a "sudden choking kinship" to one another, but at its end, "they filed back inside with lowered eyes, suddenly ashamed of their own emotion, and of seeing a man's naked soul" (251). Nighttime darkness protects them from the emotion that threatens to erupt within and among them. However, while such public displays are not sanctioned in G Company, the "feminine" is never entirely eradicated; it simply emerges in more "legitimate," nonthreatening forms. For example, Friday Clark, who is still caught up in boyhood culture of comic books and ice-cream cones, becomes a kind of Company mascot. Because he is callow, gentle, shy, and slow-witted—attributes not associated with traditional masculinity, an unspoken agreement exists between the men that picking on Friday is off limits. In a milieu where toughness and street smarts are necessary for everyday survival, Friday internalizes the feminine for the rest of the troop, thus providing a site on which affection is safely projected and a conduit through which the men's own emotional attachments to one another can be implicitly affirmed.

Even the most significant relationship in the novel, that of the central characters Prewitt and Warden is implicated in the homoerotic. The two begin as rivals, but gradually their feelings soften, and their snarls and taunts turn to declarations of love and admiration. This is not surprising if we recall Sedgwick's claim in her work on homosocial desire and erotic triangles that the bonds of rivalry between males also are "structured by the same play of emulation and identification" (23). While the relationship between Warden and Prewitt is not triangulated by a woman in the way that Sedgwick claims strengthens male bonding, at one significant juncture Lorene does mediate their relationship. When Prewitt is in the Stockade, Warden visits him, and, before leaving, he slaps Prewitt on the back, "the first frank gesture of friendship [Prewitt] had ever seen The Warden make toward him or toward anybody else" (580). For Prewitt, this gesture was "worth three months in any Black Hole in any Stockade" (580). Prewitt then asks Warden to let Lorene know he is in prison; Warden agrees, but mischievously suggests that he and Lorene might end up going out. Prewitt admits his impotence here, replying, "All right, then go down to the New Congress and tell her and take her to bed while you're there" (581), but, at the same time, he has just acknowledged the great value of Warden's friendship.

Even before this Prewitt realizes, "there was a closeness between him and The Warden, an understanding, tacit, never spoken of, but closer and stronger than even what he felt for Maggio .... Maybe that was what it was about The Warden: honor; yet Maggio had honor, too, and was with him more often and had done more for him, than Warden, yet there was not as warm a closeness, not as great a love" (316). The two men have a chance to express this "love" one night on bivouac. In the middle of the night, in the middle of a road, they drunkenly embrace, declaring neither of them has ever had a better friend. Thinking they might be run over by a truck, they solemnly shake hands, "bravely choke back the unmanly tears of parting," and sitting "straight as soldiers" wait to die (536). While the comedic elements of this passage ostensibly safeguard this scene against any hint of mutual erotic desire, the comedy obscures the emotional resonance beneath their rivalry: the two declare each other to be the "best fuckin soljer in the Compny ... the *ony* fuckin soljer in the Compny" (537–38). This declaration not only resolves the tension between the two, but also marks the emotional climax of the key relationship in the novel.

Such a potent scene cannot take place, however, before Prewitt slays the sexual Grendel (the homosexual male) once and for all, so that buddies everywhere are free to love one another. Prewitt finally agrees to accompany Maggio to the Tavern to meet Hal, Maggio's "regular queer," and Tommy, Prewitt's prospective date. As the evening progresses, Prewitt acts increasingly hostile toward Hal and Tommy, whom Jones gives few redeeming qualities. Prewitt is intent on exposing them as "pseudo": outwardly respectable, but inwardly decadent; seemingly intellectual, but in reality shallow and selfish; appearing sensitive, but, in fact, predatory. He equates their "falseness" with un-Americanness and inwardly rages that they undeservedly live in middle-class comfort, while he, Prewitt, "a loyal American," has known nothing but poverty. Prewitt wants to make visible the masquerade of the deceitful, monstrous homosexual, thereby naturalizing his own form of masculinity, as well as justifying his heterosexism. If Prewitt can stabilize the arbitrary boundaries between the real/false and the heterosexual/homosexual, then he can continue to believe that his own masquerade of sex and gender is coherent and that the intimate relationships that he forms with Maggio, Warden, and other buddies can remain above scrutiny. As Richard Dyer notes, "if things are natural, they cannot really be questioned or scrutinized and so they fade from view" (*Matter* 134).

The boundaries between the "masculine" and "nonmasculine" are marked by slippages, however. For one, the homosexual tryst is the novel's most erotically charged scene, more so than the famous beach scene between Warden and Karen. Jones teases readers with the possibility that the four men eventually will engage in sex. Furthermore, Prewitt is symbolically linked with Hal and Tommy, his image ghosted by these forbidden "Others," so that we begin to suspect that Prewitt's virulent homophobia is an intense fear of his own unresolved homoerotic feelings. Both he and Tommy had been homosexually raped as boys, but when Tommy admits this, Prewitt goads Tommy into confessing that he really wanted it and therefore is evil. He appears to be displacing his own rage onto Tommy, as if it will somehow erase his vulnerability to such "unmanly" penetration. Prewitt also berates Hal for deserting Maggio, when, in a drunken confusion, he runs out into the streets in his underwear. Moments later, though, Prewitt deserts Maggio as well. Rather than risk being caught by MPs, Prewitt watches in hiding as they beat Maggio senseless. Moreover, while Prewitt claims to hate the corruption of homosexuals, he blackmails Hal out of forty dollars before leaving him. The opposition between the "grotesque" or "nasty" homosexual and the "clean" and "pure" masculinity that Prewitt imagines himself to project clearly breaks down here, and the demons he makes visible in the "other" become visible within himself.

Corporal Bloom: "No such things as Jews"

According to David Desser, the figure of the Jew often becomes "a kind of 'free floating ethnic signifier,' a signifier of Otherness across a wide spectrum of discourses"; historically, "Jewishness" often has been marked in Euro-American, Christian, patriarchal cultures in terms of gender, racial, and sexual difference (391). In the novel, the Jewish corporal, Isaac Bloom, consistently symbolizes Otherness as the repository of a range of differences that explicitly threaten the construction of ideal male identity. Because Bloom is also homosexual—hegemonic masculinity's most threatening Other—it is neither surprising that he is the most hated man in the troop nor that he commits suicide, for self-annihilation by a figure representing Otherness serves to reinforce the claim that hegemonic masculinity is normative and just. Because Bloom is abrasive and fails to bond with the other males, bonding being a sign of "good" masculinity, he is made to seem responsible for his own alienation and death, thus sparing the troop any responsibility for his misery. More precisely, the source of his personality "flaws" is Bloom's assertion of his "Jewishness." Sergeant Choate states that Bloom would be all right if he could "forgit for a while he was a Jew .... Hell they call me Indian, dont they? Well, I am a Indian, aint I? Well, Bloom's a Jew, aint he?" (553). The irony here is that Choate, a Choctaw Indian, implies that differences are devoid of cultural and political meanings. Being accepted as one of the guys, according to Choate, requires the simultaneous acknowledgment and denial of difference, or the creation of a kind of happy, psychic pluralism.

Significantly, Bloom takes his life soon after he receives a beating from Prewitt in an hour-long spectacle of violence witnessed by the entire Company. Prewitt insists Bloom's Jewishness had no bearing on the fight; instead a common condition of alienation was at the root of their mutual rage: "He had fought Bloom because he had had to fight somebody, or else bite himself and go mad, the same reason Bloom had fought him, two men on the edge and ridden raw, and they got in a fight for the amusement of all concerned, except themselves, and fought each other, and that was all" (557). Not only does Prewitt naturalize violence as a component of masculinity here, but his conception of Bloom as simply another misfit like himself obscures how Bloom's "Jewishness" signifies in the troop.

Bloom's suicide monologue presents a counterdiscourse to Choate's and Prewitt's insistence that his Jewishness does not matter. Bloom has internalized the troop's definition of "manhood," but he realizes the impossibility of inhabiting two mutually exclusive identities: the ethnic "Other" and the coherent, masculine "Self." In a moment of self-pity and self-castigation, he realizes that "he didnt have what it took" to become "accepted as a man" (636). His standard-bearer of manhood is, of course, the rear rank superman, Prewitt, whom Bloom sourly describes as "perfect." He admits the futility of having spent his Army career trying to "prove to them a Jew was no different than anybody else ... that there were no such things as Jews" (633–34). His strategy had been to align himself with the particular tropes of power signifying manliness: "When he had seen how fighters were respected in the Company, he had become a fighter. When he had seen how noncoms were looked up to and liked, he had become a noncom" (633).

By blowing his head off, Bloom attempts to recuperate his sense of manhood, but, even in this desperate final act of autonomy and self-definition, Bloom seems to confirm his subordinate, feminized position rather than verifying it. His suicide is sexually charged with phallic imagery: He looks at his Springfield rifle "affectionately" and "rubbed his hand pleasurably along the stock," noticing "the long sleek streamline, very slim but with the potent bulges all in the just exactly right places to give it that pugnaciously forward-looking eager look" (635). Significantly, the Springfield rifle becomes metaphorically linked with Prewitt in Bloom's final ruminations (635), compounding the implication that Bloom desires to be fucked and fucked over by Prewitt. In a brutal act of oral penetration, in which sex and death are commingled, Bloom places the barrel in his mouth. He then accuses himself of being "queer," therefore "monstrous." Recalling his relationship with Tommy (the same Tommy who dates Prewitt), he thinks: "You did it and you liked it, and that makes you a queer ... You don't deserve to live" (638). In a pathetic attempt at "recovering" his (heterosexual) masculinity, his final thought is half-plea, half-rallying cry: "Dont forget the steaks and whores and beer, boys ... dont ever forget that" (639).

His corpse and splattered brains become raw spectacle, which functions as another kind of brutal domination of the Other as the troop files past his mutilated body in disgust and anger. His suicide does not elicit sympathy, for, even in death, Bloom violates the men's sense of troop unity, as well as breaking the illusion that masculinity is coherent, whole, and unpenetrable. Bloom's final thoughts, however, reveal his desire to be accepted as a "man," an impossible struggle, given masculinity's exclusionary codes. Hegemonic masculinity holds out the promise of full enfranchisement to all males, but it cannot fulfill that promise since masculinity is mediated by race, ethnicity, and sexual preferences, however much these coordinates are obscured by the homogenizing rhetoric of "steaks and whores and beer."

It is finally the homosexual dimension of Bloom's Otherness that implicitly threatens to disrupt this all-male community's buddy relationships. His death underscores the extreme intolerance of hegemonic masculinity for homosexuality. Getting his sergeant's stripes and becoming a boxer—two rituals of induction into "real manhood"—fail to secure his acceptance, because, in his own words, "Isaac Nathan Bloom was a Jew, and ... everybody else knew it too" (635). Because "Jew" circulates with the mutually reinforcing categories of gender and sexuality, Bloom is unable to actualize "normative" masculinity. In this respect, Jones's novel reproduces a homosexual/ heterosexual dichotomy, which "acts as a central symbol in *all* rankings of masculinity" (Carrigan, Connell, and Lee 174).

However much the text stabilizes this dichotomy in Bloom's case, its arbitrariness is made apparent if we consider how Prewitt and Bloom's antagonism is implicated in Prewitt and Maggio's friendship. Recall Prewitt and Bloom's fight: Whereas Prewitt, one of the novel's privileged voices, assures us that the fight is motivated by the mutual desire for a "natural" outlet for their frustration, the hostility functions more symbolically. That is to say, Bloom and Maggio, as counterparts who share outsider status in the troop, are linked to Prewitt through their hero worship of him. The significant difference, however, is that Maggio's attraction to Prewitt, as well as his position as ethnic Other, authorize Prewitt's masculinity because the two men form a tight, homosocial bond, which, as Sedgwick reminds us, functions to repress homosexual desire. In contrast, Bloom's sexuality is less easily contained than ethnic difference; therefore, he constitutes an unconscious threat to Prewitt. Being buddies with Bloom would set up an ever-present potential for homosexual desire to leak into the homosocial bond. Bloom, then, becomes a scapegoat of Otherness to be publicly and violently punished by Prewitt. However, because Maggio's ethnicity does not disrupt the buddy relationship in the same way that Bloom's Jewishness (read homosexuality) does, Prewitt can safely love, defend, and mourn his friend. This symbolic component of Bloom's punishment suggests that the construction of male gender identity clearly depends upon sexual containment; more precisely, by conflating gender and sex, "masculine" is able to mean "heterosexual." Prewitt's violent, if subconscious, response to Bloom's homosexuality indicates that such conflation is not a natural phenomenon, but one produced socially, in this case, through surveillance and policing.

Hollywood's *Eternity* omitted Isaac Bloom's story and the novel's cruising scenes, therefore repressing homosexuality in a different way. Restricted by the Production Code from representing homosexual acts or characters on the screen, the film simply makes same-sex relations "unspeakable." However, despite "sanitizing" the narrative for general viewing, the film did not necessarily eradicate this "transgressive" content. Rather, casting Montgomery Clift as the narrative's pivotal character—who not only structures the antagonisms and homosociality between men but whose affections swing between Lorene, Maggio, and Warden—allows for the emergence of a homosexual subtext. It is possible that extratextual associations with Clift's image recast the male relationships within the film in a new light. As noted earlier, Clift's appeal to fans was based on his "softer," youthful masculinity, with its mixture of both male and female gender cues, and his new theatrical style of acting, marked by hesitations, subtle gestures, and intense stares. His star image and performance style produced strikingly different screen characters, men who were sensitive, psychologically tormented, and vulnerable. While this projection of interiority was in stark contrast to the thick-shelled, physical heroes, who, before the fifties, had dominated screen representations of masculinity, Clift's new "look" in the Hollywood male did not simply feminize him, thus situating his image in a binary relationship that reconstructed the period's gender dualism of masculine/feminine. This argument, put forth by Steven Cohan in *Masked Men*, points to the possibility that the Clift persona disrupted this opposition, instead producing an instability in the representation of gender and sexuality and, at the same time, introducing "the transgressive dimensions of 'the new look' of the era's young male stars" (262–63).

Cohan's investigation of Clift's screen performances and fan discourses generated by the extraordinary interest in Clift in the early fifties tells us that he often was referred to or represented as a "boy" (who was not a man), this becoming a marker of sexual difference—a position historically assigned to the female figure. However, Clift's "boyishness" did not function to guarantee the opposition of man and boy (or not man), thus subordinating boy to man. Instead, Cohan argues, the "boy" was not only celebrated both on- and off-screen, but constituted "an important reconfiguration of masculinity in the movies of this period because [this] 'new look' challenged the conflation of 'gender' and 'sexuality' underwriting the symbolic economy with which 'boys' were made legible as the opposites of 'men'" (*Masked* 203). In short, the "boy" signified an alternative brand of "maleness" as opposed to "femaleness," as was so apparent in Clift's performance opposite he-man John Wayne in *Red River*.[13] Moreover, because the visual treatment of Clift's "boyishness" was infused with erotic imagery, Clift was able to dramatize a category crisis in the traditional ground of gender representation, creating, at once, a positive, alternative masculinity, which appears to critique hegemonic norms, and an erotic figure of a sexy young body, which appealed to both men and women (*Masked* 203). Coupled with his performativity (his intensity and interiority or emotional excess) and his androgynous dimensions, Clift's "boyishness" implied a bisexuality or strong hints of sexual uncertainty, however muted or understated.

Because *From Here to Eternity*'s Private Prewitt exhibits many of the attributes associated with traditional masculinity—he is, after all, a tough, individualistic lone wolf, a reading of Clift/Prewitt as a "boy" in the way Cohan reads Clift in *Red River* or *A Place in the Sun* (1951) may appear to be less applicable to *Eternity*. However, in keeping with the "difference" Clift's star persona connoted, we can still see hints of the sexual uncertainty that Clift projected in Hollywood's *Eternity* as well, primarily in scenes where Clift/Prewitt openly performs in front of other males. Because the narrative is propelled forward by the Treatment, much of the action centers on men watching Clift/Prewitt being abused in public spectacles of power. At these moments he oscillates between signifying the object of contempt, which delineates the powerful and powerless, and the object of identification. Still in the role of the younger man—the "boy"—who defies an older authority figure, Clift/Prewitt seems to solicit desire from the other soldiers, who become increasingly invested in watching him—and we cannot forget that Clift was a beautiful actor to watch. His passive aggressive resistance to the Treatment fosters a desire in the spectators through a masochistic offering up of his diminutive, vulnerable body for physical abuse, which simultaneously situates his own desire as nonactive and nonaggressive. Further, his body, like that of the female in traditional representation, becomes marked by its penetrability and instability. Both his passivity and his performativity (he is always acting out some exhausting punishment, such as scrubbing floors, marching in circles, crawling in the mud, running laps) situate him as the subject of desire, generating a positive response from the others: to be like him and to like him. While the "hostesses" at the New Congress Club assure us with their overt ogling that Clift/Prewitt is desirable to women, the soldiers' fixation on his performance, intensity, and passivity alerts us to the transgressive resonance of the Clift persona.

According to Richard Lippe, Clift's star persona "involves a potential to find its greatest gratification through homosexual relations," and in *From Here to Eternity* his "deepest emotional commitments are to other men—the boxer friend he blinded accidentally, and Sinatra, who cultivates his friendship and unguardedly provides Clift with affection and support" (40). Although the film, like Jones's novel, features heterosexual romance, this seems more like a safeguard against any overt suggestion of homosexuality because both male protagonists ultimately demonstrate their love for the army and the company of men in preference to their female lovers. In short, the film affirms that there is "an insurmountable division between the sexes" (Lippe 40), allowing close male bonds—whether marked by mutual affection or antagonism—to sustain the emotional connections between human beings.

The film's scenes of parting and mourning—Maggio's death, Prewitt's death, and Prewitt's leaving Lorene—illustrate Lippe's point. When Clift/Prewitt walks out on a sobbing Donna Reed, he never looks back, his former obsession with her suddenly dissipated by the prospect of returning to G Company. He sheds no tears because these have already been spent playing Taps for his dead buddy, Maggio. The taps scene, perhaps the most powerfully emotional one of the film, is played by Clift with tears streaming down his cheeks and his eyes registering despair and pain. Maggio's death scene, which rivals the few tender moments between Warden and Karen, shows Clift cradling the dying Sinatra, who clings to Clift like a frail child. The scene is shot straight on, at medium-close range. Clift keeps his face just inches from Sinatra's, never moving his eyes from Sinatra's face. According to a Clift biographer, screenwriter Daniel Taradash labored over this scene in order to make it one of the most moving in the film. Taradash envisioned that "Maggio was to die in Prewitt's arms and wordlessly show that he loved Prew most of all; Milt Warden was to come to understand the difference between what is truly human and worthwhile and what is barbaric; and Prew was to be spotlighted as the only man left capable of love in an oppressive environment" (LaGuardia 112).

When Prewitt dies, Donna Reed is given the final scene in the film, as Lorene is in the novel, to grieve for her "fiancé." Transforming him in death to satisfy her own fantasy of respectability, Reed/Lorene tells a stunned Karen Holmes (who knows of Prewitt through Warden) that he was a bomber pilot who died heroically at Pearl Harbor. Given Karen's shocked look, such a story announces itself as one more disingenuous aspect of heterosexual romance, while implicitly authenticating Prewitt's love for Maggio as genuine. Lorene's fabrication is emphasized more so by its juxtaposition with Warden/Lancaster's mourning over Prewitt's dead body. Lorene fantasizes a hero's life, but Warden is given the task of assigning "real" meaning to Prewitt's life and death, both eulogizing him as a good soldier but chastising him because he "just couldn't play it smart." Once again, the homosocial bond is privileged as "truer" and more significant than male-female relationships. In other words, masculinity is authorized in these scenes, not by heterosexual relations, but by homosocial ones.

Warden's qualified eulogy, however, perhaps could be read as a revision of the tender pièta of Prewitt and Maggio, which recalls Biskind's conventional reading of the film that claims the organization man comes out on top. That is to say, Warden never lets himself weep for an underdog; he knows where to draw the line, and so, by implication, does the film. If we contextualize Warden's eulogy in the novel's cruising scenes, which clearly implicate Prewitt in the homosexual elements of troop life, and in the film's projection of Clift's bisexuality, we could make the argument that both the film and the novel must finally draw the line between Prewitt and Warden. Prewitt carries the taint of the underdog—the man on the "bottom"— the man who always gets screwed. In other words, while both narratives allow for male protest, pity, and buddy love, they finally pull back and remind audiences to "play it smart" like Warden, to win every time.

Such a recuperation of the transgressive elements, however, negates the powerful signs in both novel and film that suggest the "top dog" must follow "the hard compulsions under which gender configurations are formed" (Connell *Masculinities* 76). Warden must continually suppress his own "unmanly" desires in order to contain the gender and sexual diversity within his troop and himself, which, in turn, maintains his status and legitimacy as the hegemonic male. Hating the officer class, though, he is clearly drawn into the nonhegemonic circle of Prewitt, a circle less inclined to organize itself in terms of hierarchy and oppositional differences. While Warden's growing affection for Prewitt is allowed to leak out in the scene where they drunkenly embrace in the middle of the road, Warden's emotions in the final scene threaten to overwhelm his self-control as he kneels over Prewitt's dead body. Disciplining his tendency to mourn openly in front of the MPs who are waiting off to one side, Warden springs up and bellows, "Whatta' you men lookin' at? Haven't you ever seen a dead man before?"

Warden's contentiousness belies his feelings of loss for the loved object, which are inscripted visually by the film in the final shot/reverse shot with Clift and Lancaster. The camera moves in for a close-up of Lancaster/Warden's face as he kneels over the dead private. The reverse shot, a close-up of Clift/Prewitt's face in death, shows what momentarily arrests Warden's movement: a beautiful face that offers itself up for contemplation, like an eternal Sleeping Beauty. The wind flutters his hair, and his face, a mixture of delicate and strong features, reflects back a perfect calm. The violence with which Warden must refuse the feelings engendered by this beautiful love object by bellowing at the MPs implies that it is not Prewitt who is tainted, but a social order that systematically punishes difference, especially the homoerotic dimensions of same sex relationships, in order to sustain the privileged positions of certain men over others.

Despite reformulating the novel by filtering out the complexity and multiplicity of masculinity, Hollywood's *From Here to Eternity* also fails to contain or suppress completely the gender and sexual fluidity that threatened the stability of these categories, upon which Cold War ideology was dependent. As much as both the novel and the film possibly construct a satisfying image for postwar viewers of an organization man who is at once tough, fair, individualistic, *and* company-minded, thus offering a symbolic resolution to the culture's perceived "crisis" of male power and authority, neither text is able to fully erase the complications, indeed, the disturbing elements of the very gender norms they attempt to reinforce. Considering the cultural discourses that conflated masculinity and heterosexuality and signified national security risks in the image of the homosexual, the implications of introducing homoeroticism into the relationships between G Company's soldiers are clearly subversive. Moreover, in terms of the "naturalness" of hegemonic masculinity, the various social fields of masculinity in both narratives give structure to male power hierarchies. Take away the oppositional differences of class, ethnicity, age, sexuality, and so forth, which characterize contrastive masculinities, and it becomes difficult to locate the position and authority of the hegemonic male.

3

"Madame Butterfly with a Social Conscience": Gender, Race, and National Identity in James Michener's *Sayonara*

Perhaps no other writer in postwar America wrote as prolifically about Asia for popular audiences as did James A. Michener. Beginning in 1947 with his Pulitzer Prize-winning *Tales of the South Pacific*, Michener first introduced his recurring theme of universal brotherhood and interracial love between East and West. Four years later he published his best-selling *Return to Paradise*, consisting of a series of paired essays and short stories about various locales in the South Pacific, followed by *The Voice of Asia*, a collection of eleven interviews with people of different Asian countries. In 1953, Michener returned to an Asian setting in his Korean War novel *The Bridges of Toko-Ri*. Michener also published four books on Japanese art and numerous magazine articles on Japan and other Asian cultures.[1] His most extensive was a double-length feature article for *Holiday*'s August 1952 edition, which provided a literary travel tour of cultural institutions, customs, and the countryside of Japan.

By 1954, when *Sayonara* was approaching best-seller status, Michener's reputation as "the warm voice of Asia" was firmly established.[2] Accordingly, *Newsweek* prefaced its review of *Sayonara* with the following acclaim: "No popular writer has done more than James A. Michener to interpret, in friendship and understanding, Asia to the Americans .... In seven years he has introduced the world of the trans-Pacific into almost every American home. Through him his countrymen have seen the far-off little houses by the canals and heard the flutes at night" ("Again" 92). On the whole, contemporary reviews of *Sayonara* focused on Michener's sympathetic treatment of interracial romances between U.S. servicemen and Japanese women and their resulting personal and cultural tensions. This was a particularly relevant subject at this time, for, taking into account the number of marriages alone, over 10,000 U.S. servicemen had wed Japanese women since the Allied occupation began in 1945, despite cultural differences, racial prejudice, and the legal hurdles erected by U.S. immigration policy. The American government had initially refused to permit its soldiers to marry Japanese women, but, because this policy was difficult to enforce, these marriages were allowed at three different, although brief periods of time during the occupation.[3] Passage of the McCarran-Walter Act in late 1952 permanently legalized such marriages and granted permission to servicemen to bring their Japanese brides and children, if any, to the United States. While visiting Japan during the early 1950s, Michener observed the hardships and stress that American-Japanese couples encountered, particularly due to the restrictive and racist U.S. military policies. Sayonara—a revision of the Madame Butterfly story in which Air Force Major Lloyd "Ace" Gruver and Japanese actress Hana-ogi find "transcendent" love—was ostensibly Michener's attempt to call attention to America's racial intolerance and its presumptions of cultural superiority. Time magazine accordingly dubbed Sayonara "the new Madame Butterfly" with a "social conscience" ("New Madame" 114).

Michener's call for racial tolerance was timely not only because it echoed the legal and political efforts being made at home by civil rights leaders, but because race had become a volatile issue, indeed an ideological sore spot, in the Cold War discourses of anti-communism. The "othering" of nonwhites, particularly within its own geographical boundaries, presented an image gap for the United States that the Soviet Union was quick to exploit as a way of embarrassing its enemy and proving to the rest of the world that American claims to democracy were at best unreliable. In turn, the U.S. applauded each advance in racial justice as a sign of democracy in action; the 1954 Brown v. the Board of Education decision, for example, was celebrated as evidence of a victory over discrimination in the world's leading democracy (Oakley 92). However, Brown also generated opposing views on race and communism. Segregationists claimed integration was "aiding and abetting the communist cause" by fostering race mixing, which ultimately would mongrelize the nation and thus weaken it in the fight against communism (Oakley 196). According to this logic, fighting communism was ultimately the white man's burden.

Even within more liberal discourses, race was intricately bound up with gender in signifying "America" during the Cold War (after all, the white masculine subject symbolized the strong nation). Therefore, the call for racial justice conflicted symbolically with the campaign against communism. That is to say, if white male hegemony presented itself as the obvious means of spreading western democracy, this situated nonwhite forms of masculinity both at home and abroad as subordinate "Others" in the dual dichotomies of gender and race. As William Pietz's insightful discussion of Cold War discourses reveals, the discursive construction of western superiority and Cold War rhetoric relied on colonialist and orientalist discourses. Specifically, as a means of distinguishing the "civilized" heritage of the West from Soviet totalitarianism and communist ideology, prominent Cold War intellectuals and top policy makers, such as State Department policy planner George Kennan, concluded that communism was indeed rooted in "traditional oriental despotism plus modern police technology" (Pietz 58). The Russians in this paradigm were characterized as having "natural and instinctive urges" of the ancient oriental psyche, which created "an atmosphere of oriental secretiveness and conspiracy." This depiction of eastern peoples as cautious, insecure, deceitful, even savage, served to make an explicit contrast with the West's rationality and faith in the dignity of the human spirit and truth (Pietz 59–60). As Pietz makes clear, racist constructions of the East were bound up with political ideologies and western identity. Moreover, the project of democratizing nonwestern nations, such as Japan and those of Southeast Asia, was inseparable from U.S. economic and cultural imperialism, which necessarily subjugated nonwhite cultures and economies. It would appear, then, that appeals to racial equality at home during the Red Scare implicitly clashed with imperatives to maintain U.S. global power and authority, made legible in the figure of the Anglo-American male.

Paradoxically, while the hegemonic aims of the U.S. during the Cold War could be described as a masculinist project steeped in colonialist discourses, the work of convincing the American public of the ideological and economic soundness of these aims very often appropriated feminine discourses of sentiment and sympathy to win "consent" for them, an argument that Christina Klein makes in her extensive study on middlebrow culture's role in fostering public acceptance of Cold War policies. "The language of sentiment," Klein states, "became during the 1950s one of the preferred modes for understanding America's global expansion of power into Asia, and as such it served as one of the prime devices for denying American imperial aspirations" (18). Various discourses of the feminine, such as family, sentiment, and sympathy, as they appeared in middlebrow culture, worked to "decenter masculinity and violence in its constructions of national identity and the global imaginary" (Klein 19). Americans were offered a utopic vision of cross-racial and cross-national unity, notes Klein, in a wide range of popular texts and entertainment, including magazine articles, songs, movies, essays, and plays, which undoubtedly functioned to promote American foreign policy in terms that were compatible with the national self-image as anti-imperialist, democratic, and open to racial and cultural differences. The discourses of gender—a more easily manipulated category—were used to resolve ideological conflicts within expansionist policies that could not be easily resolved otherwise.

Michener's *Sayonara* offers us insight as to how these various discourses—gender, race, anti-communism, and global hegemony—converge and compete both in the narrative and in postwar culture. Clearly, the language of sentiment looms large in the novel's efforts to negotiate and resolve the conflicting aspects of these discourses. Using the Korean War and the Japanese occupation as its backdrop, *Sayonara* attempts to reconcile the problems inherent in advocating interracial, cross-cultural harmony and, at the same time, maintaining strong national security and instituting economic internationalism. However, much as Michener's reputation as the "warm voice of Asia" promoted a certain liberal-mindedness toward miscegenation and helped to shape America's postwar global imaginary in the language of mutual friendship and understanding, these goals appear to be at odds with *Sayonara*'s subtle orientalism and, perhaps less evident, the novel's endorsement of America's national and international interests during the height of the Cold War. The aim of this chapter, then, is to examine how these contending forces in both the novel and the 1957 film adaptation become manifest in the narratives' interracial love story.

The following section focuses solely on the novel in order to illuminate how its thematic concerns functioned in concert with specific Cold War issues pertinent to historical events of 1953 and 1954. I begin with the claim that, while race is an important element in the novel's romances (indeed this is how book reviewers tended to judge the novel), gender is the social coordinate that organizes the narrative's relationships, with interracial romance exploited as a means of raising, then resolving, what postwar culture perceived to be a "crisis" of masculinity, precipitated in part by the Red Scare. In the novel, the issue of racial tolerance ultimately becomes subsumed by the need to realign the "official" image of nation with white western male subjectivity, represented by the central character, Major Gruver. By contextualizing the novel in U.S. foreign-policy directives regarding

Asia, we can see how its conceptualization of masculinity functioned to advance values and attitudes requisite to the success of postwar America's hegemonic aims, namely, to establish an economically integrated, free world market in Asia. The next section examines both Michener's and Hollywood's *Sayonara* in conjunction with America's efforts to establish positive relations with Japan as a means of advancing U.S. foreign-policy objectives, which meant calling for racial tolerance toward the Japanese. However, the novel and film generated contradictory messages: Both *Sayonaras* were purportedly invested in improving interracial, cross-cultural relations, while, at the same time, engaging in a masculinist project of controlling and dominating a feminized Asian "Other."

The final two sections consider Hollywood's commercially successful adaptation of *Sayonara* (1957),[4] which reinforced the novel's more conservative politics, but which also drew out the ideological valences of the narrative. While the novel ends with Gruver's return to his military obligations, the film concludes with a transgressive act—his marriage to Hana-ogi. Thus, the film appears to provide a critical commentary on the novel's recuperation of white male subjectivity along with a more progressive outlook on miscegenation. However, the film functions more like a palimpsest in relation to the novel, both writing over it (to correct it?) and yet unable to erase the novel's ambivalence toward privileging racial harmony (in lieu of white male hegemony) within the climate of Cold War politics. The final section explores how the star text of Marlon Brando (Major Gruver) complicates *Sayonara*'s representation of a stable, white male identity, which Michener so abruptly recuperates in the closing moments of the novel. While extratextual associations accruing around Brando's star persona, as well as his performance style in the film, may have functioned to authenticate his character, Brando's use of disguise and masquerade in a series of films prior to *Sayonara* makes problematic any firm assurances that masculinity itself is an inherent quality that exists "naturally" as opposed to existing inside representation. Brando's star image, then, contributes to a sense that gender is more complicated in terms of its ontology than either *Sayonara* or mainstream notions of gender in postwar America seemed to suggest.

U.S. Foreign Policy and Michener's *Sayonara*

The Russian challenge to the West is a challenge to us to be Asia's good angel—the angel who will guide Asia's feet out of the Communist paths of destruction by showing her a Western way of peace. (Toynbee 354)

What we need to do is to recapture the kind of crusading spirit of the early days of the Republic when we were certain that we had something better than anyone else and we knew the rest of the world needed it and wanted it and that we were going to carry it around the world. (Secretary of State John Foster Dulles, 1954)[5]

In the years immediately following World War II, the U.S. embarked on what historian Thomas McCormick calls a "hegemonic project" to organize and manage global power and establish a world order of economic internationalism, which would sustain the growth of capitalism (xiii). Such a project was inscribed by a geo-imaginary, or a mode of articulating global regions in symbolic terms, that structured East and West in an asymmetrical, binarized relationship that endured until the mid-1970s.[6] This undertaking could also be defined symbolically in terms of gender, as a masculinist project involving a drive for universal power and authority over the world economy, although in the popular press it was articulated either with the kind of paternalism and missionary zeal exhibited in the above statements by Toynbee and Dulles, or, as Klein argues, in the language of sympathy and sentiment. In the Asian arena, this venture compelled Japan to defer to the leadership of the American government, which had undertaken the reconstruction of its former enemy with the aims of creating economic stability and exacting Japan's ideological commitment to global capitalism. This would not only dissuade Japan from playing the communist card, but also would elevate Japan to regional role model, showcasing the advantages of a pro-capitalist system of economic development (McCormick 88).

One of America's primary initiatives in reindustrializing Japan and make its exports competitive in world markets was the National Security Council policy, NSC-68, which effectively quadrupled military spending from $14 to $53 billion in two years. Japan would benefit from NSC-68 through military subcontracts and the provision of goods and services to U.S. military personnel. Industrial growth for Japan also depended on integrating economically underdeveloped nations of the Asian periphery (Taiwan, Korea, Vietnam, Indonesia,

Philippines) into global capitalism, for these nations were sources of Japan's raw materials and primary commodities. However, as McCormick points out, "much of the periphery, especially the Asian rimlands, was destabilized by war and revolution" (97), which impeded the development of Japanese economic regionalism and made them vulnerable to communist influence or rule. Thus, an important objective of NSC-68 was military pacification and political stabilization of rimland nations (McCormick 99). Reconstructing Japan, then, had far-reaching consequences for the entire Pacific region and for America: For the next twenty years it would involve the U.S., as hegemon of world capitalism, in a military contest for economic control of the rimlands. In terms of gender and race, this contest could be seen as a reformulation of nineteenth-century orientalism, which Edward Said defines as "a Western style for dominating, restructuring, and having authority over the Orient" (3).

While the Korean War helped President Truman's cabinet obtain initial authorization from a fiscally conservative Congress to implement NSC-68, the war's resolution did not allay policy makers' fears that Japan might eventually be forced into accommodation with communist nations in Asia.[7] The stability of the entire region of Southeast Asia seemed threatened by what Secretary of State John Foster Dulles called "other Koreas" and the realization of the domino theory. "Saving" the rimlands, though, was not an easy proposition to sell to the American public because it would most likely entail American involvement in the kind of limited, localized, and expensive war that characterized the Korean War—routinely called the "no-win war" in the press. As fifties historian J. Ronald Oakley points out, following the rout of American troops by Chinese communist-led troops in North Korea in 1950 and 1951, "the [American] people's hearts were no longer in the war. Neither the soldiers nor the public could see much point in risking lives to take hills, little towns, or rice paddies of no apparent value" (93). Given both the high economic stakes of the containment policy in Asia and the unpopularity of committing American soldiers to such "no-win wars" as Korea, maintaining ideological and fiscal support for NSC-68 was seen as a vital and difficult task for government officials. America's hegemonic project, and particularly the military values underwriting NSC-68, presented an image problem for policy makers: The imperatives of being a power wielder and a world policing agent clashed not only with the nation's democratic ideals, but also with the reluctance of many Americans to make the personal sacrifices necessary to support the nation's military machine.

While an extended explanation of the strategies by which government officials attempted to reconcile these ideological conflicts are beyond the scope of this chapter, I would like to advance an account of how Michener's *Sayonara* was in dialogue with history at this time. The novel offers, if not a clear justification of official ideology, then a clarification of the values that supported it, values appealing to the nation's sense of duty and responsibility for world peace and containing communism. *Sayonara* performed important cultural and political work by endorsing the (masculinist) military aims of NSC-68, while, at the same time, attempting to bridge the gulf between East and West with the (feminine) language of sympathy, sentiment, tolerance, and respect. Michener's Major Gruver ostensibly manages to effect both of these objectives—bolstering support for global hegemony and economic imperialism and calling attention to the need for racial tolerance and cross-national unity—which suggests that the white, western male subject could unproblematically reconcile these competing aims within his image.

At the outset of the novel, the narrative is clearly motivated by the racist policies of the U.S. Air Force, which strongly discouraged military personnel from marrying Japanese women and expressly forbade officers from being seen with them in public. While stationed in Osaka during the Korean War, both Major Gruver and an irreverent enlisted man in his Company, Private Joe Kelly (reminiscent of the mercurial Maggio in *From Here to Eternity*), confront official sanctions and personal affront when they fall in love with Japanese women. However, running through *Sayonara* is a preoccupation with both male vulnerability and the instability of male hegemony. Particularly for Gruver, the impulse behind his desire for a more "feminine," that is, more man pleasing, Asian lover is the psychological vulnerability to which he feels subject in relationships with emasculating American women.[8] Prior to his assignment in Japan, Gruver finds the notion of "good average guys" marrying "yellow girls" repulsive and incomprehensible (7)[9]; all Japanese women appear alike to him: dumpy, fat, and slant-eyed with red, round faces. When he learns the implacable Kelly is determined to marry Katsumi, Gruver tries to change his mind, using a picture of his own fiancée, General Webster's blond and beautiful daughter Eileen, as his most potent tool of persuasion. Despite this powerful signifier of racial "purity" and

Americanness and despite the legal prohibition barring Kelly from bringing Katsumi back to the States, he is resolved to marry her. Later, by observing the newlyweds' happiness, Gruver comes to learn the "secret" of why so many American men "had braved the fury of their commanders and their country to marry [Japanese] women" (147): They "make their men feel important" (52), unlike American women who clog their husbands' lives with dreary details of "Junior's braces and country club dances and what kinds of car [they] bought" (17).

Gruver soon develops cold feet about marrying Eileen, who has arrived in Japan for their wedding. Fearing she will become like her domineering mother, who, according to Air Force gossip, was the voice behind General Webster's decisions, he retreats to the air base in order to avoid courting Eileen. He convinces himself that his retreat "had something to do with the fun of living with a gang of men that you can never explain. The relaxation, the freedom of running down the hall in your shorts, the common interests in a common problem" (81). When Eileen insists that "a man has to surrender himself sometimes," Gruver thinks, "Mrs. Webster, frankly, had scared the devil out of me and now I could see the same marital tendencies in her daughter" (62). Later he admits, "something had happened in American life to drive men ... away from such delectable girls" as Eileen (138).

The novel does not say precisely what that "something" was that had happened in American life, but postwar readers could have readily supplied the answer from Philip Wylie's widely circulated *Generation of Vipers* (1942), which asserted that American wives and mothers (or "Moms") had surreptitiously converted the nation into a matriarchy of domineering, power hungry, omnipresent wives and mothers. Indeed, Gruver reinforces this image of the castrating American female in his assessment of the wives he encounters in the Osaka P.X.: They were "hard," "efficient," "discontented," "driven by outside forces" (137). Although Eileen is "a dish, even for a general's daughter" (13) and "absolutely adorable with the fresh bright charm that only American girls ever seem to have" (60), lurking beneath her charm is her similarity to Mom: Nancy and Eileen Webster invoke for him what Wylie called "the bride at every funeral and the corpse at every wedding" (198). The oscillation between glorifying and demonizing American women was entirely consistent with efforts to shore up masculinity during the Red Scare, which took the form of constructing discrete boundaries to protect males from emasculating influences, especially "Mom." According to Michael Rogin, targeting the feminine was one means of locating a visible enemy or a visible cause of security breaches at a time in which "real" invisible communist subversives could not be easily recognized or marked (245).[10]

Gruver's sentiments that marriage and domesticity compromise masculine integrity and independence and foreclose to men the pleasure of living in an all-male community are ones that we recall pervaded Jones's *From Here to Eternity*. However, as Brandon French maintains, Jones's novel provided "an honorable escape from domestic life" in having the male protagonists pledge their primary allegiance to the Army (59). In *Sayonara*, the immediate solution to such loss of independence is not to evade marriage *per se*, but either to surrender without a battle to a Nancy Webster or to evade marriage to *American* women. As Gruver comes to believe, a Japanese wife like Katsumi safeguards masculinity, for Katsumi was "one of the most perfect women [he] had ever known, for she had obviously studied her man and had worked out every item of the day's work so that the end result would be a happy husband and a peaceful home" (165). Gruver, too, becomes infatuated with Japanese "femininity" and breaks his engagement with Eileen to pursue Hana-ogi, whom he finds passive and submissive, yet exotic and tantalizing.

Because Gruver continues to disobey orders by fraternizing with Hana-ogi and teeters on the brink of giving up his Air Force commission, he ruptures the solidarity within the upper ranks of the military. As a result, he intensifies male vulnerability and the instability of male hegemony. It is this rift within hegemony that drives the narrative forward as much as, perhaps more than, the military's racist policies designed to discourage Japanese-American romances. The novel's conclusion heals this rift, emphasizing patriotism and commitment to duties and obligations: Gruver and Hana-ogi are forced to say a forlorn "sayonara" so that Hana-ogi may continue as "Number One Girl" in the all-female Takarazuka theatre and Gruver, more reluctantly, can remain with the Air Force. Despite Gruver's distress over parting with Hana-ogi ("I wanted to fling myself upon the floor and weep" [242]), he squelches in himself what might be perceived as "feminine" weakness and realigns himself with the military. Relinquishing his personal desires, he tells himself, "I was forced to acknowledge that I lived in an age when the only honorable profession was soldiering, when the only acceptable attitude toward strange lands and people of another color must be not love but fear." In the next instant, when General Webster informs Gruver that he will be promoted to lieutenant-colonel, he "instinctively salutes" (243), signaling both his capitulation to military directives, and, more importantly, the resuturing of power and authority within the upper ranks of male hegemony. This obvious cementing of institutional-based ties between hegemonic males was entirely compatible with the culture's efforts to stabilize and reinvigorate masculinity during the Red Scare.

Gruver's return to the Air Force and commie-fighting signify a kind of male identity that was in step not only with America's self-image, but also was in keeping with the kind of assurances the U.S. felt was necessary to project to its free world allies: that America was very much at the helm in orchestrating and protecting a global, capitalist system of production and free trade. While Michener's *Sayonara* did not formulate a specific scenario of Cold-War policy, it served as an imaginative terrain that forged the requisite (masculine) interests, attitudes, and values that would foster the success of American foreign policy and international economic designs.

Once Gruver and Hana-ogi embark on a clandestine affair, he undergoes a metamorphosis from a gung-ho commie-fighter and white racist to a softer, gentler, more sensitive male, content to wear a kimono around the house and remove his shoes at the door. His final assertion at the end of the narrative that "the only honorable profession was soldiering" appears to have supplanted this new masculine identity. However, both of these somewhat contradictory images—the tough Cold Warrior and the sensitive lover—held symbolic importance in relation to foreign policy. Gruver's transformation to a socially aware, liberal humanist advanced an image the U.S. wanted to project to itself and to the rest of the world as tolerant, humane, and correct.[11] At the same time, his recommitment to the Air Force endorsed a sense of rightness for the military muscle America would need to realize its global designs. Gruver, then, appears to reconcile military values with a more tolerant sensibility; such a reconciliation was precisely that which would have eased the image problem created by implementing NSC-68.

Gruver's eventual return to warplanes and to Eileen Webster is motivated by several factors. As a West Point graduate and the son of a four-star general, he has a promising future as top brass. More compelling than personal gain, though, is the issue of national security. When General Webster discovers Gruver secretly living with Hana-ogi, in true military fashion, he calls in the big gun—Gruver's father,

General "Hot Shot" Harry Gruver, an apologist for American racial and ethnic purity, who tries to talk sense into his wayward offspring. "Son," says Hot Shot, "I've watched our men marry German girls and French girls and even Russian girls. Invariably, if you know the man, it's a sign of weakness. They're all panty-waists. Strong men have the guts to marry the girls who grew up next door. Such marriages fit into the community. They make the nation strong .... Leave it to the poets and painters and people who turn their back on America because they're afraid of it to go chasing after foreign girls" (161). Hot Shot makes clear the connection between national identity and masculinity in this passage. A strong nation depends on strong men who have the "guts" to marry American girls. More is at stake than just one officer's career: As the Air Force's pinup flyboy, Gruver and, by extension, a future *Anglo-American* wife represent the kind of racial and cultural purity that conservative ideologies in the postwar era equated with national security and Americanness. After all, Harry says pointedly to Ace, "y'can't send half-Jap boys to the Point" (160). Fifties audiences might recognize, too, Harry's implications about "panty-waists" and foreign women. Though his remarks are made in the context of heterosexual marriage, his label for men who are not "masculine" enough to marry American women implicates them in homosexuality. In the context of demonizing homosexuals as security risks at the height of McCarthyism and anticommunist hysteria, Harry aims here for a powerful rhetorical effect on his son. Foreign women carried a double stigma: As women, they were the demonized feminine "Other" of Cold War hysteria and, as foreign, they were implicated in un-American political theories (read Marxist ideology).

Gruver is not immediately convinced by his father's sermon, but he begins to realize the significance of marrying Hana-ogi. He would be relinquishing more than his career; he also would be abandoning his nation. As he wanders through Osaka, Gruver recalls a recent radio broadcast explaining why Texan Democrats were supporting Eisenhower for president. "Suddenly, there in the dark streets of Osaka, Eisenhower became the symbol of what a major in the Air Force might become: a man ready for many different kinds of action if his country needed him" (176). He is confronted, then, with the dilemma of either fulfilling a patriotic duty by hazarding marriage to an American wife or endangering his career, yet securing his sense of manhood and personal fulfillment by remaining with Hana-ogi. Ike's symbolic power and Harry's binarized rendition of gender and nation (manly/Anglo-American/heterosexual/patriotic versus unmanly/foreign/homosexual/security risk) fail to persuade Gruver, for the next morning he heads for the U.S. Consulate to process the papers for marrying a Japanese woman.

Gruver's subordinating the needs of the state to his own interests and desires emerges as a central conflict in the novel, one that resonates with Cold War hysteria: Public and private interests are no longer in step with one another. This situation, of course, constitutes one of the paradoxes of Cold War ideology. That is to say, within a capitalist system, individualism is ostensibly allowed to flourish, and the private life of an individual is supposedly sacrosanct; in contrast, communism is seen to efface all individuality. However, as Rogin argues, one of the consequences of demonizing those associated with communism (homosexuals, "Mom," the Left) was the collapse of the arbitrary boundary between public and private. Not only did private lives come under the scrutiny of the national security state, which Rogin claims mimicked the very kinds of controls that American anti-communists attributed to communist leaders, but public discourse and the very processes of government became restricted as well. At the height of the Red Scare and the interventions of the national security state, public and private meshed closely with one another. Harry Gruver demonstrates this phenomenon when he indicates that such "private" issues as choice of marriage partner and sexual preference are indeed very public matters in the name of national identity and security.

Because Gruver continues to assert his individuality and ignore the apparent danger around him, his superior officers must bring him back into line. In keeping with the kind of paternalism that characterized U.S. foreign policy, Generals Webster and Gruver, Sr., manipulate events behind the scenes, conspiring with the owner of the Takarazuka theatre to end the romance. Hana-ogi is hidden away and transferred to another city, while Gruver is given immediate orders to report stateside. A promotion is the reward for his "compliance," and a trip to the airport with Eileen sweetens the deal. The novel ends by suggesting that the American Way of Life (represented by the white, middle-class, nuclear family, and, by implication, capitalism) will be secure after all.

Gruver's subjugation of personal desire to return to the business of war also parallels the process of consensus formation that dominated postwar American political processes. The now liberal Ace forms an alliance with the hard-line conservative military leaders, in order to present a united front, or in Arthur Schlesinger's words, "a vital center" in preserving democracy and fighting communism.[12] More pressing national and international issues, then, co-opt Ace's personal desires and campaign to overcome racism. This show of consensus suggests a support for the rightness of NSC-68 and contemporary foreign policy in Asia as well, which did not always have complete support at the congressional or constituent levels. While Michener's *Sayonara* does not directly involve itself in demonizing communists or communist sympathizers, which was an integral part in sustaining ideological support for capitalism and American political processes, it does uphold the importance of the military. The ending seems to suggest that while the top brass may be a little coldhearted and a lot racist, ultimately they have the best interests of Gruver and the nation at heart. That *Sayonara* was published approximately six months after the end of the Korean War does not diminish its historical significance, nor does it render Gruver's return to the Air Force a moot point. Foreign-policy leaders were well aware that Korea was likely to be only the beginning of what was, in fact, a prolonged military effort to open Southeast Asia to free markets and promote Japan's economic stability.

The novel promoted particular values—patriotic commitment, duty, and obligation—that function as the ideological glue that sustains hegemony. Such values constituted a recurring theme for Michener as well; he introduced this theme in *Tales of the South Pacific* and foregrounded it in *The Bridges at Toko-Ri*, which was published six months before *Sayonara*.[13] In *Toko-Ri*, Korean War bomber pilot Lieutenant Harry Brubaker comes to realize that, despite his resentment at having to fight a war that nobody supports, "all through history free men have had to fight the wrong war in the wrong place" (37). "Nobody ever knows why he gets the dirty job. But any society is held together by the efforts ... yes, and the sacrifices, of only a few" (40). Brubaker's commanding officer, Admiral Tarrant, however, worries whether America has become too indifferent to stick out the struggle and make the sacrifices necessary to keep the Cold War from escalating; such indifference, he thinks, may lead to the dire possibility of having to confront the Russians on the banks of the Mississippi (44). The supporters of NSC-68 could not have hoped for better public relations spokesmen than Tarrant and Brubaker. Although Gruver makes different kinds of sacrifices in *Sayonara* (Brubaker dies after the air strike on the formidable bridges at Toko-Ri), the two novels thematically are mutually reinforcing in their support of U.S.

commitment to containment. In terms of masculinity, they send a clear message: The "real" man does not shift the burden elsewhere for his own personal comfort and pleasure.

America's Cold War Romance with Japan

Nancy Webster: It's not that I dislike Japanese. Goodness, they're wonderful people. So clever and all that. Even in the short time I've been here they've shown me unusual courtesies. But a conquering army must retain its dignity.

General Webster: I agree, but those yokels in Washington say we've got to woo them now. Nancy, you ought to read the directives I get! (Sayonara 34)

This exchange between General and Nancy Webster alludes to the diplomatic balancing act that the U.S. felt compelled to perform in its role as both Occupier and potential free-world ally of Japan. Because Japan's ideological commitment to global capitalism was the linchpin in America's hegemonic designs, U.S. policy makers were prepared "to woo" Japan, an undertaking that received extensive coverage in the popular press between 1950 and 1954. Ironically, this entailed obscuring some profound contradictions inherent in occupation policies toward Japan. The American effort to democratize Japan was, in John W. Dower's words, "schizophrenic"; "visions of 'democratization' that would have seemed extreme if proposed within the United States went hand in hand with severe authoritarian rule [by General Douglas MacArthur and his command]" (26–27).[14] For instance, introducing democratic reform coexisted alongside some of the most repressive labor laws imposed on Japanese workers by occupation policies (McCormick 89). A more striking example is that after an all-*American* task force had written a new democratic constitution for Japan—which was then given only 48 hours to adopt it—General MacArthur proudly declared it "the product of enlightened Japanese thought" (Wheeler 713).[15] Any Japanese opposition to America's restructuring had to be "breathed voicelessly," as one Japanese journalist put it.

For those back home, imposing democratic reform on Japan was couched in the language of paternalism—reproducing the historical racial paternalism of western expansion—as evidenced by such weekly magazine articles as "MacArthur: Father and Leader of Postwar Japan"; "Japan's Still under Our Wing"; "Free Japan, a U.S. Headache";

"Japan: Free-World Responsibility."[16] However, at the inception of the Peace Treaty with Japan, Ambassador William J. Sebald delivered a self-congratulatory speech on behalf of the American government for building a "new partnership with Japan," which "demonstrates that an oriental nation and people can work on a basis of equality, co-operation, and understanding with an occidental nation and people" (493). Not surprising, though, Sebald's rhetoric of unity and equality was offset by his anxiety over Japan's proximity to communist nations. The ambassador warned, "even today the menacing power of Soviet Communism is dangerously close to Japan," whose level of scientific knowledge, technical skill, and managerial capabilities was especially enticing to Soviet Russia (493). Doubts lingered as to whether Japan would resist the inducements made by Russia and China to move it closer to the communist orbit. *The Saturday Evening Post* fretted that "since Japan is in Asia and must get along on some terms with her neighbors, this pressure can become tremendous, and could even kindle the fires of the dreaded 'big war'" ("We Have" 12).

American fears were augmented by a wave of anti-American sentiment that swept Japan shortly after occupation forces withdrew. Since Japanese people no longer had to "breath voicelessly" their resentments, anti-American books—*Children of the Atomic Bomb, Children of Military Bases,* and *Military Base Japan,* for example—became instant best-sellers; conversely, Japanese writers expressing pro-American views found it increasingly difficult to find publishers. Movies, such as *Orphans of Mixed Blood* and *Towers of White Lilies,* about the killing of Japanese schoolgirls by American soldiers during the Okinawan invasion, were box office hits, and newspapers avidly reported anti-American news items, particularly trouble connected with American military bases ("Anti-American" 76). Japanese journalist Atsushi Oi reported that during the elections of 1953, anti-Americanism became a determining political force: Many Japanese politicians who had pro-American records were defeated, whereas those who spoke openly against America won their bids for election (31). While an undercurrent of resentment and opposition to the U.S. did exist, it would be misleading to suggest that the Japanese were univocal in their anti-Americanism. Many Japanese, sick of war and distrustful of the militaristic attitudes that had spurred their nation into war, had cooperated with occupation policies and were eager to begin rebuilding their communities and lives (Dower 23–24).

In light of the fragile balance between competing interests in Asia and the wide range of Japanese responses to the process of democratization, "wooing" Japan became central to American political and economic investments. One of the strategies proposed by the State Department to secure Japan's alliance was intercultural exchange, which government officials deemed essential for bringing the "two peoples closer together in their appreciation and understanding of each other and their respective ways of life." The State Department concluded "ways should be found to allow each country to benefit from the experience and accomplishments of the other through a free and voluntary interchange of ideas and information" ("Consideration" 493).[17] During the occupation, many Japanese people were exposed to western thought and institutions, and, although this hardly qualified as "free and voluntary" interchange, such exposure served the Cold-War strategy of opening up the East in order to turn it toward the "free" world. As Christopher L. Connery points out in his discussion of the U.S. geo-imaginary and its role in "naturalizing" the idea of an open world market, postwar policy makers believed that "the principle structural impediment to the international open market was inwardness" (37). (The paradox, Connery states, in promoting capitalist universalism was that a truly open market ran counter to the existing asymmetrical, hegemonic relationship between East and West).

Along with opening up Japan, policy makers recognized the importance of changing American attitudes as well. The State Department report likewise indicated that Japanese culture remained obscure to Americans. Restating this point in *Commonweal,* John Cogley claimed that "knowledge of the Orient was vague and fragmentary; there was plenty of myth, superstition, dubious generality" (254). Aside from Pearl S. Buck novels, much of what Americans knew of Asians was through stereotypical figures of popular culture: the grinning Confucius; the tireless, aloof Chinese laundryman; Hollywood's Fu Manchu, Mr. Moto, or Madame Butterfly—all roles played by Western actors (Cogley 254). The U.S. government was well aware of the importance of private citizens and cultural producers in educating Americans about Asia and its crucial role in the global community. Indeed, as Klein's research indicates, foreign-policy makers looked to the private sector to help them translate their political and ideological goals into terms that would promote a sense of obligation to Asians as part of the world community and participation in foreign affairs. In other words, they counted on writers, musicians, and filmmakers to convince the "hearts" of Americans as well as their minds (10).

As one of these key cultural image-makers, Michener's emergence on the literary scene as an enthusiast of Asian cultures appeared at an auspicious moment for the American government. As a case in point, *Sayonara*'s saccharine romance and the wordless fascination between the two lovers (neither speaks the other's language) function as a metaphor for the terms by which Japan is "wooed" and the conquering army retains its dignity. Michener's use of romance to signify the forging of peacetime relations was entirely compatible with General MacArthur and his staff's efforts to present U.S. presence in Japan as a "partnership," or a kind of "ideological romance between the two countries" (Simpson 51). Carol Chung Simpson notes, "the Japanese woman became a significant figure in this representation, in which the white American soldier was depicted as 'husbanding' the Japanese woman's emancipation from the formerly oppressive Japanese patriarchy" .... "Tales of schoolgirl crushes and fleeting occupation romances between white American GIs and Japanese women quickly became the literal manifestations of this new partnership, even though they dangerously blurred the line between a mutually beneficial partnership and an illicit, interracial affair" (51). Simpson adds that as long as the romances between U.S. soldiers and Japanese women remained a "distant metaphor for the inevitability of U.S. dominance in Asia, they could serve a stabilizing function by casting the American mission in Japan as benevolent. However, when these romances ended in marriage and the Japanese woman came home, as it were, her presence in America provoked palpably discomfort" (51–52). Michener's novel reinforced this mindset by breaking off the romance and preventing Hana-ogi from coming "home" with her American husband, but the romance itself does attempt to foster positive feelings between the former enemies.

Initially, Gruver demonstrates his good faith through persistent efforts to court Hana-ogi so that she abandons her deep hatred of Americans and succumbs to his charm. Gruver, in turn, becomes her willing pupil, receiving—along with the reader—a travel tour of sorts, in which various Japanese customs, its countryside, and theatrical world are introduced to him. This aspect of the romance is undoubtedly why A. Grove Day calls Michener's novel his "love letter to Japan" (79)[18] and why George Becker claims that *Sayonara*, along with Michener's numerous publications on Japan, had the potential to

impart to the American public "the first intimation that there was
something to be admired about Japan" (50). One of Michener's goals,
says Becker, was purportedly "to bring Americans to a better
understanding and appreciation of Japanese life. This was a task of
importance, for feeling against the Japanese in the Pacific Coast states,
as well as among the men fighting in the Pacific, understandably ran
very high" (49) Michener apparently hoped his readers would identify
with Gruver, who becomes increasingly charmed by Japanese culture
so that his "early ideas about the Japanese enemy were swirling in
confusion" (122). His transformation appears all but complete when he
declares to Hana-ogi, "Now I've come to an alien land among people I
once hated and ... you have made a shred of heaven here" (130).

    However, we might ask with what did Michener's "love letter to
Japan" acquaint American audiences? Michener's revision of the
Madame Butterfly story ostensibly presents East and West on more
equitable terms—love being the universal equalizer and the lovers "the
timeless human beings without nation or speech or different color"
(*Sayonara* 115)—and the discourses of sentiment and romance appear
to dissolve the boundaries of nation, race, and culture. Along with
Sayonara's gesture of creating more positive feelings toward Japan,
however, it restores traditional racial and gender boundaries between
East and West as well. Moreover, benign as *Sayonara*'s travel-tour
enthusiasm may seem, its construction of Japan has more to do with
western tradition than with any "realistic" depiction of Japan. Japan is
made "knowable" either as an exotic Other or by demystifying it, what
Said calls "translating its foreignness or taming its hostilities" (103),
both processes containing Japan in colonialist discourses.

    Michener also wrote another contemporary "love letter" to
Japan—"Japan"—an article for *Holiday*'s August 1952 issue, written
just before Michener began working on *Sayonara*. It is perhaps no
coincidence, then, that his novel shares certain elements in common
with his travel article. *Holiday*, a new publication in the 1950s, both
fostered and capitalized on the postwar tourist boom; national and
international tourism had mushroomed in this decade primarily due to
economic prosperity and the promotion of travel as a leisure time
activity for the middle classes. Klein's research shows that government
officials were quick to see the political advantages in promoting
tourism as a means to break down "barriers of mutual understanding"
in face-to-face encounters with peoples of other nations (308). As a
result, in 1954 and 1955, President Eisenhower "vigorously promoted

international tourism as a part of [his] educational campaign to win public support for his foreign policy." For one, tourists' dollars functioned as economic resources for foreign countries, which would then enable them to buy American goods; therefore, "the figure of the tourist became the visible embodiment of the abstract ideal of commercial exchange and free trade" (Klein 301–2). In addition, tourists could represent America as peace loving, goodwill ambassadors (Klein 305).

Michener's *Holiday* article, given its function of commodifying Japan in the burgeoning marketplace of travel and tourism, was a rhetorical performance designed to construct Japan as a site of desire and to fix the tourist's gaze on it. The article begins, as if it were part of an anthropological venture, by urging "you" to "look for the little-known soul of Japan" in an "utterly exotic, un-Western terrain" (27). By initially using second-person address—"You will be captivated by the gaudy colors"; "You can't wait. You dive your chopsticks into the skillet" (27, 29)—Michener defers his own narrative agency in order to create (in "you") a sense of familiarity and closeness with Japan through a kind of virtual excursion. The "you" also positions the reader as the subject of experiences so that (s)he becomes implicated in the double move the article attempts to perform: Japan's differences are either "tamed" by giving them a certain (Western) "normalcy," or they are constructed as exotic and fascinating.

Supplanting wartime images of the Japanese as devil figures was especially important for *Holiday*'s purposes as well. "Japan" assiduously avoids or minimizes references to WWII and its political, social, and, literally, its nuclear fallout. However, the effect on Japan is feminizing: America's recent enemy becomes a "delicate civilization," a "land of exquisite beauty and a people dedicated to its cultivation" (27); its typical home produces "the effect of tranquillity and art" (28). "National character" is manifested in Japanese gardens and homes, which are art conscious, unostentatious, controlled, and contained by custom and law (28). As a commodity for tourist consumption, Japan is portrayed in a supremely flattering light as a pleasing spectacle, perhaps explaining Michener's overuse of superlatives and effusive language. Although this language may have alerted readers to a certain fabrication of Japan, the article's status as descriptive, therefore "factual," and instructional, coupled with Michener's reputation as an authority on Asia, work to authenticate this discursive representation. However, *Holiday* and Michener participate in constructing what Paul

Lyons calls a "fetishized history," which is not the avoidance of history, but a construction of history that "breaks up otherness in order to assimilate it to the gazer's needs" (52).[19] Furthering the needs of the Cold Warriors, Michener's recovering Japan as a "delicate civilization" served to ameliorate wartime stereotypes of the Japanese as underhanded aggressors.

Potentially, *Sayonara* promoted tourism right along with *Holiday*'s "Japan." As mutually reinforcing texts, the travel article authorized the novel's representations of Japan and, in turn, the novel recalled many of the magazine's descriptions of Japan. *Sayonara* similarly romanticized Japan. Despite Gruver's initial scorn for Japanese culture and people, he becomes enchanted with its "crowded life, the tiny shops, the paper doors with small lights shining through" (68). *Sayonara*'s Japan is one of flowered lanes, beautiful lakes, and cherry blossoms (36), and the little alley by the canal where Gruver and Hanaogi live gives him "a warmth and goodness" and "strength" he has never known, with its "hilarious," "black-bobbed children" and "teeming masses of people" (170). However, despite the beauty of its ancient countryside, Japan is "tragic, doomed" by its "fundamental secret: too many people." A "thin sliver of useless land" tended by an old man's gnarled fingers and bending back is a "tragic triangle" which sustains his large family (114).

The "tragedy" of Japan is offset by its women, who, from Gruver's point of view, are near-mythic, poetic beings, ever graceful and gracious. Notably, too, *Sayonara*'s Japan is curiously emasculated, literally without males, which resonates with the *Holiday* article's avoidance of the country's wartime militarism. Aside from the bent old men tending narrow strips of farmland and the occasional doorman or shopkeeper, Japan seems to be a nation of women who continually capture Gruver's inquisitive gaze. The sight of a "delicate woman" hurrying in "little running pintoed steps" is "exquisitely charming" (71); the "make-believe" geishas who walk "extremely pin-toed" in a "sing-song motion" and pretend to be certified professionals so Americans can experience the "real thing" are amusing (44). The procession of Takarazuka actresses crossing the Bitchi-bashi [bridge] from the theater to their dormitories present to him "the most curious and lovely group of women in the world," and as one "strange, lovely girl" in particular passes by, Gruver "felt as if [he] had been brushed across the eyes by some terrible essence of beauty, something of whose existence [he] had never before been aware" (68). Though not a physical beauty according to Gruver, Katsumi Kelly still captures a lovely, ancient "essence" in her "time-christened movements over the charcoal stoves the Japanese women have used for centuries" (109).

Like "Japan," *Sayonara* depicts Japan as a nation of ancient and bizarre rituals, curious customs, and fantastic spectacle—all awaiting consumption by the fortunate western traveler. Both texts—"Japan" less explicitly—align the reader with a masculine fantasy of Japan as nonthreatening female, graciously and delicately available, open to being explored, open to having "her" secrets discovered. *Sayonara's* "romance" with Japan is largely mediated through depictions of women who are one more aspect of the spectacle, but assume an added significance as figures of some "eternal feminine." Completely entranced, Gruver waxes: "I concluded that no man could comprehend women until he had known the women of Japan with their unbelievable combinations of unremitting work, endless suffering and boundless warmth—just as I could never have known even the outlines of love had I not lived in a little house where I sometimes drew back the covers of my bed upon the floor to see there the slim golden body of the perpetual woman" (146–47). Gruver's inability to conceive of Japanese women other than as monolithic types points us to Said's assertion that traditional western conceptions of the East tend to be "static, frozen, fixed eternally" (208). *Sayonara's* female figures are contained by a discourse of femininity that renders them nonthreatening through their capacity for self-sacrifice, endurance for pain, and service to others. Perhaps more problematic, though, is that Michener's use of interracial romance and exotic Japanese femininity to symbolize the forging of peacetime relations with Japan reinforced the gendered metaphors already well established by occupation forces in terms of the sexual linking of conqueror and conquered. Dower observes in *Embracing Defeat* that "the enemy was transformed with startling suddenness from a bestial people fit to be annihilated into receptive exotics to be handled and enjoyed. That enjoyment was palpable—the panpan [Japanese prostitute] personified this. Japan—only yesterday a menacing, masculine threat—had been transformed, almost in the blink of an eye, into a compliant, female body on which the white victors could impose their will" (138).

In certain respects, though, *Sayonara* refutes such traditional notions of Asian women in its deliberate alteration of the Madame Butterfly story, perhaps in keeping with the postwar climate of reconciliation with Japan and the novel's liberal sympathies with interracial romances.[20] The most significant plot change in Michener's version is Hana-ogi's (the Butterfly figure) refusal in the end to marry Gruver. "I Japanese. I always Japanese. I never be happy nowhere," she insists (204). Because she is not in the role of the cast off lover, neither is she compelled to commit suicide, as did traditional Butterflies.[21] Michener's Hana-ogi, then, is less a passive victim, and neither is Gruver a ruthless, arrogant Pinkerton. Nonetheless, Gruver is still stunned by her refusal: "It was incomprehensible to me that any Japanese girl, living in that cramped little land with no conveniences and no future, would refuse America" (181). Assuming all romances between Asian women and American men were somehow incarnations of the Butterfly tale, he attempts to restructure their relationship along these lines, saying to Hana-ogi, "I'm a West Point honor man. In the story [Madame Butterfly] you're supposed to beg me to marry you. Hanayo-chan, please beg me" (203). Because Gruver must do the begging, *Sayonara* appears to debunk the western male fantasy of superiority and irresistibility.

By imagining that Hana-ogi has some agency in articulating her own desires and goals, Michener offers us an important reminder that the simple binary terms in which the West historically has structured its relations with the East is perhaps too reductive. In *Sites of Desire/Economies of Pleasure: Sexualities in Asia and the Pacific*, Margaret Jolly and Lenore Manderson argue for reassessing the assumption that an all powerful [western] male gaze had full power to script the colonized as victim or reshape their consciousness. The authors contend that in examining cross-cultural exchanges in sexualities, we must consider the dialogic relations between western males and eastern (colonized) females. In this sense, Michener's fictional rendering, at least momentarily, accounts for both Hana-ogi's "looking back" at Gruver and her female resistance as well as accommodation to male domination.

The novel undermines its critique of the traditional Butterfly in several ways, however. In the first place, paperback publishers were unable to resist capitalizing on the familiarity with (and desirability of) the western male fantasy of the Butterfly stories; the cover of the 1955 Bantam edition enticed readers by asserting that *Sayonara* "probes unflinchingly into the question of why so many American men prefer the tender and submissive women of the exotic East." In addition to casting aspersions on Anglo-American women before readers open the book, the cover established at the outset the requisite active masculine/passive feminine dichotomy that structures the relationships between both Pinkerton and Butterfly figures as well as West and East. Moreover, these binarized relationships are ones that fitted most readily into dominant ideologies of race and gender: A "transgressive" relationship between a white male and a nonwhite female was permissible, even desirable, but *Sayonara* never imagines the more "transgressive" possibility of nonwhite male/white female romances.

Furthermore, while Hana-ogi's refusal to marry Gruver may have opened up alternative configurations of gender, race, and national identity, the narrative encourages readers to identify with the first-person narrator, Gruver. He offers such a doggedly grim view of her future prospects without him that her rejection of romance seems almost inexplicable, even though Hana-ogi gives sound reasons for her refusal, one being American racism: "We read about Japanese girls in America—what happened in Cedar Rapids," she tells him (204). American audiences were reading such articles as well, in magazines like *The Saturday Evening Post*, which documented the social obstacles, loneliness, and occasional cruelties encountered by many Japanese wives who came to America with their G.I. husbands.[22] However, Hana-ogi does not stay with Takarazuka simply because of fear of cultural dislocation and racism, for even in her own culture she would be oppressed. Having been sold by her father into concubinage as a young woman, Hana-ogi knows that "Japanese men are very cruel to wives like [her]" (204). Given the harsh realities of patriarchal control of female identity and sexuality—whether in the East or West—Hana-ogi's decision to stay in the Takarazuka seems to be a discerning one. Moreover, Hana-ogi is "Number One" in Takarazuka and firmly committed to her art and the company that saved her from prostitution.

Still, Gruver overrides all these reasons, telling readers Hana-ogi will be committed "to the inverted world of the Takarazuka girls and the green, flowing skirts" (204), relegated to being "the glorious outline of a woman, imprisoned in little rooms or on mammoth stages—loved only by other women" (203).[23] Because dominant postwar gender ideologies prescribed that emotionally healthy women place heterosexual romance and marriage ahead of other values and interests, Hana-ogi's career choice may have seemed inappropriate. (Even Hana-ogi expresses the fear that when her star power is finally extinguished, she may end up begging outside the stage door). Readers may have asked, what woman would willingly choose such a life over marital bliss with Major Gruver? His perspective, though, may belie an attendant fear that female identity and sexuality will remain outside the control of men. It is entirely possible that audience members might see Hana-ogi's choice as an important message about female autonomy, career options, and choosing the company of women over the "natural" choice of heterosexual marriage. Again, though, this perspective goes against the narrative grain, which renders her decision "unnatural," emotionally arid, and ultimately heartbreaking, rather than one based on the material realities of being female in a patriarchal culture.

Michener's novel supplies a further critique of the Butterfly tale through the Takarazuka theatre's restaging of it in *Swing Butterfly*, which inverts the traditional western male fantasy of the East. As Takarazuka's male impersonator, Hana-ogi plays Pinkerton as an arrogant buffoon whose propositions are deftly refused by Butterfly, while another Japanese woman warrior single-handedly fights off an entire shipload of American sailors. *Swing Butterfly* foregrounds both the power relations between East and West from Japan's perspective and the undercurrent of resentment and distrust that Japanese felt toward Americans during the occupation. Accordingly, the play presents a fantasy of resistance and reversal of western domination, in which the white male subject becomes the object of Japanese female scrutiny. Initially, Gruver is disgusted by the ridicule of American military men, but once he is smitten with Hana-ogi, his attitude changes. *Sayonara* acknowledges Japanese sentiments, then, and imagines America's acceptance of them through Gruver's transformation.

However, Takarazuka's social critique is finally depoliticized by Gruver's assessment of the performance in purely aesthetic terms; Hana-ogi's staging of Pinkerton becomes an "exquisite performance," rather than an artistic rendering of a political situation (231). Thus, *Swing Butterfly's* female-identified fantasy exposing the colonialist attitudes of racial and sexual dominance is contained by Gruver's discourse of aesthetics.[24] Nevertheless, his reification of Hana-ogi as artist cannot entirely erase the doubly transgressive meaning that she presents in *Swing Butterfly*: As Pinkerton, she crosses the boundaries of both gender and nation to demonstrate that "white masculinity" is a particular kind of performance. In order to construct her "American," Hana-ogi "studied with intimate care [Gruver's] mannerisms and now reproduced them in burlesque form. When she lit a cigarette she mimicked [him], when she propositioned Madame Butterfly it was [Gruver] trying to kiss her on the Bitchi-bashi" (231). Even as this drag performance calls into question the naturalness of this particular male identity by suggesting that it is built around a series of gestures, mannerisms, dress, and other trappings of masculinity, Gruver still tries to read behind the masquerade: Hana-ogi's impersonation always makes her look all the more "essentially feminine" to him (94).

Michener's revision of the Butterfly story also contains the subversive implications of *Swing Butterfly*. While his plot changes seem to put the dichotomies of gender and nation on more equal footing, thus constructing a more historically relevant story, the narrative still does not fully alter these same hierarchies that structure the Madame Butterfly tale. Even though Michener's Pinkerton/Gruver is not compensated by Butterfly's child or her ultimate sacrifice (suicide) for his love, he still seeks compensation for his lost love by subjecting Hana-ogi to the realm of the eternal. As such, the traditional male fantasy of sexual dominance is reincarnated as a male fantasy of transcendent love, and the Butterfly as sacrificial victim is reincarnated as the eternal woman: "As I watched Hana-ogi I knew that in the future, when even the memory of our occupation has grown dim, a quarter of a million American men will love all women more for having tenderly watched some golden-skinned girl fold herself into the shimmering beauty of a kimono. In memory of her feminine grace all women will forever seem more feminine" (221). The object watched here—Hana-ogi/some golden-skinned girl—becomes the universal standard-bearer of femininity by virtue of her being a passive, eroticized object. The (American) male subject/voyeur reaffirms his own status as active lover, along with reinforcing national and racial boundaries. Memory, in Gruver's conception, becomes an important link between the place called "Japan" and the body of the Japanese female. Just as the "memory of her feminine grace" takes on meaning through its association with "the memory of our occupation," Japan is feminized by its link to its "golden-skinned girls."

Although the urgency of "wooing" both Japan and the American public had diminished somewhat in 1957 when Hollywood's *Sayonara* was released, America's stake in maintaining a positive relationship with Japan was still a foreign-policy objective. Like the novel, the film version, under Joshua Logan's direction, reinforced Michener's attempts at creating cross-cultural harmony through its visual representations of Japan. The opening credits appear over wide-angle shots of Kyoto's beautiful Imperial Gardens; delicate raindrops disturb a pond surface, while a haunting soprano voice sings Irving Berlin's "Sayonara," creating an exotic, romantic mood. Throughout the film, audiences capture glimpses of a colorful marketplace, quaint neighborhoods full of animated children and delicate paper houses, Kobe's wild, rocky coastline, the annual star festival, and the lush gardens surrounding the Takarazuka theater. Along with Gruver, we learn the ritual welcoming of guests in a Japanese home and watch an ancient tea ceremony, tempura cooking, Bunraku puppet and Kabuki performances. Like the novel, Hollywood focuses on the feminine charm of Japanese women, represented by the sweet, painfully shy Katsumi, and the graceful, young Takarazuka actresses—particularly the luminous Hana-ogi—who are part of the poetic spectacle of Japan as they cross a bridge from the theater to dormitory.

However much America's former enemy was humanized by Logan, several of the film's casting decisions not only clouded the film's purported message of racial tolerance, but also galvanized Japanese animosity against the U.S. To Logan's and producer William Goetz's credit, Miyoshi Umeki was signed to play Katsumi; Umeki won an Academy Award for best supporting actress, the first awarded to an Asian American. Even so, Logan initially offered the leading role of Hana-ogi to Audrey Hepburn (who turned it down), prior to discovering Miiko Taka, a second-generation Japanese-American secretary, at a Los Angeles cultural festival. Seeking Hepburn for this part was entirely consistent with Hollywood's systematic discrimination in casting, which inevitably denied Asian actors leading roles. As Eugene Wong points out, "If the role of an Asian character is major, despite the system of role segregation which keeps Asians in Asian roles only or minimally in nonwhite roles, there is no guarantee that an Asian will secure the role because the system of major/minor role stratification can at any time serve to displace the Asian with a white actor or actress" (14).

Casting Ricardo Montalban as Nakamura, a famous Kabuki actor, had further racist implications. Creating Asian features cosmetically, Wong claims, broadened the exclusion of Asian actors on the whole (27),[25] so filling an Asian role with the Mexican-born Montalban reinforced the institutional restrictions on Asian actors and, at the same time, presented audiences with a less threatening ethnic counterpart for the role. Interestingly, Montalban himself was "othered" by Hollywood's insistence on Euro-Americans for leading parts. Prior to *Sayonara*, Montalban filled a variety of ethnic roles—Mexican, Brazilian, Spanish, Arabian, Italian, Native American; with the exception of a few of his early MGM films, he was not given roles as the romantic lead. Montalban functioned in the film industry as a kind of ethnic cipher or variable, able to fill any ethnic role with the help of make-up and costumes. The Japanese press also delighted in taking potshots at Logan's choice of a Mexican to play a ranking Kabuki performer. Moreover, when Logan planned to hire a Japanese Kabuki star to substitute for Montalban in the dance sequences, one Japanese writer remarked that it "was much the same as 'asking Ethel Barrymore to be a stand-in'" (Capote 73). Many Japanese were antagonistic to *Sayonara*'s appropriation of the Takarazuka and Bunraku puppet theaters, as well, seeing this as "degrading [their] finest artistic traditions" (Capote 73).

The film industry, according to Wong, also has been long guilty of sexually neutralizing Asian or nonwhite actors; Asian male romances with white women are "cinematically foreclosed," which effectively ensures white male sexual dominance over all women and neutralizes the Asian male as a sexual rival of white males, "whether or not their potential sexual partners are white or Asian females (26–27). *Sayonara* appears to be on the verge of challenging this prohibition (something Michener's novel never even considers) by adding a subplot featuring an understated romantic interest between Eileen Webster (Patricia Owens) and Nakamura. Even so, the film backs off from this "transgressive" representation; Nakamura refrains from active pursuit of Eileen, always displaying restraint and a courtly manner, which, of course, contrasts with Brando's persistent chase of Hana-ogi, which ends with his "conquest." When Nakamura does finally find himself on a moonlit patio with Eileen, instead of proffering a kiss, he compliments her, quickly reassuring her that he is "not necessarily making love to [her]." After this scene, their relationship is not mentioned again. Nakamura is further desexualized as the shoulder on which Eileen can cry, once she hears of Gruver's "illicit" romance.

In addition to the casting problems associated with Montalban, Logan had difficulty finding an all-girl opera company. Because the Takarazuka had been deeply offended by Michener's libel in the novel, the troupe would neither cooperate with the film company nor lend its name to the production, which left Logan to find his own dancers and call them the Matsubayashi Girl Revue. However, in, his staff went about casting calls for the Matsubayashi in typical Hollywood fashion another gross misreading of Japanese culture, particularly with regard to women as nonpublic figures: They distributed posters around Kyoto advertising that *Sayonara*'s producers were seeking "the one hundred most beautiful girls in Japan." When the posted date arrived, however, not one prospective actress showed up (Capote 74). Logan managed to find enough extras, but the finished product reflected less of the original Takarazuka than Hollywood's idea of a stage spectacle. Several American reviewers noted this, commenting that the Matsubayashi numbers looked like "Oriental week at the Music Hall" (Hatch 484) "the stage show at the Radio City Music Hall when the Rockettes are cutting loose" ("Variation" 90), and "an overdressed girlie show" (Rev. of *Sayonara*, *Time* 16 Dec. 1957, 95).

Both the novel and film appear to be invested in representing Japan as a now friendly, peaceful civilization, full of exotic wonders, time-honored traditions, and beautiful, submissive women. Presenting Japan in this vein was, of course, timely, considering the U.S. government's aim to harness Japan to America's ideological aims for global dominance. However, both narratives contain contradictory messages: advocating tolerance for racial and national "Others," while reproducing traditional power hierarchies between East and West. Pleasing as Japan is made to seem in the two *Sayonaras*, its representations are consistent with the positional superiority, underwritten by racial and gender dichotomies, that the West historically has claimed over the East. Perhaps because, as Said reminds us, there can be no apolitical knowledge or disinterested involvement of West in the East (191), the constructions of Japan in Michener's and Hollywood's versions were marked by an orientalist vision. Furthermore, because the *Sayonaras'* liberal impulses for racial equality and cross-cultural harmony were given shape and impetus within Cold War ideologies, qualms about Asian loyalties to the U.S. and its project of global hegemony continued to reverberate around the edges of the narratives' more progressive aims. In one respect, however, the film does attempt to reconcile the competing interests that the novel unsuccessfully juggles, by supplying a "corrective" to the novel's recuperative ending, which, we recall, whisks Gruver "safely" back to the States, away from the seductive "Orient."

Hollywood's Happy Ending

While remaining sympathetic toward its Japanese-American couples, the novel implies that, given the persistence of racism and cultural differences, interracial marriages were perhaps not a good idea after all. When Marlon Brando read the script for the 1957 film version of *Sayonara*, he objected to this implication, prompting him to name as one of the conditions for playing the role of Major Gruver that the story conclude with the marriage of Gruver and Hana-ogi.[26] Director Joshua Logan resisted at first, saying, "if he marries her, then it becomes a typical Hollywood happy ending." Brando countered, arguing that "people of different races are marrying all the time. Why avoid the issue? Face the fact that an American Southerner could marry a Japanese girl" (Thomas 119). Brando's viewpoint prevailed. In the final moments of the film, Gruver and Hana-ogi (Miiko Taka) head for the U.S. Consulate to be married, leaving fifties audiences with the promise of romantic union and presumably a lesson on racial tolerance. Hollywood's happy ending marks another significant difference from the novel as well. Three zealous reporters from the *Stars and Stripes*, who are eager to make the marriage the latest news, confront the happy couple. "The big brass are going to yell their heads off about this," shouts one reporter. "Got anything to say to them, sir?" After a calculated pause, Gruver replies, "Yeah. Tell 'em we said 'sayonara.'" Brando's cheeky response signals a rupture within the white male power structure when Gruver, the Air Force's "Number One Pin-Up Boy," declines further advancement in the military. Whereas the novel's conclusion reverses its course, revitalizing hegemonic masculinity and its stake in the Cold War, the film ending offers a more progressive outlook on interracial marriage and appears to destabilize the solidarity of hegemony.

Brando's insistence on script changes, effecting a more open view of interracial marriage and racial tolerance, corresponded to an historical shift in the late 1950s, characterized by a "national penchant for soul-searching" and "critical self-evaluation" of domestic issues (Miller and Nowak 16–17). With the end of McCarthyism, with no "other Koreas" in immediate sight, and with the rhetorical shift from anti-communist "containment" to "peaceful coexistence" with the Soviets, Americans had become more introspective about persistent internal problems—race relations being a primary concern (Goldman 284). According to historian J. Ronald Oakley, this period of national reassessment inaugurated the decline of the Eisenhower consensus that had dominated mid-fifties politics and the increase in criticism against conservative approaches to social problems, which tended to deny them altogether or delay implementing democratic solutions (332). Nineteen fifty-seven—the year the film was released—also registered major advances in civil rights activism: Newly forged organizations and initiatives by black leaders stepped up pressure to enact civil rights legislation and enforce compliance with the *Brown* decision.

As if in accord with this particular set of historical circumstances, the film version redirects the novel's ideological and historical contexts, eliminating or downplaying certain elements that explicitly contextualized the novel in the discourses of anti-communism, such as Hot Shot Harry's character and the allusions to "Momism." Deemphasizing references to the Red Scare allowed the film to foreground the issue of race prejudice. In addition, the film's revised ending registers symbolically the difference between 1954 and 1957, which seemingly fulfilled the promise of liberal politics—that achieving civil rights was a matter of gradual, but certain progress. To this end, Brando's insistence on playing Gruver as a Southerner, complete with a "corn-pone and chittlin's accent,"[27] endorsed the belief that even the most hardened racist could be transformed through love and understanding of a racial Other. No doubt, too, the publicity surrounding Brando's own interracial and ethnic romances also lent a certain legitimacy to the film's interracial couples. Several months prior to the film's release, Brando married "Indian" actress Anna Kashfi.[28] However, even before this event, most of the women Brando dated were foreign or non-Anglo—Movita (aka Maria Castenada), Rita Moreno, Pier Angeli, and Josiane Marian-Berenger.

Civil rights was still a Cold War issue, however. The film's Cold War backdrop gave a larger historical purchase to this issue, placing racial conflict beyond the nation's geographical boundaries. Indeed, the eyes of the world were on such incidences as Little Rock, the Soviet Union, in particular, being anxious to take advantage of America's most volatile racial incident of the decade. As noted above, white America's racial intolerance was antithetical to the project of spreading global democracy and economic "goodwill." Cold War anticommunism also hovered at the edges of the narrative; the film's Korean War setting supplied thematic cohesion between 1954 and 1957 with regard to continuing political instability in Asia and U.S. image problems abroad. In this sense, the film maintained historical links to the larger concerns of the Cold War. At the same time, though, it highlighted the historical distance between the novel and the film. In other words, Hollywood's version drew out the political valences of the narrative. We might ask, however, in light of the film's "corrective" ending, what kinds of intervention was *Sayonara* making in the politics of race and gender?

Carol Chung Simpson's research on the crisis of cultural pluralism in the mid-to-late 1950s offers a compelling explanation as to why it was possible or even necessary to rewrite the novel's ending. Noting a shift in the popular press coverage from early fifties articles portraying the "tragic strains" and "the futility of Japanese war brides' futures in America" to mid-fifties stories emphasizing "greater tolerance and even celebration" of their coming to America, Simpson links this image change with white America's need to "redeem rather than to agitate the fraught racial landscape" (68–69). Given the tension and anxiety of the moment as a result of such high profile events as the Montgomery Bus Boycott and the Emmitt Till murder, Americans waited with uncertainty as to how and when racial integration would come about. "This is the point," states Simpson, "at which popular representations of Japanese war brides' relations with exclusively white males became screens for the imagining of a successful racial integration in postwar life and for the re-establishment of the illusion of white innocence" (70). Interestingly, it was none other than James Michener who authored one of the war bride articles. While his 21 February 1955 *Life* magazine story on Frank and Sachiko Pfeiffer recounted the initial difficulties the racially mixed couple experienced, Michener ultimately produced what Simpson calls a "study in triumph of racial tolerance in the postwar period and the amazing potential of white middle-class America to forgo the legacy of racial prejudice" (75). The depiction of Japanese-born Sachiko as a "model minority" helped maintain the illusion that white America could "[approach] the issue of racism ... without ever taking up the historical and political threat to white privilege posed by the *Brown* decision" (Simpson 74).

If indeed the representation of the war bride provided a screen for imagining the successful resolution to racial integration, the 1957 *Sayonara* offered further support. However, its happy ending did not convince everyone that the film presented a forthright, astringent critique of racial intolerance, or, more precisely, enabled a cogent intervention in the forces promoting racism. Film reviewer Robert Hatch was skeptical of its facile resolution of racial conflict through romantic union: "At the end Brando and his girl are on their happy way home to Dixie—I would dearly love to see her pushing a basket down the aisle of a supermarket" (484). Hatch targeted the liberals' faith in the sentimental idea that racial conflict can be overcome relatively easily through a little wishful thinking or by a misinformed bigot catching a love bug. More surprising were Marlon Brando's remarks. His initial attraction to the script was its potential to make a serious statement about racism, prompting him to inform the press upon his arrival in Tokyo for on-location shooting that "[*Sayonara*] strikes very precisely at prejudices that serve to limit our progress toward a peaceful world." However, weeks later Brando trashed the film, calling it "a long ... romantic wallow" (Shipman 60) and, elsewhere, "this wondrous hearts and flowers nonsense," which was incapable of saying anything meaningful about race (Capote 68). If some filmgoers had doubts about the film's efficacy in making a serious social statement, Brando's cynicism would hardly make them believers.

While the film's happy ending seemingly disrupts the power hierarchies of race and nation in the metaphorical union of the lovers, this disruption may come at the expense of gender equality. Hegemonic masculinity appears to be fractured in light of Gruver's "sayonara" to the top brass; however, patriarchy still remains in place. For one, Gruver's masculinity "crisis," brought on by his war weariness and engagement to Eileen, is mitigated—as in the novel—by his affair with a more submissive, exotic eastern woman. Hana-ogi also relinquishes her career and prestige as "Number One Girl" in order to be wife and mother of Gruver's children, which reinstates traditional postwar gender roles. Furthermore, because Hana-ogi—the gendered Other within Cold War discourses—is both a racial and cultural Other, the assurances that racial and national differences are nonconsequential is somewhat problematic, an argument Gina Marchetti makes in *Romance and the Yellow "Peril."* "It is somewhat ironic," Marchetti states, "that Gruver learns racial tolerance through the sexual subjugation of a woman, who sacrifices her independence for his enlightenment. The didactic point of the narrative blurs, and the viewer may begin to wonder if by putting Hana-ogi back into her proper 'place' as a woman, Gruver is not also symbolically putting the racial and national other into its 'place' as subordinate to white America" (137). Thus, the representations of gender, race, and nation in the closing moments of the film potentially reinscribe the discursive formations of the Cold War, while purportedly foregrounding the culture's focus on the emerging civil rights movement and the waning moments of anti-communist hysteria. As in the novel, the hegemonic male becomes racially enlightened and exhibits a "softer" style of masculinity, an image that clearly was in keeping with mainstream demands on postwar males. Moreover, as Marchettti indicates, the symbolic linking of gender, race, and nation within representation makes it difficult to dismantle successfully one power hierarchy (race, for example) while leaving another hierarchy (gender) in place.

Hollywood's *Sayonara* does furnish, however briefly, a subversive representation of gender in the Japanese theatrical world with its female and male impersonators in the Kabuki and Matsubayashi theaters. According to Marjorie Garber, transvestite figures challenge the notion of stable gender identities by creating category crises through their crossdressing, thus producing the undecidability of signification (37). "Transvestitism tells the truth about gender," Garber claims. "Gender ... exists only in representation—in performance" (250). By playing the men's parts, Hana-ogi presents "man" as a construct; likewise, the Kabuki actor, who crossdresses for female roles, presents a highly stylized idea of femininity. As Roland Barthes points out in *Empire of Signs*, "The Oriental transvestite [of Kabuki theater] does not copy woman, but signifies her. Femininity is presented to read, not to see" (53). Perhaps it is this troubling of an essentialist notion of femininity that causes Gruver's acute discomfort when he attends Kabuki, a spectacle requiring him to gaze at a female figure who is, in fact, male, and which then prompts his ill-mannered remark to Nakamura that Kabuki could use "a few Marilyn Monroes."

In addition to creating a gender disturbance, Hana-ogi's cross-dressing also hints at a disruption of "normative" (hetero)sexuality. Significantly, when Gruver first sees Hana-ogi, she is in drag, and he is instantly enthralled with her. Thus, her performance produces what Marchetti calls "an even more forbidden homoeroticism." As their love affair progresses, however, Hana-ogi ceases to appear in drag, instead dressing in traditional kimonos and behaving demurely and more submissively (Marchetti 136). Thus, while she initially occupies a subversive space as a cross-dressed, racial, *and* sexual Other, her disruptive potential is muted by reinstating traditional gender practices. In this sense, Hana-ogi's transformation becomes symbolic-ally linked with Japanese submission to American authority, and the theatrical world with its production of gender performativity is left behind in the realm of the "foreign" as the two lovers head for America.

Marlon Brando's Gruver

Performativity itself is underscored in Japanese theater, most notably in Takarazuka, Kabuki, and Bunraku productions.[29] Interestingly, the casting of Marlon Brando, one of the fifties foremost Method actors, juxtaposes this western style of acting, which purportedly authenticates representation by conflating actor and character's inner emotional states, with the explicit refusal of inwardness and illusion in Japanese theater. Using Bunraku puppets to illustrate the fundamental difference in theatrical modes, Barthes argues that the Japanese puppet show foregrounds the illusion of theater, whereas western stage productions present "the illusion of totality originating in the body" (59). The West presents a "metonymic contagion of voice and gesture, body and soul, which entraps our actors," giving audiences a fantasy of originality and "depth through the elaboration of copy" (Barthes 55). In contrast, says Barthes, "what is expelled from the [Bunraku] stage is hysteria, i.e., theater itself; and what is put in its place is the action necessary to the production of the spectacle: work is substituted for inwardness" (62). Method acting ostensibly works to present "authentic" emotion as opposed to signs; certainly, this was how fifties film critics described Method performances. However, "authenticity," which supposedly lays claim to some "inner truth" of character and actor, may not necessarily be the only or final effect. As Virginia Wright Wexman claims, Method techniques (outlined in chapter 2) also emphasize theatricality so that performativity and style override the "truth" of character. Moreover, Method acting serves to construct a (male) subjectivity that is vulnerable, ambivalent about male power and authority, and conflicted about gender identification (Wexman 161, 167). In this sense, the Method advanced the potential for understanding gender as complex and multiple rather than coherent and unified.

It would be remiss, though, not to point out that in *Sayonara* Brando's trademark gestures—his manner of articulating confusion, indecision, angst, or inner pain—conceivably "authenticated" his character as a divided protagonist, one caught between his status as a hegemonic male and his rejection of rigid, racist, military values.

Furthermore, in certain respects, Brando proved to be a good fit with Gruver, meaning that Brando's public persona was in close accord with the various signs of his character. Even so, as I will show in the following discussion, Brando's star text also held the potential to offer multiple articulations of male gender identity through his association with masculine masquerading and performativity, which work to demystify the coherence and "authenticity" of identity, similar to the way Japanese stage impersonators subverted gender and sexual identities.

In terms of Brando's potential to conflate star and character, extratextual aspects of his image and his performance in *Sayonara* both contributed to this possibility. During the mid-to-late fifties, Brando became associated with social causes, aspiring to use movies and his own production company, Pennebaker Productions, to say "important things to a lot of people about discrimination and prejudice" (Capote 65). *Sayonara* appeared to be an apt vehicle through which he could begin saying some of these things (at least for those unaware of Brando's disparaging remarks about the film). In addition, Brando's image as "sensitive, but two-fisted" ("The Master" 19) was well suited to Michener's Gruver, who was alternately pulled between the opposing forces of military obligation and personal desire. Brando's early fifties image as an inveterate iconoclast may have continued to reverberate with Gruver's nonconformity as well. True, Brando's late fifties star text was rarely linked with his earlier characterization in fan discourses as "The Rebel" or "The Slob"—monikers he earned by his inclination to be "rude, moody, sloppy, prodigal" (Martin 90)—and from such shocking, sexually alluring portrayals as Stanley Kowalski in *A Streetcar Named Desire* (1951) and Johnny in *The Wild One* (1954). However, Brando's association with a "sense of otherness," which meant rejecting the "bland, politesse of middle-class America" (Schickel 36), may have had a residual effect in *Sayonara*. For example, when Gruver, recalling his previous decision to forgo an acting career in order to enter West Point, confesses to pal Mike Bailey (James Garner) that "just lately, [he's] been thinkin' about a whole new way of life," audiences might have associated this trace of "otherness" with fan magazines' claims that Brando himself was a man in search of his identity. (In a twist on art imitating life, Brando, in fact, left Shattuck Military Academy only later to pursue an acting career).

Brando's star text acquired new dimensions in the mid-fifties as he actively sought to divorce himself from his youthful image as rebellious, rude, immature, even primitive. He was fairly successful in achieving this transition "from rebel to quiet, melancholy man," as evidenced by one fan magazine's assertion that "The Magnificent Brat has grown up" ("Quiet" 18). Likewise, the *Woman's Home Companion* assured its readers that, in contradistinction to his crude, black leather-jacketed image, Brando was "in fact sensitive, intelligent, and articulate" (Ardomore 22). Elsewhere, he was called "an exemplary new domesticated Marlon Brando [who] has replaced the surly, old savage one" (Ager 24). Nonetheless, according to the fan discourse, Brando tamed was still "a man in search of his own identity," again, an image consistent with Michener's confused ace pilot. The self-questioning, newly domesticated film star echoes his character's increasing uncertainty about the dominance, control, and violence associated with traditional forms of white male identity. In the opening scene of the film, after taxiing his jet to a standstill, Gruver stays seated in the cockpit, brooding, staring straight ahead. Signifying his inner turmoil with a familiar Brando gesture—sighing and wiping his hand over his mouth and chin, Gruver says to Kelly (Red Buttons), "There was a guy with a face in one of those planes today." This antiwar stance, coming at the beginning of the narrative, clues audiences that Brando's Gruver is different from Michener's: He is less likely to "snap to" in the closing moments of the film and return to the business of war.

Other key scenes in the film perhaps underscored Gruver's "naturalness" and "interiority," making credible his transformation from hard to soft masculinity. When Gruver is left alone with Hana-ogi, her initial silence flusters him to the point where he launches into a nervous monologue fraught with Brando's trademark hesitations and repetitious speech. Attempting a typical American come-on ("Did ... did anyone ever tell you, Miss Ogi, you are one fahn lookin' woman?"), he encounters her blank stare, which elicits a stammering apology about his "embarrassin' American manners." Realizing that he has tried to dominate their meeting and treat it as a typical American date, he relinquishes control, stammering and mumbling, "You got to tell me ... where to go from here .... cause I don't know what to say ... I'm runnin' outta' things to say." His image is further softened when Brando/Gruver later sheds his military uniform for a kimono. In this particular scene, he waits for Hana-ogi at Kelly's home, whistling softly as he waters a houseplant, then reclines on the floor—Japanese style—dreamily smoking a cigarette. His kimono, the watering can, the cigarette, and his reclining posture all signal a different style of masculinity: sensitive, nurturing, relaxed, introspective.

Just as plausible, though, these scenes register a kind of performance or masquerade that calls into question any essential notion of gender identity. It goes without saying that actors must undergo cosmetic makeovers and sartorial transformations, hence effect a kind of masquerade. Such theatrical artifice also may have suggested that a "real" self or actor stands behind—separate from—the make-up, costume, gestures, and so forth, since "the masculine self has traditionally been held to be inherently opposed to the kind of deceit and dissembling characteristic of the masquerade" (Brod 13). As Steven Cohan puts it, "the cosmetic aspect of screen performance ... runs against the grain of the traditional assumption that masculinity is the essential and spontaneous expression of maleness;" however, acting "blows the cover of a 'natural' man in its technical acknowledgment that gendered sexualities are constituted out of fakery and spectacle" ("Masquerading" 221). By masquerade, then, I mean something beyond the obvious fact that acting—playing a role—requires dressing up and impersonation, which places in opposition a fixed, constant, masculine "self" and a role constructed through various disguises. Rather, masquerade calls attention to the surface effects, fabricated by props, gestures, mannerisms, and diction, which function in concert to gender the body. In short, masquerade does not express gender; rather, gender *is* masquerade or performance.

Brando/Gruver's discarding his military uniform, which symbolically armors the male body and furnishes the trappings of hegemonic authority, for a kimono hints at the sartorial and gestural components of gender. Through the change of clothing and mannerisms, the performativity of gender is made more explicit. Furthermore, Gruver's desire to find "a whole new way of life" suggests he has been masquerading as a major, using position and authority to make the man. In a striking example early in the film—Gruver trying to convince Kelly to give up Katsumi—we see that his hegemonic status is largely constituted by discursive effects, the trappings of power, and the "consent" of subordinate males. Still in his flight suit, a signifier of rank and power, Gruver pretends to effect a casual manner with Kelly by having a talk over a cup of coffee. However, his obvious discomfort with his own authority is made visible in typical Brando-esque gestures, such as his attempt to dump out the dregs of an obviously bone-dry coffee cup. For each objection

Gruver raises about interracial marriage, Kelly fires back a sound retort: His family won't care, because he "ain't got any family; he is passionate about Katsumi, but maybe Gruver doesn't "feel as strongly about his girl" (clearly striking a nerve with Gruver). When Gruver shows him Eileen's picture, Kelly (looking at Mrs. Webster's image instead) says nastily, "She's kinda' beat up, ain't she?" once again throwing Gruver off his mark. With Kelly clearly in control, Gruver becomes less articulate and more confused, as if lost in a maze. Finally, when Kelly subtlely dismisses Gruver (reversing military protocol), we begin to realize that hegemonic masculinity is a symbolic construction, dependent on who has discursive control.

Gruver puts on his official voice one other time with equal unsuccess. When Mike Bailey is reprimanded by General Webster (Kent Smith) for bringing a Japanese woman to the Officers Club, provoked, he fails to address Webster as "sir." Gruver, adding his own reprimand, demands, "Don't you know there's such a thing as insolence through manner?" Later Bailey mocks Gruver with these words when he orders a drink: "Don't you mean 'scotch and soda, *sir?*'" Sheepishly conceding his pomposity, in the next few minutes Gruver confesses to Bailey that he is having doubts about military life. The rigid masculinity demanded by the military becomes an increasingly difficult performance to sustain. Thus, when he must masquerade as an officer, his speech becomes hesitant and repetitious, accompanied by twitches of his mouth or shakes of his head. According to Graham McCann, Brando, as in his other film roles, "conveyed how the traditional toughness and tight-lipped invulnerability of the male hero were actually defense mechanisms as opposed to emblems of masculinity" (111).

Film reviewers were not unaware of Brando's masquerading in *Sayonara* (despite that his Method techniques supposedly naturalized performance). *Time*'s film critic had difficulty seeing Gruver in terms other than Brando's theatricality: His Southern accent "sounds as if it was strained through Stanislavsky's mustache" and his big love scene with Hana-ogi is marred by "much too much Brandoperatic declamation." Furthermore, the reviewer called attention to performance per se by criticizing Brando's failure to collapse star and part—that is to say, his apparent failure to establish a convincing correspondence between his own authenticity and his character's authenticated life: "Brando has to pretend to take the situation seriously, and it plainly bores him. He has some fun now and then monkey-see-monkey-doing like the Japanese, but he seems to find it unsatisfying to have to scratch himself through a kimono" (Rev. of *Sayonara, Time* 16 Dec. 1957: 94–95). This "monkey-see-monkey-doing" occurs, for instance, when Gruver first visits Kelly and Katsumi's home. He imitates Katsumi's gestures in the ritual exchange of saki cups, but barely conceals his amused condescension or his flair for the theatrical by pretending to wash his ears and underarms with a serviette. Although the *New Yorker* found his southern accent "absolutely legitimate, even to the generic drawback of occasionally ... making him sound like the end man in a minstrel show," we might remind ourselves that minstrel shows are themselves highly conventional, theatrical performances. The review goes on to praise Brando's "excellent acting ... when he is articulate and not giving the impression that there's something loose in his haid" ("Variation" 89–90). Again, these remarks refute the "naturalness" of acting, suggesting otherwise his obvious masquerade of a good ol' southern boy.

Brando/Gruver's hamming it up as Hana-ogi makes her daily walk across the Bitchi-bashi further illustrates his production of a gendered, sexualized performance. One day he slouches on the bridge railing, tipping his hat to the object of his desire. The next day he lounges on a flat, sloping tree trunk; on the following day, he hides behind it, gratified that Hana-ogi pauses to look for him. Imitating her own gender performance of the aloof, icy, stage actress, Gruver playfully mimes a snooty woman as she passes him by. His penchant for the dramatic does not go unnoticed by Hana-ogi; later she admits to him: "I have been watching you too." Presumably, so has the audience. The camera seems not so much interested in Hana-ogi as the object of the gaze here as it does in Brando/Gruver. Not only does this interest underscore the use of the body to produce the effects of a particular form of masculinity, but it also theatricalizes masculinity as a sequence of poses. Furthermore, the Bitchi-bashi scenes overturn the traditional binary of active male subject versus passive female object, which governs who gazes and who is looked at. By making the male body desirable, the film problematizes the stability of traditional masculinity, similar to the way Burt Lancaster's masculinity is destabilized in *From Here to Eternity*'s beach scene.

Even before *Sayonara*, Brando's film appearances were characterized by masquerade, particularly in the mid-fifties and after. "Masquerade," Cohan maintains, "turns out to be the central motif of Brando's career" (*Masked* 249). From starring as a Mexican revolutionary in *Viva Zapata!* (1952), Mark Antony in *Julius Caesar* (1953), Napoleon in *Désirée* (1954), an amiable gambler in *Guys and Dolls* (1955), to an Okinawan interpreter in *Teahouse of the August Moon* (1956), Brando appeared in strikingly different roles and costume disguises. Although these films did not foreground the erotic dimensions of Brando's body as did his earlier film, *Streetcar*, in which Brando appeared to be "impersonating his virility rather than embodying it" (Cohan *Masked* 249),[30] *Julius Caesar* did give audiences a chance to see Brando's bulging biceps protruding from his toga. One reviewer, however, criticized Brando's over-reliance on bodily gestures to produce his Roman statesman: "Brando, as Mark Antony, plainly shows he needs a bit of speech training before he can graduate into an acting league where the spoken word is a trifle more significant than the flexed biceps and the fixed eye" (Rev. of *Julius Caesar*, *New Yorker* 13 June 1953: 65). While this critic was faulting Brando for his failure to master Shakespeare's blank verse, he also pointed out Brando's techniques of performing masculinity with muscles and gestures, affirming Cohan's claim about Brando's impersonating virility.

Although Brando received his share of critical praise for his acting in the mid-fifties, he also was faulted, most notably for his blatant theatricality, specifically his "failure" to disguise his acting. While critics felt the "naturalness" was missing in his various impersonations, by drawing attention to the cosmetology, speech patterns, costuming, gestures, and mannerisms that Brando used to construct a range of characters, these reviewers also drew attention to his patent masquerading of masculinities. Of his acting in *Viva Zapata!*, at least two reviewers complained that Brando's gestures and diction too often recalled Stanley Kowalski of *Streetcar*.[31] Several critics drew a bead on Brando's make-up. *Life*, for one, stated, "Brando is betrayed ... by the Twentieth Century-Fox make-up men who let his unlined American-boy cheeks belie his role as a hard-bitten outlaw" (Rev. of *Viva Zapata!* 25 Feb. 1952: 59). Whereas these criticisms suggest that Brando failed to make a convincing Mexican revolutionary, they imply, too, that masculinity is the result of what one does in terms of processing the body. Surely, this implication is made explicit in *Life*'s description and accompanying photograph of how Brando was transformed into Zapata: "An Indian look was given Brando by make-up men, who enlarged his nostrils with plastic bands, glued up corners of his eyes, [and] pasted on a drooping black mustache" (Rev. of *Viva Zapata!* 25 Feb. 1952: 59).

Costuming and gestures were again important in creating Brando's Napoleon and his Okinawan Sakini, two distinctly different masculine personas. Brando himself vaunted the theatrical fakery that helped produce his Napoleon: "Most of the time I just let the make-up play the part" ("Tiger" 65). Critics noticed more than his reliance on make-up, however. *Time*'s reviewer maintained, "Not that [Brando] really plays Napoleon ... he beetles his brow and pots his belly in the manner of the official portraits" (Rev. of *Désirée, Time* 29 Nov. 1954: 76). Another critic noted, "he is stiffly posed in every scene, and it must be said that he is seldom more than Marlon Brando in a Napoleon suit" ("The Emperor" 39). In a contrasting observation, which nonetheless still emphasizes performativity, *Newsweek* stated, "he looks more like Napoleon than Napoleon himself, with a result that sometimes borders on burlesque" (Rev. of *Désirée, Newsweek* 29 Nov. 1954: 97). Brando's appearance in *The Teahouse of the August Moon* garnered similar reactions from the critics, who focused on his highly theatrical performance and his drastic change of voice, cosmetics, and gestures to effect Sakini, a humble, but wily Okinawan interpreter. Brando, *Newsweek*'s film critic observed, "is almost completely hidden from view by heavy makeup and a mode of performance so highly stylized that he seems not to be an actor so much as a dancer giving an ingenious and difficult imitation" ("Brando as Rogue" 98–99). The *New Yorker* was less approving: Although Brando "is made up to look like a relative of Dr. Fu Manchu, and babbling pidgin English at a great rate, he never succeeds in hiding the fact that he's really an All-American boy" ("No Time" 145). What is noteworthy in this last statement is the displacement of one well-known masculine masquerade—the All-American boy—by another—Dr. Fu Manchu.

What may be significant in Brando's impersonations of Sakini and perhaps in his performance of Emiliano Zapata, is the implication that "race" is also a kind of masquerade, which can be produced through a processing of the body, just as different forms of masculinity can. Moreover, by juxtaposing Brando's performances of nonwestern characters with his range of white, western figures, we can begin to see the raciality of whiteness, meaning that whiteness is produced as much through various signs of "race" as is nonwhiteness. In other words, Brando's series of mid-to-late fifties roles helped to make "white" appear as a race, in contradistinction to the dominant discourses of Anglo-American culture, which naturalized and thus erased from representation the signs of whiteness; this naturalization and erasure, in turn, situated whiteness as the center in determining position and difference of all other racial groupings. Brando's masquerades, which show that his white characters rely on costume and body markings as much as his nonwhite ones, may have exposed the fact that whiteness is also the product of certain representational practices.

While Marlon Brando might have played a crucial role in *Sayonara* in authenticating his character, his association with masquerade and theatricality implies that gender exists in the realm of representation as opposed to the (fictive) realm of the "natural." The visual spectacle of Brando—as Roman statesman, Mexican outlaw, European emperor, underworld gambler, Okinawan interpreter, southern officer—alerts us to the performative dimensions of masculinity, showing that gender identification does not depend on some authentic, natural embodiment of masculinity. Rather, it depends upon the display of a range of effects produced on the body. As reviewers repeatedly brought to the public's attention, Brando's blatant theatricality held the potential to overpower the notion that Method acting collapsed star and part, and, while some reviewers found this failure to collapse actor and role as one of his shortcomings, they inadvertently shed light on masquerade itself as a production of particular gendered identities. Both Brando's use of the Method and masquerade ultimately contribute to the complication of gender norms and representations of race in *Sayonara* —in some respects lending credibility and authenticity to Gruver, but otherwise problematizing the notion that masculinity is a self-evident, stable category of gender. Furthermore, if gender itself is none other than performance, this, too, calls into question the gender hierarchy that structures the romantic relationships in the film. As we see through Gruver's loss of control of speech and meaning at times, hierarchy is constructed and maintained by particular discursive posturings of authority and power.

In conclusion, at first glance, Hollywood's *Sayonara* appears to leave a positive impression of some of the political and social challenges facing America in 1957: The relationship with Japan was entering a new era, the Red Scare had lessened somewhat (otherwise would not Gruver have returned to shooting down MIGs?), and racial harmony seemed obtainable. However, the film produced its share of uncertainties in terms of its representations of gender and race, categories which were intricately interwoven with these Cold War issues. Perhaps filmgoers did not leave the theater fully articulating *Sayonara*'s representational inconsistencies, but they may have sensed in watching the film and through their knowledge of extratextual material—casting problems, film reviews, Brando's response to the film itself—the kinds of ideological conflicts that were embedded in this text. That is to say, what may have appeared to be a seamless closure, promising racial harmony, both internally and externally, is qualified by the film's uncomplicated resolution of racial conflict and its unmediated vision of Japan, which fails to dismantle the West's historical construction of the East as a subordinate, feminine "Other."

Try as it might, then, the film narrative did not fully rescue the novel from its failure to reconcile its own competing interests, namely, easing the masculinity "crisis" and resolving racial conflict. Michener's novel, in particular, makes explicit the historical links between gender, race, and nation, justifying in the final chapters the reinstatement of white hegemonic masculinity, while offering up an image of symbolic racial integration through the white soldier's memory of the "yellow-skinned girl." Miscegenation and racial integration can be imagined by whites, even longed for, but still not openly or freely practiced. In this sense, the novel served as a kind of contemporary index in 1954 of the national initiatives set in motion by the *Brown* decision: Many Americans recognized the urgency in achieving racial equality, yet were not certain as to how the obstacles to integration could be over-come. One such obstacle, as I have argued, was the Cold War insistence on fortifying representations of nation through certain images of masculinity—white, middle-class, virile, and heterosexual—which necessarily excluded an array of "others" and effectively white-washed national image in order to present a coherent America, impervious to communist subversion.

Both novel and film, however, play a role in registering the inherent contradictions of Cold War ideology and serve as testimonies to the incongruities and conflicts that were embedded in the discourses of race and gender, particularly when these discourses became inextricably bound to representations of nation. The two *Sayonaras* demonstrate how much remained at stake in the act of representation itself, indeed how much was at stake in making images of nation cohere around particular images of gender and race during the Cold War. However, if the stakes were high, the *Sayonaras* also demonstrated the very impossibility of stabilizing representation, perhaps because these texts so clearly imply that representation is grounded in history and culture. In the following chapter on *Giant*, which preceded *Sayonara* by two years, this emphasis on the historical and cultural grounds of representation is made even more explicit. Not attempting to ease the masculinity "crisis," *Giant* exposes the racism and sexism that were underpinnings of the mutually reinforcing images of masculinity and nation.

4

"Slipping from under Me Like a Loose Saddle": The Degeneration of Dynasty in Edna Ferber's *Giant*

In both *From Here to Eternity* and *Sayonara*, the governing thrust of each novel centers on formulating acceptable styles of masculinity that are congruent with mainstream cultural and political needs in representing nationhood. This concept entails revising rigid and oppressive forms of patriarchy, represented in these texts by hard-line military men. Focusing just as keenly on male subjectivity, Edna Ferber's *Giant* (1952) reproduces this critique of hard masculinity within the context of a dynastic family rather than the military. Ferber's novel, however, registers ambivalence toward, even distrust of male power, whereas neither *From Here to Eternity* nor *Sayonara* ultimately questions male prerogatives to act as agents of institutionalized forms of power. Both novels evoke the mythology of endangered masculinity that had become central to postwar discourses linking gender and national identity and then resolve the masculinity-in-crisis they create, echoing the national strategy to diminish Cold War anxieties. Unlike *From Here to Eternity* or *Sayonara*, *Giant* introduces a feminine perspective that appears to be instrumental in refocusing its formulation of masculinity. In fact, Ferber's novel presumes the "crisis" lies elsewhere—not in a masculinity that needs shoring up, but in the very notion of traditional gender formations.

Gender is not only one of the central preoccupations in Ferber's "Texas novel," but it informed its literary production and reception as well. Intrigued by the larger-than-life aura of everything Texan and the lore of the West, Ferber visited Texas in 1939 to begin collecting raw material for a book. The Lone Star state lived up to her expectations as "virile," "brash," and "larger than life," but after her tour Ferber shelved a prospective novel about Texas (Gilbert 176). Despite her success with other regional novels, *So Big* (1924) and *Cimarron* (1929), and her popularity as a best-selling author, Ferber later claimed after seeing Texas that writing about this state was "a man's job," more specifically, a job for "some two-fisted hemingwayish novelist" (qtd. in Gilbert 176). This perspective on writing, sexual difference, and Texas, however, may have functioned as a shrewd rhetorical position for Ferber as a writer, situating her as "a woman battling the odds in a man's world."[1] Specifically, after thirteen more years and several more trips to the region, she produced *Giant,* a muckraking saga of the cattle-wealthy Benedict family, whose dynasty, ruled over by Jordan "Bick" Benedict III, is challenged by the encroaching oil industry as well as by the reassessment of "progress" in terms of human value and civil rights. Ferber's story traces the gradual decline of Bick's ironclad reign over his family, his ranching community, and local politics. His authority is questioned not only by his eastern liberal wife Leslie, but also by his two children, who reject the status quo of which Bick is a part. *Giant* was enormously popular, placing sixth on the annual best-seller list and chosen as a Book-of-the-Month-Club selection in October 1952. One year later, *Reader's Digest Condensed Books* published an abridged edition. Aware that *Giant* would complete his film trilogy on America's geographical and economic transitions, along with *A Place in the Sun* (1951) and *Shane* (1953), director George Stevens began preproduction for a film version in 1953. Released in 1956, Hollywood's *Giant* captured ten Academy Award nominations[2] and was a top moneymaker for that year, third behind two other "big" pictures, *The Ten Commandments* and *Around the World in Eighty Days.*

Although readers nationwide launched the novel to best-seller status when it first appeared, "a fair share of Texas ... failed to find in *Giant* the substance for amusement" (Nichols 30). Rather, they felt impugned by Ferber's descriptions of their state as a carnival of wealth for flamboyant cattle and oil barons and a seedbed of race prejudice against Mexican Americans. One Texan complained, ironically, that by appropriating the Texan "art" of "embroidery of fact," Ferber gave into a "passion for hilarious exaggeration," and "the irresistible impulse to turn everything into a 'tall tale'" and, therefore, got his state all wrong (Gilbert 187–88). Ferber herself reported receiving hundreds of letters that ranged from "choleric" to "vicious"; some suggested she be shot or lynched for maligning their state (Nichols 30).

Sam Nugent, a particularly vexed reader from Austin, Texas, objected not so much to what was perceived by some as Ferber's regional "rabbit punch," but to her "bias in favor of Woman" and her "tidy little feminist world" in which "men are only excess baggage." In a letter to the Dallas *Morning News,* Nugent complained that the newspaper's book reviewer did not underscore forcefully enough that "Miss Ferber may be provoked because Texas is not a 'womaned' state" (qtd. in Gilbert 190). Like Ferber, Nugent conceptualized Texas as a masculine State/state, yet he felt compelled to defend its honor by discrediting Ferber as a kind of male basher. Nugent may well have correctly identified the "bias" in Ferber's body of work, perhaps pegging why her literary representations of male identity differed from those of her postwar contemporaries, Jones and Michener. Ferber's niece and biographer, Julie Goldsmith Gilbert, points out that she was "a precursor of the Women's Liberation Movement by depicting every single one of her fictional heroines as progressive originals who doggedly paved large inroads for themselves and their 'race.' Her male characters, on the other hand, were usually felled by their colorful but ultimately ineffectual machismo" (12). Ferber's feminism likely contributed to her popularity as a writer and, therefore, extended beyond the personal to address the social—points that Nugent overlooked. Moreover, by suggesting that Texas was not "womaned," Nugent called attention to precisely what Ferber aimed to critique: a concept of hegemonic masculinity that is so polarized, exclusive, and hard that it forecloses expressions of difference, creativity, and human compassion.

Curiously, the Texan response to the film version was quite different. In general, the agitation over Ferber's (mis)representation of Texas gave way to their enthusiastic attendance at the movie theaters.[3] John Rosenfield, film critic for the Dallas *Morning News*, noted there were "anticipated difficulties" over unflattering depictions of Texas but that "all the fears now seem groundless. [*Giant*] is accepted for what it is, mighty entertainment" (Gilbert 152). A vice-president of the movie theater chain, Interstate Circuit, reported that "[he] had not heard anyone say that *Giant* misrepresents Texas .... A valid controversy never hurt movie business ... but I guess we won't have one" (Gilbert 153). Certainly, we cannot determine precisely why some Texans considered the film "mighty entertainment" and the novel an occasion to lynch Ferber at an autograph party. However, this shift in reception, particularly from those who felt a strong allegiance to their state, may function as a rudimentary gauge of ideological differences between the novel and the film. If we consider gender to be one of the central categories informing Ferber's representation of Texas, we might ask what this shift means at the level of gender.

The burden of both the novel and the film seems to be to convince cattle baron and family patriarch Bick Benedict that his form of rule is oppressive and destructive. However, the novel offers a more stringent critique of patriarchy, which in this case operates through the feudal structure of the dynastic family. Dynasty is primarily concerned with preserving power through land holdings, inheritance, and lineage and exerting its power and authority over the lives and affairs of local populations within its range of influence. Because the dynastic family, according to Virginia Wright Wexman, is central to the American myth of national origins and identity (76–77), the novel appears to be deconstructing this myth as well, by exposing its suppressed elements—the marginalization or destruction of nature, nonwhite inhabitants, and the feminine. The construct "Texas" and Bick's Reata ranch, then, serve as the setting for events and people who have been obscured and/or obliterated in the mainstream narrative of American "history." The novel has a more pronounced investment than the film in situating gender overtly in the realm of politics. In other words, the novel exposes the political techniques of patriarchy, or those strategies and practices by which traditional gender hierarchies are produced and sustained, as well as how these hierarchies intersect with the categories of race and class.

Although the film also proposes to critique hard masculine ideals, it minimizes the harshness of its "giant," Bick Benedict. In fact, it is quite tempting to agree with Peter Biskind's claim that, in keeping with many postwar cinematic depictions of the family, Hollywood's *Giant* "feminizes Bick"—mainly through wife Leslie's influence—and thus reconstitutes patriarchy as a matriarchy, in which "mother knows best."[4] Whereas male subjectivity in the film does undergo a transformation, making it more compatible with dominant discourses in the 1950s that glorified the companionate marriage within a privatized nuclear family, Biskind's idea of patriarchy reconstituted as matriarchy is not entirely convincing. True, certain plot and structural changes in the film function to produce a softer, more benevolent Bick, and clearly the star persona of "gentle giant" Rock Hudson[5] moderates Ferber's swaggering, hard-headed cattle baron. However, if patriarchy in Hollywood's *Giant* is domesticated, it also is ultimately revitalized. The film narrative, after all, belongs to Rock Hudson's Bick, who not only survives, relatively unscathed, the transition from a cattle to an oil-producing economy, but also learns to temper his racism, therefore, conceding that gradual racial integration is the right course of action. Patriarchy is not so much overturned by matriarchy as it survives by becoming softened on hard-line race issues. By recuperating its own critique of patriarchy, the film not only offers a more simplified understanding of the novel's gender politics, but also brings into sharper focus the novel's confrontation with patriarchy. In short, the film produces an alternate reading of the novel and a context through which to read it.

Even so, the casting of James Dean, who stars as Bick's archrival Jett Rink, complicates this reading of the film, a subject addressed in the final section. Narratively, Jett functions to authorize Bick's relatively untrammeled masculinity. However, Dean's sudden death prior to *Giant's* release created a nationwide furor over this rising young actor, causing audiences and reviewers alike to focus on Dean's screen presence despite that he had appeared in only about thirty minutes of *Giant's* three hour and eighteen minute running time. In addition to this publicity explosion, Dean's star persona overrode his narrative role as the foil to Bick/Hudson's hegemonic masculinity by providing a resistance to middle-class propriety and to the notion of gender identity as a stable, fixed entity. Whereas the film's recontextualizing of masculinity through both Rock Hudson and plot alterations tends to defuse the novel's troubling of male hegemony, the hype surrounding James Dean reintroduced the question of gender instability, perhaps opening up an alternative space for viewers' identification.

Historical and Geographical Contexts

In the courtyard square facing the street was a monstrous plate-glass case as large as a sizable room made of thick transparent glass on all sides. Within this, staring moodily out at a modern world, stood a stuffed and mounted Longhorn steer. A huge animal, his horn-spread was easily nine feet from tip to tip. (Giant 114)

Spanning nearly three decades, *Giant* chronicles the economic and social transitions of two generations of the Benedict family, the first beginning with the marriage of Texas ranch mogul Jordan "Bick" Benedict III and Virginia blueblood Leslie Lynnton in the early 1920s. Although Leslie looks forward to living in Texas, much of what she discovers about her new home is distressing. Not only does she become the target of Bick's older sister Luz's hostility, but the love interest of his insolent, sullen cowhand, Jett Rink. In addition, Leslie encounters a host of social ills: racial prejudice against Mexican Americans, the feudal organization of ranch life, and, what affects her most personally, a social structure that replicates the old saying that "in Texas the cattle come first, then the men, then the horses and last the women" (54).[6] Not surprising, Bick, a conservative traditionalist, and Leslie, a liberal reformer, are often at cross-purposes, though they do stay married and raise two (three in the film) headstrong children, Jordy (Jordan IV) and Luz II. Both offspring ultimately disappoint their father by not loving Reata as much as he does and by rejecting many of the values and social practices that have structured ranch life for decades. Bick's cattle dynasty is further eroded by Texas's transition to an industrial-based economy; once Jett strikes oil on his small scrap of Reata, he becomes an instant millionaire and succeeds in getting his rival Bick to sell him drilling leases on Reata.

Ferber's use of Texas as a geographical and historical context for *Giant* furnished postwar readers with a point of entry apropos to her social critique. Images of grandiose exaggeration and hypermasculine excess have been central to the construct "Texas" in American culture, and Ferber did not hesitate to reproduce these impressions. Postwar Texas had become known for, and by, its tall tales: Only rich and poor millionaires inhabited Texas, a land of Cadillacs with Longhorn horns mounted on the grill. Texan mosquitoes were the size of dragonflies. Canaries sang bass. Even today, a tall man in a big Stetson—size being an obvious trope for phallic superiority, iconizes Texas. Perhaps Texans have diligently fostered such associations, creating a collective fantasy of Texan wealth and power; however, non-Texans also have willingly used these images to contain the contradictions of national identity. That is to say, the line can easily blur between the American living the "good life" and the "ugly American," whose brash manners, excessive wealth, and conspicuous consumption are an international embarrassment. Texas conveniently serves as a site on which Americans can displace a national sense of distaste and chagrin, while at the same time retaining their pride in economic abundance, cultural "superiority," and "progress."

Texas, though, has cultural significance beyond being, in Ferber's words, "the crude uncle who has struck it rich" (Gilbert 174). It has long been associated in the popular imagination with the West, an association reinforced in the 1950s by the proliferation of Western films and perhaps made more favorable (for some) by the symbolic alliance between the West and national identity. As a mythic space, the West has functioned historically as a repository for white America's claims to a unique national identity based on rugged individualism, manifest destiny, and empire building. According to Wexman, at the core of westward expansion and empire building is the image of the "family on the land" and dynastic marriage. Although this image has been idealized as the small family farm, more often in Westerns it is depicted as the sprawling ranch. Ranching occurs on a more grandiose scale, Wexman notes, and therefore is represented as a more "heroic" enterprise; paradoxically, though, it "involves a division of labor spearheaded by a capitalist entrepreneur," which, in fact, portrays a less egalitarian enterprise of large tracts of land owned by only a few (81). Despite its rapid industrial and urban growth, postwar Texas was still able to summon the memory of the mythic West, with its wide open space, colossal size, and its symbolic correlates of individual freedom and opportunity for conquest.

Giant readily draws on the iconography and thematic concerns of the mythic West and the Western: It has ranchers, cowboys, horses, cattle, sprawling landscape, and a taciturn male figure whose rugged individualism is constantly threatened by the demands of community and family. However, *Giant* stops short of being a full-blown Western, primarily because Ferber focalizes the narrative through her central female figure, Leslie Benedict. According to Jane Tompkins, Westerns insist on being models for men "by emphasizing the importance of manhood as an ideal .... *the* ideal" (17–18); therefore, the "power and presence of women [are] proportionately reduced" (45). In *Giant*, the exclusively male world of rancher Bick Benedict is pervaded by his headstrong wife Leslie, who imports to Texas and their marriage those things signaling "feminine" in Westerns and, therefore, must be carefully guarded against: Eastern culture, domesticity, and (by far the worst) the encroachment on male time and power. *Giant*, then, is both Western and anti-Western, evoking familiar generic icons and themes but then redirecting its conventional story "about men's fear of losing their mastery, and hence their identity, both of which the Western tirelessly reinvents" (Tompkins 45). Ferber's novel insists that the male protagonist must reconsider what mastery and identity mean in relation to other social groups and institutions. In short, Western and family melodrama converge in *Giant*—male-identified genre meets women's fiction. The imaginative terrain "Texas"—the West—is transformed from a site of male struggle against masculine elements, in which courage and endurance are timelessly celebrated, into one of conflict between male and female "voices."

My point about *Giant* being both Western and anti-Western is underscored by comparison to a well-known postwar Western,

Howard Hawks's film classic *Red River* (1948). Both tell a story of empire building through the determination and rugged individualism of a family patriarch. Both involve father-son conflict in which the father tries to impose his unadulterated will and hard masculine ideals on his son (an adopted son in *Red River*), whose resistance to the father threatens the continuity of his cattle empire. *Red River* ends with patriarch Tom Dunson's (John Wayne) empire intact, only now he shares it with his son Matthew Garth (Montgomery Clift), who has succeeded in tempering his father's iron-fisted rule with his own sense of fair play and acknowledgment of others. Matthew's marriage to girlfriend Tess (Joanne Dru) insures the succession of the ranch to future heirs. Historically, *Giant* seems to pick up where *Red River* leaves off, bringing the nineteenth century into the twentieth. The Dunson-Garth type ranches in Ferber's saga are giving way to modernity and the burgeoning oil industry. Moreover, Bick's son Jordy is not interested in reforming his father's undemocratic rule, unlike *Red River*'s Matthew Garth; instead, Jordy rejects ranching altogether. The great Benedict dynasty is ending: The heir apparent has abdicated, oil derricks overrun the pasture, and the vaqueros (cowboys) are riding off into a late-capitalist, urban malaise. Whereas *Red River* resecures dynasty, *Giant* leaves it in decay. Finally, while the moral center of Westerns is often represented in the male cowboy hero—Matthew Garth in *Red River*—Ferber assigns this role to Leslie, whose liberal ideals come to mediate ranch life.

Giant is more than simply a story of Texas in transition. It registers some of the major shifts occurring at mid-century—from rural to urban/suburban; from an agricultural to an industrial-based economy; from an ethos of inner-directed, aggressive individualism to outer-directed, corporate team playing. The novel does not infuse these transitions with the nostalgia often associated with mythic or heroic ideals of America. Instead, it passes the "History" of the West through the prism of Leslie Benedict's consciousness, opening up a spectrum of histories. "History" is opened to question and put on display, much like the Longhorn mounted in the glass case at the center of Bick's town: the once free-ranging, rugged animal signifies the grandiose project of Western settlement, yet it stares moodily—not triumphantly—back at the modern world.

Too Much Bull on Reata Ranch

Bigger. Biggest ranch. Biggest steer. Biggest houses. Biggest hat. Biggest state. A
mania for bigness. What littleness did it hide? (Giant 223)

Ferber's novel relentlessly foregrounds its exposé of the dynastic
family as mythic ideal by focalizing the narrative through Leslie
Benedict's critical voice and by focusing the narrative at the outset on
Texicanus vulgaris.[7] Chronologically, the novel begins at the end, on a
day in the early 1950s as the Benedicts—Bick, Leslie, their adult
children Luz and Jordy, and his Mexican-American wife Juana—
prepare to attend an ostentatious gala commemorating the new "Jett
Rink Airport." Bick and Leslie have gathered an entourage of relatives,
friends, celebrities, and foreign dignitaries to accompany them on
Reata's private plane. This eclectic group serves to introduce the
central characters and to make pointed distinctions between Texans
and non-Texans and Americans and non-Americans: European nobility
clashes with brash American nouveaux riche; Old World monarchy
contrasts with American democracy; Texan swagger invites non-Texan
scorn. The gullible Hollywood starlet's query, "What's Spindletop? Is
that a mountain or something?"[8] arouses Texans' muffled hilarity;
Vashti Snyth's Texan femininity—"shrill as a calliope whistle"—offsets
Leslie's Virginian poise and understated elegance. These binary
oppositions serve as a point of departure by constructing recognizable
types for the reader, but they also reinscribe familiar assumptions
about American democracy that the narrative then proceeds to
question.

Ferber devotes particular attention here to the King and Queen of
Sargovia, exiles from their minuscule European monarchy. Dowdy,
enervated, reserved, and bewildered by finding themselves without a
kingdom but contemptuous of the idea of work, the King and Queen
serve to authorize American openness, vitality, and industry.
Juxtaposed to this sallow royal couple is another ruler—Bick
Benedict—"tanned to a warm russet," "broad-shouldered" with a "lean
hard body" despite his encroaching middle age. However, Bick
possesses the same "detachment, the aloofness, the politely absent-
minded isolation of royalty," as do the King and Queen (28), which
implies that he, too, has ruled irresponsibly by distancing himself from
the consequences of power. Leslie, of course, recognizes this similarity:
"I'm one of a family of rulers, too, by marriage. The Benedicts of

Texas. I wonder how soon we're going to be deposed" (42).

The narrative soon targets what is eroding the Benedict dynasty. Upon arrival at the gala, Bick and Leslie must intervene for one of their guests, a South American ambassador who is mistaken for a Mexican and refused entrance. Soon after, Juana is denied service in the airport's "whites only" beauty salon. Jordy, outraged, shoots up the beauty parlor, then bloodies Jett Rink's nose in front of the celebrants. Rink retaliates by kicking Jordy full-force in the groin. He crumples into unconsciousness, whispering "morphine ... pain ... horrible." Bick turns to finish the fight, but Leslie holds him back, saying "You see. It's caught up with you, it's caught up with us. It always does" (63). The novel "ends" here, abruptly and chronologically, after a fifty-four-page slowdown of the narrative, covering less than a third of one day. The next section begins an extended flashback, reaching back to the early 1920s (where the film version begins) to recount Bick and Leslie's courtship; from there, the narrative proceeds linearly to relate the Benedict family history. The expectations of narrative at the end of this first section, then, are established through unflattering images of conspicuous consumption, racial intolerance, and, most strikingly, the symbolically castrated son (I return to this particular image later). Readers are primed to discover what the "it" is that has finally "caught up with" the Benedicts.

The film's narrative frame is altogether different, which underscores the novel's investment in social critique and satire. Moviegoers who had read Ferber's novel were cued at the outset of the film to expect a more benign treatment of patriarchy. Hollywood settled viewers into their seats with a panoramic, overhead shot of ranch hands driving cattle to a water hole. While the opening credits roll over this scene, an uplifting musical score (theme song "Giant") promises an affirmative story of epic proportions. Signs of the West— the vast, austere landscape, a cattle empire, the freedom of wide-open spaces—furnish visual shorthand for national "history." Cattle and credits then fade to a train chugging its way through lush Maryland countryside, circa 1923.[9] A young, handsome Rock Hudson (Bick), wearing a very large Stetson that links him to the cattle at the water hole, stares in amazement from the train window at a passing foxhunt, which is more shorthand telling viewers that East and West will become inextricably linked. Sure enough, seconds later, Bick sees his soon-to-be bride, the vivacious Leslie Lynnton (Elizabeth Taylor) astride Whirlwind, the horse he has come to purchase. When he murmurs, "that's one fine lookin' animal," it is not clear whether he is referring to Leslie or to Whirlwind, leaving us to wonder whether women and horses are exchangeable commodities for Bick. The next fifteen minutes are consumed with courtship: Bick and Leslie trade surreptitious glances, veiled compliments, and some heated words about Texan history. Nonetheless, soon the two are newlyweds, bound for Texas in Bick's private Pullman.

Unlike the novel, the expectations of the film at this point concern the vast cultural and geographical differences that will beset this couple in their marriage. Moreover, as the image of the high-spirited Leslie astride the even more high-spirited Whirlwind suggests, Bick may have married more woman than he can handle. While the film appears to advance the concerns of melodrama—emotional entanglements, family conflicts, and problems of identity, the stars guarantee affirmative resolutions to these problems. After all, how could the union between Rock Hudson, handsome and unruffled even when he is supposedly furious at Leslie, and Liz Taylor, a lovely-to-look-at steel magnolia, go asunder? The rhetorical question that drives the novel forward (What is "it" that catches up with the Benedicts?) never presents itself in the film.

As Ferber's narrative unfolds, the answer is revealed: "It" is the racist, patriarchal structure of the dynastic family, with its privileging of property and inheritance over social equality and justice; "it" is Bick Benedict, a paragon of the kind of hard masculine ideals that foreclose the display of emotion, physical vulnerability, or passivity and champion at all costs autonomy, mastery, and rationality. As the uncompromising ruler of Reata, Bick has little time for anything else, much to Leslie's dismay. When she says, "you just look upon life as an annoying interruption to ranching," Bick replies matter-of-factly, "Reata takes all my time. It always will. You'll be a neglected wife" (198–99). This absorption in Reata, though, is less for economic gain per se than for its being a setting in which he can actualize his desire to perpetuate his empire.

Bick's connection to the rugged terrain reinforces his assumption that his masculinity is entirely natural, more or less inherited. Indeed, he brags to Leslie that his "mother practically produced [him] on horseback" (316). When Jordy is born, Bick assumes his son will follow in his footsteps, inherently possessing the Benedict skill and daring to conquer nature and rule "lesser" beings. However, Jordy's footsteps cut a different impression. When the two-year-old is fitted for his first pair of cowboy boots, the bootmaker reluctantly gives Bick the "bad" news: "This is more the foot of a dancer; it is not a foot for a stirrup" (329). Feeling betrayed by nature itself (and presumably by the implication that the "foot of a dancer" could only belong to an "unnatural" man), Bick retorts: Jordy's foot may be flat, but "it damned well will" adjust to the stirrup (329). When Bick puts Jordy on a horse at age three, however, he screams to be taken down. Relentless, Bick vows, "He's a Benedict and I'm going to make a horseman out of him if I have to tie him to do it" (329). Again, Leslie, the moral center, chastises Bick for supposing Jordy is property. "He's not yours. He's yours and mine. And not even ours. He's himself" (329).

The film, in this case, does reinforce the novel's critique of Bick's masculinity by presenting this scenario as a public spectacle. The occasion is Jordy and twin Judy's birthday party (Judy's part is created for the film). The celebration is marred when Bick forces Jordy to ride his new pony in order to show off his aptitude for horsemanship, which supposedly reflects back on Bick's own "natural" abilities. Bick's performance backfires, however. As in the novel, Jordy wails until Leslie retrieves him. After seeing little Angel Obregon effortlessly ride the pony around the yard, however, Bick makes one more cruel attempt to display Jordy's future prowess. He mounts his own horse and, along with Jordy, races up and down the driveway. The camera moves between little Jordy, now crying convulsively, the party guests watching in tense, embarrassed silence, and little Judy, who, we can see, is the Benedict who really longs to ride the range. This spectacle, designed to prove the "naturalness" of masculinity, miscarries by displaying its performativity instead; that is, it suggests masculinity must be continually staged, its signs of mastery over nature and emotions displayed for an audience.

Later that evening, Bick's Uncle Bawley (Chill Wills) consoles Leslie, saying, "Bick doesn't know the first thing about raising children." Bawley advises her to "stay with it [her] own way." The novel—but **not** the film—tells us why Uncle Bawley seems to know more about child rearing than Bick. Like Jordy, Bawley did not want to be a rancher when he was young but dreamed of becoming a concert pianist, even studying in Europe. However, his and Bick's father chose Bawley to run the Holgado Division. They "got after him" and brought him home to rope cattle, which ruined his hands. "About that time," he tells Leslie, "Brahms was just beginning to catch on, I was crazy about his—well, you know, you can't fool around with anything like that, I sat there at the piano looking at my fingers, it was like they were tied on with wires. That was when I quit" (247). The film not only cuts this family history, but installs Bawley as a colorful parlor fixture who sits around playing *Clair de Lune* on the organ (a muted reference to his musical aspirations in the novel) and tells Leslie how much she will love Texas in fifty years. In the novel, though, Bawley exposes the squelching of creativity: "There's always been music in the family, one way or another, but the minute it shows its head it gets stepped on" (246).

Neither do filmgoers learn the significance of the nickname, Bawley (Baldwin). The novel tells us that he is allergic to cows so that his eyes run constantly, a condition that turned young Bawley's hands, instruments of artistry, into weapons of self-defense: "I like to wore out my knuckles proving I wasn't a sissy," he tells Leslie (244). Bawley's "tears"—not shed in the film—are like the return of the repressed; they serve as a repudiation to the Benedict patriarchs and as a sign for his suppressed creativity. Perhaps, too, as a reproach to the emphasis on lineage and heterosexual union, Bawley never marries, but lives hermit-like on the remote Holgado Division. Understandably, when Jordy wishes to go to medical school rather than run Reata, Bawley secretly conspires with Leslie to finance his education.

As an inner-directed, rugged individualist, Bick's brand of masculinity is more in keeping with prewar empire building than with the postwar corporate organization ethos of team-playing, outer-directedness, and conformity. However, considering that conformity had become a watchword for discontent in the discourses of postwar masculinity, particularly in reference to beleaguered organization men who were subject to the collective corporate will and network of office relationships,[10] Bick likely elicited some approval when he declares in the novel that Texas means "freedom," a place where "no one there tells you what to do and how you have to do it." Both narratives—the novel more insistently—trouble this notion of freedom, however, because "freedom" on Reata entails the exclusive ownership of two-and-a-half million acres[11] and the ascendancy and control over others, a situation that generates life-long conflict between Leslie and himself. In one of their many quarrels, Bick asserts: "Just get this. I run Reata. I run Holgado. I run the damn wet Humedo Division and Los Gatos too .... Everything in them and on them is run by me. I run everything and everyone that has the Reata brand on it" (313). This argument is played out differently in the film so as to heighten the romantic pairing of

Hudson and Taylor and to soften the hard-shelled patriarch. The argument begins when Leslie publicly criticizes Bick and his friends for excluding women from their evening political talk. In both novel and film, she charges, "You men ought to be wearing leopard skins and carrying clubs and living in caves. You date back a hundred thousand years." When a neighboring rancher then suggests the women "get their beauty rest," Leslie retorts, "Yes, send the idiot children to bed so that you massive brains can talk in peace" (308). Later on, Bick rages at Leslie for making a spectacle and insulting his friends.

In Hollywood's *Giant*, a furious Bick at this point prepares to sleep in the spare room until Leslie, looking demure and alluring, deflates his anger, saying, "Come on pardner. Why don't you kick off your spurs." Sulking, Bick approaches the bed and the scene fades to black. The next morning is played by Taylor and Hudson for quasi-comic effect: Elizabeth Taylor twirls in a shaft of sunlight, trilling, "What a glorious, gorgeous brand new day!" Off-screen, Rock Hudson groans, "Oh honey, I'm beat!" He then enters the bedroom shuffling, enervated from a night of "making up." Their argument threatens to reignite when Leslie suggests that somebody else run Reata while they take a trip. Bick launches into his "I run Reata" speech, but again softens to mush as Leslie astutely chooses this moment to announce her pregnancy. Bick is soon absorbed with the idea of Reata's (male) heir. In contrast, the novel does not exonerate Bick with a romantic interlude, nor does it imply that the proverbial "good woman" may eventually transform him. Instead Bick goes to bed furious at Leslie, who, still venturing to press her point, asks, "Who was it [that] said that thing about power?" He growls that he does not know. When Leslie remembers, she announces to her now sleeping husband, "Power corrupts. And absolute power corrupts absolutely" (314). Her husband's abuse of power is not limited to his treatment of women, however, because gender is imbricated in race similar to the way these categories intersect in *Sayonara*.

Racial Difference and Dynastic Privilege

It's not a question of skin. It's a question of money or education or both ... that's the way the race problem's going to end in the United States. It may be that the Mexican is always the peon or the migratory worker or the man who gets the dirty end ... but it's not because of the color of his skin. (City Editor, Houston Post, 1954)[12]

The City Editor's declaration that "it's not a question of skin" reflects a common assumption within postwar culture: In the wake of some initial legal reforms and the overall rise in income levels that gave nonwhites "buying power" and the "right to consume," race and class did not necessarily intersect, and racism was vanishing or even nonexistent, except in backwater areas of the South (Miller and Nowak 187–88). The editor problematically assumes the minority worker is always the "peon," the one who "gets the dirty end" because he simply does not know how to negotiate the system of work and education. In other words, the system is not at fault; rather, the fault lies with the one who gets the dirty end. Middle-class Mexican Americans were evidence, according to the editor, that race did not affect class status. Such faith in progress under capitalism, however, obscured both the psychological component of racism and the history of white supremacy authorized by genetic theories of difference.

Ferber's *Giant* supplies a corrective to the sanguine view that conditions had vastly improved for minorities. Bick's conception of Texas parallels the American myth of nation-building, which is narrativized as "history as white progress," while at the same time obscuring the land devastation, racial brutality, and misogyny inherent in this form of "progress." "Texas," Bick proudly asserts, "isn't geography. It's history" (110), a history symbolized by the six flags of Texas—Spanish, French, Mexican, the Republic of Texas, the Confederacy, the United States—hung on the walls of Reata's huge entrance. Rather than signifying contestation over land and cultures, however, these colorful signs function for Bick and his fellow ranchers as part of a seamless narrative of Anglo-American "triumphs" over hostile forces opposed to western conceptions of progress.

This narrative of progress begins with the assumption that the white male is the "natural" proprietor of the land. According to Wexman, entitlement to land in western territories was justified by two dominant nineteenth-century, Euro-American discourses that worked in conjunction with one another to rationalize subordinating of nonwhite cultures and taking their land. As noted above, the ideal of land ownership is one of these discourses. The other, scientific racism, claimed that racial differences were primarily biological and natural. As a result, non-Anglo "Others" were interpreted as inherently and unalterably inferior. Furthermore, by superimposing the categories of "civilized" and "savage" on the biological distinctions of "white" and "black," Euro-Americans further justified their privileges as a civilized people (Wexman 90). In this schema of race and civilization, Wexman claims, Mexicans were considered part Indian, thus Mongoloid rather than Castilian Spanish. Marked as such, Mexicans were depicted, like other nonwhite groups, as more primitive, both linguistically and technologically, and more childlike, nonrational, and libidinous than whites. Such attitudes toward Mexican Americans surfaced publicly during congressional hearings on Mexican immigration between 1926 and 1930. Some of the testimony recorded by the House Committee on Immigration and Naturalization in 1930 was especially vicious. One eugenicist claimed most Mexicans were "hordes of hungry dogs, and filthy children with faces plastered with flies ... human filth. [They are] promiscuous ... apathetic peons and lazy squaws [who] prowl by night ... stealing anything they can get their hands on" (Munoz 22). The discourses of scientific racism functioned in concert with the cultural imperative to acquire land, which justified usurping land from its nonwhite occupants in the nineteenth century. Because the (white) dynastic family became regarded as the model of economic, social, and racial "progress," Mexicans and Indians, who supposedly used the land "unproductively" or viewed it as communal rather than privately owned, were considered undeserving of it (Wexman 91).

On Bick's Reata, Mexican Americans live and work as house servants or vaqueros. The presence, and therefore the labor, of the house servants—those closest to the white family members—are minimized. They are "dark, shadowy figures" (173), whose manner, Leslie thinks, is "not unfriendly, but withdrawn even for a servant—strange as though they wished to be as unnoticeable as possible. They move silently, fluidly, and with remarkable inefficiency" (146). Inefficiency signified Mexicans' "inherent" laziness and inferior capabilities. Bick's sister, Luz, in both the novel and film, insists she "knows how to handle Mexicans": she must "keep after them," otherwise "they'd be squatting on their honkers all day" (152). However, inefficiency conceivably signals the servants' passive resistance to their exploitation. Mexican-Americans' contributions are rarely recognized; therefore, when Leslie thanks a young worker, Bick reproaches her for "making a fuss" over him. "We don't do that here in Texas," he says (110).

In the novel Bick credits Reata's vaqueros as being "the best horsemen in the world," yet Leslie discovers such skill is compensated at a scandalously low rate of twenty dollars a month. Bick assures her that some vaqueros become "practically part of the family." As a boy, Reata's foreman, Old Polo, slept on the floor outside Bick's father's door; Polo's son slept outside of Bick's door; even at present young Tomasa most likely sleeps in the Main House (202). While he admits this is "pretty damned foolish," Bick neither intervenes to stop the practice nor questions the social order promoting such subservience. Becoming "part of the family," then, serves to delineate who is the future patriarch—the boy sleeping in the bed, as opposed to the one curled up on the floor.[13]

Vaqueros occupy dual, but compatible, subject positions within, and for, the Anglo culture in the novel: They are desirable as cheap labor and undesirable as racial "inferiors," the ultimate threat to Anglo "purity." They are both laboring bodies and exotic backdrops, positions that at times merge. Vaqueros are the ranch's sweat and muscle and, at the same time, they give it a flair and an element of adventure. Remnants of Hispanic culture are readily appropriated as local "color" by the white culture; however, Mexican Americans are segregated in poor, filthy, disease-ridden communities. Leslie observes this paradox at the Vientecito Fiesta: "Where are the Mexicans? It's all about Spain and Mexico and old Texas. Where are they? All the people in the parade and even on the streets are what you call—well—Anglo" (334). Ignoring or missing her implication, Bick explains the Mexicans have their own celebration on another day in the Mexican part of town.

In the novel, Leslie also discovers an even more disturbing practice of Texan ranchers: controlling Mexican American votes. Her friend Vashti explains to her horrified friend: "It's real exciting at election. Regular old times, guns and all. They lock the gates and guard the fences, nobody can get out .... So they'll vote right .... So they won't go out and get mixed up with somebody'll tell 'em wrong. This way they vote like they're told to vote" (309). By assuming that Mexicans are childlike and neither highly rational nor intelligent, Bick and his cronies justify this practice. "They are full of superstitions and legends," Bick gripes. "They believe in the evil eye and witchcraft and every damn thing ... all that Mexican stuff" (210).

Perhaps Ferber's most inflammatory attack on institutionalized racism concerns young Angel Obregon's death. Angel, who willingly enlists in the Army, is killed in action during World War II and is posthumously awarded the Congressional Medal of Honor for heroism. However, the town's white undertaker refuses to handle his funeral because he is Mexican American. Leslie, acting anonymously to avoid Bick's objection, protests to the President of the United States, who then orders a hero's burial for Angel in Arlington National Cemetery (414–15).[14] Bick shows a callous indifference toward Angel, who had been Jordy's boyhood friend and loyal Old Polo's grandson. In fact, Bick cared little about Angel, dead or alive; when Angel had planned to marry, Bick grumbled about having to attend the wedding (412).

The film's treatment of this incident is markedly different, again emphasizing the ideological distinctions between the two texts. Hollywood empties out all the biting satire that Ferber pours into the circumstances of Angel's burial. Just before reporting for duty, Angel (Sal Mineo) and Old Polo (Alexander Scourby) are warmly welcomed at the Benedicts' Christmas party, although tellingly they remain physically marginalized from the festivities. Old Polo announces solemnly, "Reata's first soldier!" Sal Mineo, looking terribly young, vulnerable, and sweet, swells his chest in pride and gratitude as Leslie remarks how handsome he looks (perhaps, as one of my colleagues has suggested, reflecting her own white racial fantasy of nonwhite Otherness?). Several scenes later, Angel's family huddles together at the train station, waiting to claim his flag-draped coffin. At the graveside Mass, Bick and Leslie stand solemnly with the grieving family. After an honor guard presents the U.S. flag to Angel's mother, Bick hands Old Polo the flag of Texas, which filmgoers have seen Bick remove reverently from his own display cabinet. Old Polo nods his acceptance and a boys' choir sings the "Star Spangled Banner."

This scene carries some disturbing implications when placed in the context of Ferber's novel and postwar America. It suggests that Bick's ranch is basically benevolent and beneficent and, despite some ugly scenes of Mexican-American poverty, Bick appears to be essentially a good steward to his workers. Passing the Texan flag to Old Polo not only acknowledges the Obregons' loss but also signifies the ranch's communal nature. However, by presenting Angel's ultimate sacrifice as elegiac and with the pathos of a fallen hero, the burden of sacrifice in America's fight against tyranny abroad is shifted onto the lower class; this point is reinforced by the fact that Judy's husband, Bob, (Earl Holiman) returns home unscathed by war duty a few scenes earlier. Furthermore, Ferber's condemnation of racial discrimination in the Armed Forces and American society is eliminated. Whereas the novel marks this event as one of shame and outrageous conduct for

Reata, Texas, and the nation, the film offers a mythic scenario of harmony and a mutually caring, interracial community. The film's treatment of Angel's death also works in conjunction with its revitalizing white male hegemony. By having Bick acknowledge Angel's sacrifice, the film makes Bick's change of attitude toward Mexicans more plausible, a change that, in fact, occurs at the film's conclusion when he accepts his brown grandchild.

The critique of racism featured in both versions of *Giant*, however forthright or muted, undoubtedly referenced the more widespread problems of segregation and white supremacy in the society as a whole, which were finally beginning to find favor among white liberals after so many decades of insistence by black activists to end segregation.[15] In certain respects, both the novel and the film offered solutions to racism that were typical of fifties popular culture. As in *Sayonara*, the romantic union between a white male and a nonwhite female became the symbolic means of transcending race prejudice. The *Giant*s also espoused one of the premises of liberal reform: that whites would eventually solve the problems of nonwhite minorities. *Giant* assigns this responsibility to Leslie and her freethinking son, who chooses altruism over capitalist exploitation and breaks social barriers by marrying Juana. Both texts, typically, avoid references to or depictions of Mexican-American discontent and activism, although Ferber's novel does allude briefly to a burgeoning discontent among young Mexican Americans, who rejected ranching for urban living. Angel sneers at the idea of being a vaquero, choosing instead to work as a bellboy in Vientecito: "Vaquero with twenny [sic] or twenny-five dollars a month ... Sometimes I earn that in two days at the Hake if there's a big poker game on .... Vaquero like my father and his father and his father, not me .... Now who does that is a borlo [fool]" (385). Angel changes his cowboy duds for silk shirts, effects sideburns, and pomades his hair; he speaks in a bastard dialect of Mexican jargon, American slang, and Spanish idiom and presents himself as a macho tough—a far cry from Sal Mineo's endearing Angel in the film.

Angel's refusal to be a "borlo" references the emerging consciousness-raising moment among young Mexican Americans in the Southwest and California in the 1940s. Groups of young males, known as *pachucos*, originally formed subculture gangs in El Paso, Texas, which quickly spread throughout the Southwest and California. *Pachucos* identified themselves by dressing in baggy pants and long-tailed coats known as zoot suits.[16] Mexican-American historian Manuel

Machado points out that their "grotesque dandyism and anarchic behavior" was rooted in alienation caused by poverty and perhaps typical of adolescent rebellion; but it was also an attempt to "flaunt difference" … "to strive for separateness from the dominant Anglo culture" (80). While *pachucos* did not attack racism and injustice directly, they set a clear historical precedent for Hispanic resistance organizations of the 1960s (Machado 80).

Other than this brief mention, the novel portrays Mexican Americans as submissive, passive figures, perhaps Ferber's attempt to create verisimilitude of ranch life, in which vaqueros were isolated in rural areas and virtually dependent on ranch owners for their livelihood and education; such dependency precluded their encountering consciousness-raising ideas. Moreover, because even nonpolitical, social service organizations, such as the Mexican-American Movement, were labeled by right-wing groups as communist affiliates, Mexican-American civil rights activists at mid-century were cautious about speaking in overtly militant voices. The FBI, in fact, investigated the Mexican-American Movement in the early 1950s for subversive activities (Munoz 39). Despite the stifling political atmosphere of McCarthyism, Mexican Americans were actively forging a new social and political consciousness after World War II.[17] However, when popular texts, including *Giant*, did address race relations, they rarely acknowledged that minority groups were capable of, and actively engaged in, effecting change on their own behalf. As a result, minority activists experienced a double silencing in these mainstream representations.

While both versions of *Giant* offered a critical, albeit limited, perspective on racial issues, their messages were somewhat divergent. The novel more emphatically damned its racist characters and foregrounded race and class issues, perhaps cautioning readers against complacency and false optimism in resolving social injustices. Furthermore, it implies that token gestures are insufficient responses to institutionalized racism. For example, readers could hardly miss Ferber's profoundly ironic tone in describing the president's offer to bury Angel at Arlington, which suggests that, to a politician, a dead Mexican American may be more politically useful than a living one; that is to say, one symbolic goodwill gesture obscures a thousand injustices. The novel, then, calls readers to social activism and moral outrage, significantly at a historical moment when such activism had become muted in the public arena.

The film is more compatible with the endorsement of gradual progress and reform. The landmark *Brown* decision, which sparked controversy and resistance along with celebration and support, intervened in the years between the novel and the release of the film. Particularly in the South, *Brown* summoned a highly publicized revival of nineteenth-century "scientific" findings supporting white racial superiority and purity in order to justify segregation (Oakley 195). In addition, "interference" by the federal government rekindled the rhetoric of states' rights, particularly in the South. The film, released a year before Little Rock, implies that such federal intervention could and should be forestalled. In the final moments of the film—in scenes written exclusively for the film—Bick ends up fighting Sarge, an intractable redneck, for the right of Juana, his grandson Little Polo, and another Mexican family to be served in Sarge's roadside diner. Bick, the (southern) racist patriarch, is finally persuaded to think right mindedly and then to take matters into his own hands, in his own way. Joan Mellen is quite right in claiming the film demonstrates that "slavocracy will redeem itself" without outside interference, and, by enlisting the virile white male on the eve of the Civil Rights Movement, black and Mexican militancy can be discouraged and disparaged (234). Furthermore, Bick's manliness is not impugned when Sarge finally knocks him into a mess of coleslaw, for this beating is requisite punishment for his former abuse of power, after which he can be "resurrected." Indeed, Leslie pronounces him redeemed in the final scene: "Do you want to know something, Jordan? I think you're great. When you ... landed crashing into that pile of dirty dishes, you were at last my hero. Oh, what a fight! It was glorious! ... After a hundred years, the Benedict family is a real big success." Curiously, just before Leslie's speech, the now-reformed Bick is allowed one final "wetback" remark about his grandchild ("So help me, he looks like a little wetback"), all, of course, in the name of honesty. "There's times," he declares, "when a man's just got to be honest."

Thinking Beyond Dynasty

Hollywood's inventing the diner brawl allows for a conventional "happy" ending in which Bick and Leslie reconcile and Hudson and Taylor enhance their status as leading stars. Ferber's novel does not redeem Bick. As the book draws to a close, it is several days before the

Jett Rink airport gala, on a day when Leslie, Luz II, Juana, and Little Polo are denied service at a diner because Juana and Polo are "cholos." Although Leslie is shocked and humiliated, she makes the others promise not to tell Bick in order to avoid exciting his weakening heart. That same night, Bick muses to Leslie, "things are getting away from me. Kind of slipping from under me like a loose saddle .... I sometimes feel like a failure ... The whole Benedict family a failure" (447). Leslie agrees the Benedicts are failures, yet in a way that has nothing to do with ranches, oil, and millions. She then adds, "And then I thought about our [Jordy] and our Luz and I said to myself, well, after a hundred years it looks as if the Benedict family is going to be a real success at last" (447). Bick is deemed a "failure," but his children will be "successful" by devoting their careers to social change.

Even so, the novel does not call for radical change. Rather, it understands social progress as the inevitable, gradual result of enlightened thinking. Leslie's scholarly father, Dr. Lynnton, whose occasional appearance functions as a foil to Bick's pragmatism, tells her that change occurs with the advance of each generation: "Your Bick won't change, nor you—but your children will take another big step. Enormous step, probably. Some call it revolution, but it's evolution, really" (350). In this conceptualization, history is progress—an ostensibly seamless narrative of liberal thought and action, in which rupture, conflict, and violence are effectively diluted. This concept of history, however, contradicts how Ferber begins to problematize history elsewhere in the novel, by making visible the conflicting interests and power relations within the social fabric of pre- and postwar "Texas." By doing so, *Giant* appears to urge readers to theorize both history itself and, accordingly, the whole notion of American progress, at the very least, recognizing the distinctions and contradictions between enlightened progress and contested history.

In addition, the novel offers a way of imagining social change by going beyond exposing Bick's patriarchal destructiveness to suggest how centers of power may be challenged. In Antonio Gramsci's formulation of hegemony, he theorizes that ruling groups secure power and authority primarily by legitimating their ideas and values within public discourses in order to persuade subordinate groups to "consent" voluntarily to the dominant social order. However, consent is always provisional and sometimes precarious. In *Giant*, Bick's authority erodes when his single-minded notion that his interests and values are those of his family and workers is challenged by different conceptions of "reality." As consent is withheld, dynasty is toppled from within. Daughter Luz repudiates her father's empire in order to run a small-scale, experimental farm with Bob Dietz. Bick, furious that Bob refuses to marry Luz if it means "marrying" Reata, threatens to prevent the marriage altogether. To Bick, Bob is just a "snotty kid," a "dirt farmer" (444–45), but the ever-prescient Leslie understands that Bob's way of thinking constitutes a challenge to, and an improvement over, Bick's feudal style of ranching, which involves ravaging thousands of acres, mismanaging grazing land, and exploiting workers: "I think Bob Dietz may change the whole face of Texas—its system and its politics and its future," she prophesizes (25). Luz II, like her mother, is also confident, outspoken, tomboyish, and independent. Unlike the vacuous, childlike Vashti Snyth or the bossy, "perverted" Luz I, who "would rather work cattle than make love" (167), Luz II will be a success, according to Leslie, because she will have both career and home, run a ranch *and* have a companionate marriage. Although femininity is still defined here solely in relation to heterosexuality and the nuclear family unit, Luz does represent a female figure whose ambitions extend beyond marriage to include college and career.

As the heir to Reata, Jordy presents the most significant challenge to Bick's hegemony because he rejects both the ideal of land ownership and the continuity of dynasty through a "proper" marriage. His alternative brand of masculinity redefines the boundaries that shape Bick's notion of manhood based on competition, greed, and abuse of power. By choosing medicine, Jordy opts for a career in healing rather than exploiting Mexican Americans: "My father is always exper-imenting to get better beef," he complains, "But I want to do that with people, not animals. T.b.-proof Mexican Americans, that would be even better" (385). When Jordy joins Dr. Guerra's practice, which consists of Mexican-American patients, Leslie is proud of his decision, but Bick responds with racist invective: "Down in Spigtown with the greasers. He's no real Benedict" (446). Jordy's marriage to Juana, a further blow to his father, breaks the social "rules" by which dynasty and white culture are preserved. In Bick's world, miscegenation threatens not only to disperse family property to racial "Others," but to undermine the "purity" of white culture.

If Jordy redefines manhood in some positive ways, at least by today's liberal feminist standards, he also remains an inexplicably ambiguous figure in Ferber's novel. As noted earlier, the novel ends chronologically on page fifty-four, the day of Jett Rink's gala, when

Jordy is solidly beaten by Rink. However, as readers encounter Leslie's proclamation on page 447 that the children will be the real successes, they know already that in just a few days, Jordy will receive a "castrating" blow from Rink. If Jordy is, in some respects, the alternative to Bick, then he is, at least in this moment, cast as the hysterical, impotent son. How, then, do the final pages of the novel square with the chronological ending? Does this hint at some nostalgia for Bick after all, in that his rugged individualism and more "heroic" stature appear more resilient in a harsh world when compared with his son, who bears himself with a "shy uncertainty" and stutters in his father's presence? Furthermore, as Jett Rink proves, Jordy is virtually defenseless around tough, unscrupulous men. However, the narrative may be punishing Jordy, not for being weak, but for taking up the "law of the West" in shooting up the beauty salon and punching Jett— in other words, for responding as his father would. His excessive response, his rage, also could stand as a reproach to the world that Bick and Jett have molded. Whether we read Jordy's image as a reproach or as nostalgia for the past, his character seems to convey a patent distrust of male violence and machismo.

Hudson Is Rock-like, But "It's Dean, Dean, Dean"

Hollywood's happy ending works to smooth over the novel's ambiguity concerning male identity. The film, narratively speaking, belongs to Bick and, by extension, to Rock Hudson, and, though Bick's masculinity may be gradually softened in the film, his manliness is safeguarded, particularly by its juxtaposition with his shy, uncharismatic son (Dennis Hopper) and the reckless, alcoholic Jett Rink (James Dean), whose compulsion to surpass Bick's wealth ultimately leads to his downfall. While *Giant*'s screenwriters expanded Jett's role as Bick's rival—a relatively minor one in the novel—the script, in and of itself, does not entertain Jett as a positive or compelling alternative to Bick's hegemonic masculinity. In the first half of the film, however, Jett does have the potential to engage viewers' sympathies as an anguished, inarticulate young man without family, friends, or property. His isolation and supreme loneliness are emphasized in scenes where he broods from a distance while Bick and Leslie embrace on the front porch or picnic with neighboring ranchers. His economic powerlessness potentially offers a class-based critique of

Reata's economic hierarchy, which is underscored at Luz I's funeral when Bick and his political cronies try to prevent Jett from inheriting a small piece of Reata bequeathed to him by Luz.[18] Sensing that Reata is more than just grazing land, Jett refuses a cash trade for it. Instead he drills for oil on his arid patch, hits a gusher, and becomes one of the richest men in Texas.

Jett's sudden affluence does not induce him to eschew the values he resents in Bick; instead, he reproduces his racism and the crudest aspects of wealth in the form of conspicuous consumption and classism. As Jett approaches middle age, social acceptance eludes him, and his long-time love for Leslie remains unrequited; thus, in a pathetic, drunken wallow at his airport gala, he tries to compensate for these losses by offering a half-hearted marriage proposal to Luz II (Carroll Baker), which she gently refuses. Moments later, after Jordy confronts Jett for insulting Juana, Bick challenges Jett to "have it out once and for all." Here the film script diverges from the novel, which ends chronologically with Leslie preventing such a confrontation between them. In the film, the two rivals proceed to a stockroom to fight, but Jett, too drunk to "put 'em up," sways unsteadily. Bick snarls, "you're not even worth hitting. You're all washed up." Looking tall, handsome, and virile in his tuxedo, Rock Hudson towers over the slighter figure of James Dean, giving visual leverage to Bick's ultimate redemption. In terms of the narrative's logic, Bick's refrain from striking Jett at this moment makes sense, for his restraint heightens the significance of Bick's decision to fight the racist, diner owner Sarge in the following scenes. The film implies, then, that revitalizing Bick's hegemony is justified because he learns when to wield power—in the service of social justice—and when this is an empty, self-serving act.

The fact that the class antagonism between the two men gets played out as a gender rivalry carries some provocative implications. As Reata's owner, Bick is compelled to maintain his status as cattle*man*, while Jett continually contests his own subordination as cow*boy*. Although he is close to Bick's age, Jett is even referred to as a "boy" in the narrative. This volatile contest between "man" and "boy" erupts from mutual—albeit antagonistic—desire, which is made legible in the hostile or brooding gazes traded between the two rivals throughout the film. In scenes in which they appear together, the two either pretend not to notice one another, or they cannot stop watching each other. This desire is also expressed through physical and verbal hostility, which is also marked with phallic imagery and sexual overtones.[19] Thus, the struggle over who is "rightfully" the "man" has the potential to create what Eve Sedgwick claims is a fluid, shifting relation between the homosocial and homoerotic (5). Jett's effort to overcome his economic subordination is pitched as a battle for his right to be a man. He names his token piece of Bick's ranch "Little Reata," which is not only a grievous insult, but an audacious challenge to Bick's big Reata/Phallus. Not surprisingly, when Jett's well strikes oil, a powerful phallic stream of greasy fluid gushes from the earth, anointing Jett's body as he stretches his arms upward to receive his newfound means of economic superiority. He immediately heads for Bick's house to gloat. Once there, he brazenly fingers Leslie's blouse, provoking Bick to strike him, but Jett swiftly delivers three emasculating punches to Bick, signaling the demise of the rancher's power and the rise of a new industrial order led by oil wildcatters.

Notably, too, each generation of Reata women triangulates Bick and Jett's relationship, introducing an erotic charge into the rivalry: Older sister Luz's mixture of maternal care and secret romantic longing for the much younger Jett strains her relationship with Bick; Leslie's arrival on Reata heightens the two men's mutual suspicion, while Luz II's teenage crush on "dreamy," middle-aged Jett presents Bick with the threat of sexual "violation" of his family. Significantly, these heterosexual attractions are never developed within the diegesis; rather, they serve to focalize the male gender rivalry. (Interestingly, Ferber's novel gives little or no indication of romantic inclinations between Jett and either Luz I or Luz II).

Jett's nouveau status as oil millionaire, however, does not secure his status as "man" by the standards through which many fifties moviegoers would have understood this category. Within the psychological discourses of masculinity in postwar America, Jett's lifelong evasion of the role of husband and father would signify his "immaturity," which, in short, meant "not fully masculine." Moreover, Jett's proposal to Luz is not motivated out of love or the willingness to accept the breadwinner ethic; rather, it is motivated by his adolescent desire to shock the Benedicts. Both within the diegetic world and postwar culture, his refusing the responsibilities equated with adult masculinity may have clinched his "failure" to achieve full "manhood." Worse yet, in the context of anti-communist hysteria that aligned security risks with homosexuality, the immature male could connote homosexuality. Psychiatric theory posited, "Men who failed as breadwinners and husbands were 'immature,' while homosexuals were, in psychiatric judgment, 'aspirants to perpetual adolescence.' So great was the potential overlap between the sexually 'normal,' but not entirely successful man, and the blatant homosexual that psychoanalyst Lionel Oversey had to create a new category—'pseudohomosexuality.'" (Ehrenreich, "Hearts" 24–25). The film impedes this elision between "immature" and "homosexuality" mainly by reminding viewers of Jett's undying love for Leslie. However, more to the point, because the dominant cultural representation of the immature adult male occupied the middle ground between straight and gay sexuality, this figure was marked by instability and the potential to disturb the dominant configuration of gender and sexuality, in which "male" unproblematically became a sign for "masculine" and "heterosexual." Perhaps this explains Bick's obsession with Jett: His "immaturity" functions to authorize Bick's manhood and his power and authority over Jett, but, at the same time, Jett's status as "adult boy" may be the very thing that continues to intrigue Bick.[20]

In a film concerned with reifying the nuclear family unit and the virile male, it is not surprising that the narrative must neutralize their rivalry when Bick is about to fight Jett. By abruptly canceling out their fierce attraction, the narrative dismisses Jett as a further threat to Bick or his family and effectively censors any further hints of gender "trouble." That is, Bick and Jett's mutual desire is never allowed to emerge as a positive alternative to heterosexuality. With Jett written out of the narrative at this point, the film has left itself the task of stabilizing an "appropriate" model of male identity. The terms by which Bick had defined his masculinity—hard-shelled, authoritarian, aggressive individualism—no longer apply to postwar definitions of masculinity, and Hollywood's *Giant* complies with this shift. Largely through Leslie's persistence, Bick finally learns what a "real man" stands for: a reconciliation between hard masculine ideals and the need to be more flexible and responsive to family and others.

However much the film gives the narrative to Bick, this endorsement was offset by several factors: James Dean's unforeseen death, his use of Method acting, and his star persona, all of which reintroduce what the plot line tries to suppress—an incoherent masculinity. Director George Stevens, by his own account, admitted he was not fully prepared for Dean's acting techniques, which accentuated his theatricality and highly self-conscious performance style and threatened to eclipse Hudson's screen presence. Neither had Stevens nor Warner Bros. anticipated the effect Dean's death would have on *Giant*'s reception. Therefore, while the film attempts to recuperate male hegemony by deeming Bick a "success" and using Hudson strictly as an establishment figure, James Dean—*not* Jett Rink—complicates such a straightforward recovery.

The twenty-four year old Dean was killed on 30 September 1955, when his Porsche Spyder collided with an oncoming car on a California highway, just two weeks after the film's location shooting was completed. Before he died, Dean had appeared in only one film, *East of Eden* (1955), for which he received critical acclaim as Cal Trask, an anguished, tormented son who tries to win his stern, puritanical father's love and recognition. His second film, *Rebel Without a Cause* (1955), was still in postproduction at the time of his death. Dean was yet untested as a consistent box office draw, although teen moviegoers had begun to notice Dean in *East of Eden* and from *Look* and *Life* articles that appeared in the spring of 1955. At best, he was regarded in Hollywood circles as having considerable promise as a star, who, in columnist Louella Parsons's words, "belongs to the Marlon Brando-Montgomery Clift 'school' of acting, the professionally unwashed, unmannered, unconventional actors' group that ... flourishes under the brilliant direction of Elia Kazan" (Alexander 180).

With news of his death, however, Dean became an instant national obsession. The *Saturday Review* noted his demise "caused a mass hysteria at least equal to that caused by Valentino" (Alpert 28); *Look* confessed that "this mass demonstration of hero worship baffled even the press" (Scullin 120). Fan letters to Warner Bros. increased from a handful to more than three thousand in January 1956 alone; many fans requested photographs and memorabilia of Dean, while others wrote impassionate love letters addressed directly to their dead idol. More than fifty fan clubs sprang up nationwide, some with melodramatic names like the Lest We Forget Club. In addition, Dean—now deemed brilliant and accomplished—received several posthumous awards for his acting, including Best Actor from the Golden Globe, *Cinemonde*, and The New York Film Critics Circle, and Best Foreign Actor from the French Film Academy.[21] The media sustained the obsession with Dean, flooding newsstands with articles on every conceivable facet of his life, from the mundane details of his birthplace in Fairmount, Indiana, to intimate particulars of his love life ("The Girl James Dean Left Behind," "Is Dean a Dandy?") to macabre descriptions of his wrecked Porsche and the last moments of his life. As writers took up pop psychologizing Dean, they produced a now-familiar catalog of associations describing the young actor: Intense, shy, enigmatic, charming, moody, ill-mannered, sloppy, a bum, a crazy, mixed-up kid, and a poet.[22] Perhaps the most compelling and salable stories were those capturing Dean's words from the afterlife ("Jimmy Dean Returns!") (Alexander 270), or those claiming Dean was really alive but so disfigured he could not face his public (Parker 126).

Three days after his death, *Rebel without a Cause* opened. While Dean's reputation was built around his association with youthful nonconformity and eccentricity, the coincidence of *Rebel* and his death elevated him to mythic status as an eternal teen icon. His portrayal of a rebellious, but otherwise vulnerable, tormented, confused young man presented a symbolic channel for teens' own feelings of alienation and defiance of conformity. A year later when *Giant* was released, the Dean hype had not abated. The studio and other cast members worried that the hysteria would eclipse their performances; Warner Bros. felt compelled to release a statement saying that "publicity for ... *Giant* will be arranged around the cast as a whole" and that the studio did not want "to encourage or exploit this morbid interest in [Dean]" (Parker 127).

Despite Warner's efforts to refocus promotion on an ensemble cast, reviews of *Giant* fixated on Dean and his Method acting, regardless of whether the reviewer found his performance admirable or otherwise lacking. *The Catholic World* devoted two full paragraphs to convey that "Dean boobs it" as Rink, with his "smirking and mumbling like some juvenile delinquent who got forced into the senior class play at the local high school." In contrast, it damns Rock Hudson with faint praise, stating simply that he plays his part with "some depth and feelings" (Finley 222). Other reviews were likewise as cursory about Hudson (and Elizabeth Taylor) as they were expansive or enthusiastic about Dean. *Newsweek* thought Hudson "right for the part," but proclaimed "the picture belongs to the late James Dean," whose death emerges in the wake of this performance as "a much more significant theatrical loss" ("Young Dean's Legacy" 112). Never mentioning Hudson's acting, the *New Yorker* declared Dean the "exception to the standardized scheme of things ... who plays the role of an ambitious cowpoke with lunatic cuteness" (McCarten 178). The *Nation* also shortchanged Hudson, along with the rest of the cast, saying they "will neither astonish nor disappoint"; but the review credited Dean with being "passionate" and "coming off the screen like a blow" (Rev. of *Giant*, 20 Oct. 1956: 334). *The Saturday Review* not only featured Dean on its cover, but titled its review, "It's Dean, Dean, Dean." While Hudson is cited for being "capable as the ranch owner," the column devoted one-third of its review to Dean, applauding him as "an accomplished thoughtful actor" (Alpert 28). *Time* magazine concurred, giving high praise for Dean's "streak of genius." Focusing on his Method acting, *Time* wrote: "He has caught the Texas accent to nasal perfection, and has mastered the lock-hipped, high-heeled stagger of the wrangler, and the wry little jerks and smirks, tics and twitches, grunts and giggles that make up most of the language of a man who talks to himself a good deal more than he does anyone else." *Time* went on to proclaim the scene in which Jett proposes to Luz II "the finest piece of atmospheric acting seen on screen since Marlon Brando and Rod Steiger did their 'brother scene' in *On the Waterfront*" (Rev. of *Giant*, 22 Oct. 1956: 108).

In spite of Bick/Hudson emerging as the "success" within the diegesis, then, Dean's dramatic performance as the drunken, incoherent Rink at his gala, may have proved more riveting and memorable. While Jett is last seen sobbing "pretty, pretty Leslie ... the woman a man's got to have" as Luz II watches from a distance, James Dean may have been last "seen" as a fascinating anti-hero, a symbol of conflicted and tormented manhood. Hudson, of course, was not unaware of the professional hazards of sharing individual scenes and the limelight with Dean. During filming, he griped to his then wife, Phyllis Gates: "Stevens is throwing the picture to Dean. I know he is, dammit .... Stevens is giving Dean all the close-ups and I'm left out in the cold" (Parker 103). Although moviegoers were not privy to Hudson's private fears about his co-star's scene stealing, they could observe how Dean's theatricality and off-screen persona may have functioned to shift attention onto Dean, thus providing another gloss on masculinity, one the script ultimately refused to sanction.

Both on and off-screen Dean ushered in a new style of male hero, what fifties critic Gerald Weales called the "sad-bad-boy hero," whose tough guy persona merely provided a thin veneer of protection for his hurt and insecurity (41). Dean's role in the second half of *Giant* departed somewhat from the mixture of traumatized child and rebellious teen, which he best portrayed in *East of Eden* as Cal Trask and *Rebel Without a Cause* as Jim Stark. Dean, though, exhibited the key trademarks of his star persona—alienation, rebellion, uncertainty, sensitivity—in the young Jett Rink; his performance foregrounded his highly theatrical, self-conscious screen presence, distinguishing him from Hudson, whose acting style was rarely mannered and much more staid. Whereas Dean seemed to convey a secret, hidden "self" that was potentially interesting, Hudson merely had to "be there" in a scene. While not formally schooled in Method techniques, Dean did incorporate the trademarks of this style into his own acting, following in the footsteps of Marlon Brando and Montgomery Clift. Like all such actors, Dean employed a range of physical behaviors to signal an inner psychological state, which often suggested confusion, stress, or neurosis. Particularly in the scenes with Elizabeth Taylor, Dean's face is a pool of emotion, his body a manifestation of tortured gestures. Barely audible sighs, furtive glances, and bits of broken sentences register his discomfort and mortification. Elsewhere, Jett's confusion over both his status on Reata and his own sense of maleness is displayed by Dean's repeatedly adjusting his Stetson, sometimes pushing it back to reveal the open face of an innocent, almost wistful boy, other times pulling it down to the bridge of his nose as if to armor himself with anger and resentment. At the moment of Luz's death, Jett's grief is legible through the twitch of Dean's mouth and the movement of his Adam's apple.

The significance of this new style of acting, according to Wexman, was that it foregrounded the "conflicted nature of ... gender identifications"; that is, the Method actor projected a deep ambivalence about orthodox masculinity by exhibiting traditionally feminine qualities, such as vulnerability, emotional openness, and personal insecurity (167). The male "self" was constructed as fluid and pro-visional, rather than constituted by fixed, "normative" qualities that signaled "masculine." More importantly, Dean offered audiences notably ambiguous images of male sexual identity, publicly hinting at sexual dissent. Dean's performance in *Giant* brings a frankly sensual, erotic quality to Jett, clearly missing in Ferber's characterization. Dean does not simply sit down in a truck; he slides into the seat, slowly allowing the leather to massage his back. As he sulks at a distance from a neighborhood barbecue, he rhythmically strokes a horse's rump, finally running his hand through the length of its tail. When Leslie visits his Little Reata, he poses above her seated figure with his upraised arms stretched across a rifle, cruxifixion-style, as Graham McCann notes, like an erotic Christ-figure (159). Never moving quickly, he saunters, slithers, ambles, and unfolds his body as if in slow motion, drawing attention to his sensual, sensuous body.

This mixture of innocence and sexuality is what made Dean, the star, so compelling to fans as well. In the film, when young Luz II first meets Jett, she is fascinated by him; it is not Dean/Rink who controls the gaze here, but Luz—like so many of Dean's fans—who cannot unfix her stare from him. Offering himself as an object of erotic spectacle, Dean disturbs the traditional means through which cinematic representation has signified sexual difference—by who controls the gaze. In short, men do the active looking, while women passively offer themselves to be looked at. As object of the look, though, Dean is not simply feminized; nor does this position him simply as the feminine Other of the film's masculine Texan rancher. He mixes eroticism with an active, potent sexuality, which not only makes him attractive to women *and* men, but hints that the man-boy dualism that the film establishes has some disturbing implications for the representation of orthodox masculinity. That is to say, Dean/Rink is presented as the "boy"—the eroticized male Other to the "man," which introduces the element of sexual transgression into this gender binary. As I note above, the figure of the adult "boy" could have been read in fifties discourses of masculinity as the man who was not fully masculine or even the more deviant "pseudo-homosexual." However, as Steven Cohan reminds us, "boyishness … also had an undeniably attractive quality, fostering the postwar youth culture and exciting the admiration of the grown men who were not boys themselves" (*Masked* 238). Plausibly, the extratextual implications of Dean's fluid sexuality, when juxtaposed with Hudson's ostensible "normalcy," might have compounded the subversive inflection of Jett's and Bick's gender and sexual rivalries that permeate the film.

Dean further destabilized the notion that masculinity is something males acquire "by nature." He conspicuously constructs Rink's masculinity out of a series of props and phallic extensions. As the middle-aged Jett, he sports a trim, straight mustache, flat, oiled hair, a receding hairline, and expensive suits. He surrounds himself with beefy, stone-faced bodyguards, flashy sports cars, and nubile young women. In effect, Dean/Rink's transformation from "boy" to "man"—whereby he ends up looking totally fake—underscores the performative basis of masculinity in both its phallocentric and its theatrical implications. In the first place, the abundance of phallic imagery associated with Rink indicates that his possession of a penis does not automatically accord him possession of the phallus, a realization that, according to Richard Dyer, signals "the greatest instability of all for the male image"; that is, the proliferation of phallic symbols indicates lack because "they are all straining after what can hardly ever be achieved, the embodiment of the phallic mystique" ("Don't Look Now" 274–75). Furthermore, Dean/Rink calls attention to how the social act of self-presentation destabilizes identity because Dean *performs* a particular gendered identity rather than expresses some essence of his male "nature." Again, though, the film narrative strives to disavow such implications. When Bick repudiates Jett by growling, "you're not even worth hitting," he indicates that Jett's masculine masquerade is a cover-up for his "real" impotence and status as "non-man," which in turn helps solidify Bick/Hudson as the "real" man, securing his masculinity as natural rather than constructed from props and gestures.

My sense that James Dean posed a challenge to the film's endorsement of a less conflicted male subjectivity is not to suggest that Hudson's star power was inconsequential, for, at that time, he was considered one of the hottest new male stars in Hollywood. Hudson's handsome features, his strapping physique, and, more importantly, his own particular presentation of a new style of masculinity had gained the attention of fans (Parker 69). The construction of Hudson's star persona, like Dean's, was in keeping with the trend in postwar America that emphasized softer, less overtly aggressive models of male identity. Rather than projecting a tough exterior to mask his vulnerability and confusion, though, Hudson seemed to be devoid of inner torment or anguish. He appeared wholesome, the guy next door, who carries his elderly neighbor's groceries. Indeed, the 3 October 1955 edition of *Life*, whose cover featured Hudson looking relaxed in a workshirt, khakis, and a red neck scarf, described him as "affable," "easygoing," and "amiable" ("Simple Life" 128). Compare this to a mid-1950s still of Dean with his trademark myopic squint, which gave him a slightly threatening look, his black "beatnik" sweater, wrinkled chinos, and cigarette, all signifying 1950s style "coolness" and rebellion.

Hudson's relaxed masculinity was projected from an oversized, hunky physique; in fact, "[he] was physically the largest male star of the day," an attribute Hollywood emphasized in his films and publicity shots (Meyer 259). His body was inevitably shot at angles that accentuated his largeness or was allowed to fill the entire screen, giving the impression that he barely fitted into the frame. *Life*, for instance, emphasized Hudson's size by showing him "squeezing his 6' 4" frame into a sportscar" as he prepares to go out with Marisa Pavan

("Simple Life" 129). However, as Richard Meyer claims, rather than signaling an imposing or ominous physical presence, Hudson rarely communicated any kind of threat. His body appeared to be "available as an object of erotic delectation but without the threat of male action"; while his "stupendous proportions" secured "his manhood as similarly well endowed," he "tempered that big body with a measure of safety" (259–61). Hudson brought another kind of sex appeal to the screen: He was a "safe date" who promised not to pounce (Meyer 263), whereas Dean's smoldering sexuality contained a certain ominous, barely restrained, bisexual quality.

Giant capitalized on Hudson's big body. In the opening scene, he fills the frame of the train window as he watches the passing foxhunt; as he descends from the train, the camera silhouettes his massive shoulders and back in the doorway. Many of Hudson's subsequent shots were angled from below, accentuating his size and height. However, the film manages to contain any threat of unrestrained sexuality or violence associated with his body by placing him in relaxed poses: he stretches out (fully clothed) on a chaise lounge by his newly installed pool; pajama-clad, he talks with Leslie while reclining in his bed; in the final scene, he is recumbent with his head in Leslie's lap. Most dramatic is the ritual punishment he receives from Sarge.

While Hudson's oversized physical proportions could alone iconize the tall, powerful Texan, his good-guy image seemed hardly suited for Ferber's tough boots-and-spurs man. Perhaps for this reason, Hudson had not been George Stevens's first choice for the part. Tough guys Gary Cooper, Clark Gable, and William Holden had all expressed interest in the role. Stevens had settled on Holden (Parker 97), whose experience with dramatic roles in films like *Stalag 17* (1953) and *Sunset Boulevard* (1950) had not only earned him critical acclaim and power as a box office draw, but made him more appropriate as Ferber's hard, unyielding rancher. However, Hudson's agent, Henry Willson, recognized that *Giant* was going to be a big-budget, prestige production, so he approached Stevens about his client. After seeing a prerelease screening of Hudson in *Magnificent Obsession* (1954), which elevated Hudson from a B-movie actor for Universal to Hollywood's hottest property, Stevens agreed to test him. Before *Magnificent Obsession*, Hudson had appeared in nearly two dozen films, but his roles were minor or lightweight (recall his wooden performance as a Native American in *Taza, Son of Cochise*, 1954), and he had no experience with dramatic roles. Interestingly, Stevens coached Hudson for the role of Bick by having him watch films of Hollywood's veteran tough guy: Gary Cooper.

The overlay of Hudson's star persona onto Bick not only modifies Ferber's character, but fosters the film's recuperation of Reata's patriarch. The audience may have noted the gap between extrafilmic impressions of "nice-guy" Hudson and his character's Texan authoritarianism, but more likely than not, his star persona helped to resecure Bick's image in the end, so that he could function, in Barbara Klinger's words, as "the ideological anchor of sanity" just at a time when social and political upheavals seemed imminent (109). Although *Giant* did not require Hudson to play a romantic lead as he had in *Magnificent Obsession* and *All That Heaven Allows* (1955), he continued to represent a brand of masculinity that was relatively uncomplicated and psychologically untroubled. Because of this, Hudson subsequently was used in films as the foil to tormented, neurotic males, beginning with Dean's Jett Rink and continuing with Robert Stack's tortured Kyle Hadley in *Written on the Wind* (1957).[23] Hudson's "stalwart normalcy," Klinger maintains, provided "the moral and psychological counterpoint to the deep chaos and social rebellion represented by the psychoanalytical male" (109), who often was played by actors associated with Method techniques. His image of "normal," clean-cut masculinity was carefully fabricated in media representations, remaining virtually unchanged until 1985, at which time his illness with AIDS and his homosexuality' were simultaneously revealed. The stability of Hudson's pre-1980s persona also may have eased anxiety generated by the Cold War discourses of male weakness and, most ironically, the specter of homosexuality. Using Hudson, then, to symbolize American modernity in *Giant* provided a more sanguine view of "progress" than Ferber's novel allowed.

Hudson's on-screen wife, Elizabeth Taylor, compounded the film's investment in reifying the family and modernity, the two being mutually reinforcing in Cold War ideology. Instead of using Taylor to focalize the narrative as Ferber's Leslie did, the film engages her in a marital drama with Hudson, in which growth and adjustment will ensure the marriage's success. Taylor/Leslie functions to make both Reata and Bick compatible with the postwar ethos of family life and companionate marriage. One of her projects is to glamorize the interior of Bick's drab Victorian monstrosity, an imposing, masculine structure that interrupts its dry, flat surroundings as incongruously as a bull standing his ground on a deserted highway. Leslie transforms its heavy dark beams and paneled walls into an elegant white and pastel domicile, and then she tackles her tough Texan husband, changing him into ... well ... "Rock Hudson." By the film's end, they are full partners in marriage, a clear sign in the 1950s that the family was indeed the central unit of social stability and security and, again, a striking departure from Ferber's use of family to satirize national identity and a monolithic version of history.

While Taylor was given some substantive moments in which she gives Leslie some spirit and conviction, she generally added to the film's visual romance with glamour and style. Modernity did not look garish or overdone in *Giant*. It looked plush and beautiful. Taylor/Leslie's association with interior decoration added to what Karal A. Marling sees as the visual and symbolic importance of the house in the film. *Giant*, claims Marling, is "a celebration of interiors over exteriors, Liz Taylor's domain over Rock Hudson's, perhaps, the bright modern home and all the artful paraphernalia that fill it over issues, 9-to-5 careers, and an inconvenient, dark, and dingy past" (3). If modernity, fifties style, also meant consumption, Taylor, both on- and off-screen, symbolized the kind of radiant beauty and material comforts that consumers could hope to approximate through their own purchases of cosmetics, clothes, and luxury items. Indeed there was "a public obsession with [Taylor's] beauty" in the early fifties; she was "lissome Liz," "luscious Liz," "lovely Liz," and as one fan put it, "it's been enough to see her serenely aristocratic face above her voluptuous body" (Sheppard 113). Although *Giant* gave Taylor an opportunity to develop her talents as a serious actress, whereas her prior screen roles had not (with the exception of *A Place in the Sun* [1951]), she also brought to the film her association with rich girl roles and being the rarefied beauty that caused men to vie for her love. MGM, with which Taylor was under contract, had done little to alter this persona; they "apparently valued [her] to be dressed, lit, and photographed to maximum advantage. The scripts were of secondary importance" (Sheppard 131). *Giant*, of course, required Taylor to age almost thirty years and be convincing as the mother of Dennis Hopper and Carroll Baker; however, applying a powdered hairpiece and clothing her in mustards, browns, or greens did not seem to detract from Taylor's trademark look as stylish, tasteful, and expensive. As Leslie Benedict, Taylor was not so much a cipher for liberalism as she was the female counterpart to Hudson—a symbol of postwar success.

Considering Hudson's popularity and his pairing with Taylor, it would be overstated to claim Dean completely stole the show from Hudson. After all, Hudson was nominated for best actor along with Dean's posthumous nomination, and he was voted most popular male star by *Look* in 1955 and *Photoplay* in 1957, the years right before and after *Giant*'s release (Klinger 99). Perhaps more to the point, casting Dean and Hudson in *Giant* juxtaposed two markedly different, but appealing styles of masculinity. Hudson helped to valorize domesticity and reassure audiences that Bick Benedict could absorb the tensions of modernity and continue to represent American "progress." However much Bick's masculinity is reformed, though, this does not constitute a stringent critique of patriarchy. As Robert W. Connell so aptly reminds us, "The political risks run by an individualized project of reforming masculinity is that it will ultimately help modernize patriarchy rather than abolish it" (*Masculinities* 139). James Dean pulled the film in a different direction ideologically. His incoherent brand of masculinity suggested there was a breakdown in consensus over what constituted masculinity. Dean did not confront patriarchy in the same way in which Ferber's satiric bite tore at the fabric of oppressive structures, but he did mediate the film's seamless closure by hinting that the difference between the "boy" and hegemonic "man" was not simply gender opposition, but perhaps gender trouble. Dean pointed to a way of looking beyond modifying patriarchy. Rather he appeared to be taking a prolonged, self-absorbed, inward look at the male "self," finding more questions than certainties.

Despite the gender instability Dean's image brought to the film, its narrative worked to restore the dominant gender ideologies of the 1950s. By adding scenes at the end, written exclusively for the film, Hollywood's version registered the postwar refurbishing of masculinity as more relaxed, sensitive, and outer-directed. We need to be cautious about seeing these attributes as an improvement ("progress") in gender relations because they can just as easily suggest that patriarchy does not need to be dismantled, only modified in accordance with changing times. Hollywood shows that hegemony can survive, as Gramsci suggests it can, by making concessions to subordinate groups and co-opting or accommodating alternative discourses, in order to retain its legitimacy and authority. The film makes this process of struggle and conflict somehow look benign, perhaps because it treats Bick's masculinity like biography or a linear history: Viewers focus on his gradual transformation to a nice-guy, a change that follows a pattern similar to that in *From Here to Eternity* and *Sayonara*, in that all three males are able to negotiate institutional or social pressure that ask them to change, while not having to relinquish their hegemonic status. Recall that Sergeant Warden remains in charge of G Company because he tempers his individualism with the organization ethos and that Major Gruver transitions from a racist bomber pilot to a racially sensitive officer.

By contrast, the novel *Giant* offered a more ambivalent view of male identity. Ferber's Bick is as anachronistic in postwar America as a claw-footed Victorian bathtub in a Levittown home. Jordy is an ambiguous figure in that he rejects a dominating, controlling style of masculinity, but also appears to be somewhat "unheroic" and emasculated. Unlike the film, Ferber provides no definitive model of male identity, yet this may be precisely the point. Perhaps the novel's (chronological) ending—"It has finally caught up with us"—signals that a renegotiation of what constitutes masculinity is in order. As the novel implies, renegotiating masculinity entails confronting some of the culture's established certainties, not only about gender, but about race, American history, and the mythology of the West. Beyond this, we can conclude that masculinity itself is the result of negotiation; clearly, Bick's brand of masculinity is defined, not through his transformation, but through its presentation as a social process of contestation, involving the containment of Others through violence, bullying, and staging spectacles of power. By focusing on Texan "history," Ferber's *Giant* exposes that these "certainties" arise from specific, historically rooted discourses that sustain the interests of hegemonic groups, especially white males. In this respect, the novel stood apart from other contemporary best-sellers that took male gender identity as their central subject. Ferber's text did not radically alter patriarchy, but with its turn from a masculine to a feminine perspective it complicated established gender norms of the postwar era.

5

Contesting the Feminine Mystique: Gender Performance and Female Identity in Patrick Dennis's *Auntie Mame*

In 1955, a *Houston Press* writer claimed, "if [*Auntie Mame*] achieves best-sellerdom, and I expect it will, either the foundations of the Republic will be undermined, or we'll again become a happy, singing, laughing nation and howl ourselves out of this Time of Troubles."[1] The overstatement of undermining the Republic notwithstanding, the speculation that *Auntie Mame* might achieve best-sellerdom proved to be a profound understatement. The novel became a runaway hit perhaps because the amazing Mame, in her nephew Patrick's words, "seduced thousands" (24).[2] *Auntie Mame* was the number two annual best-seller in 1956 and had only slipped two places on the list in the following year (Hackett 198). Mame's flamboyance and charm continued to delight postwar audiences as evidenced by the enormous popularity of the novel's multiple incarnations. The 1956 Broadway production, starring Rosalind Russell as Mame, played to sell-out crowds; two years later, Warner Bros. released the film version, again starring Russell. Equally successful, the film *Auntie Mame* received four Academy Award nominations and placed as the top moneymaking film of 1959.[3] Still, Americans were eager for more of Mame. Author Patrick Dennis produced the obligatory sequel *Around the World with Auntie Mame* (1958),[4] which was the fourth-ranking best-seller of 1958. Ten years after the original Broadway play, Jerome Lawrence and Robert E. Lee, who also adapted the novel for the stage, teamed with lyricist Jerry Herman to create the 1966 Broadway musical *Mame*, starring Angela Lansbury. This, too, became a film in 1974 with Lucille Ball trying her hand at playing the high-powered aunt. The irrepressible Mame still appears to have plenty of lifeblood, however. The musical has since had two major stage revivals in 1983 and 1996, and, according to *Publishers Weekly*, Universal Pictures acquired the film options in 1997 for *Auntie Mame* and *Around the World with Auntie Mame*.

Spanning over four decades, this chronology speaks for *Auntie Mame*'s remarkable entertainment value. The popularity of Mame in the 1950s is even more impressive considering that the central subject is a female who is rarely a passive, feminine object. Underlying the construction of gender identities in mid-century America, the assumption persisted that gender identity followed unproblematically from sex, so that a biological female should naturally possess feminine qualities, such as receptivity, passivity, and objectivity. In this regulatory scheme, Auntie Mame represented an "unwomanly" female. Her attitudes and values contrasted sharply with those underpinning what Betty Friedan described as the "feminine mystique," the ideal of feminine fulfillment that had widespread cultural currency in postwar America. For women invested in this ideal, Friedan states: "Their only dream was to be perfect wives and mothers; their highest ambition to have five children and a beautiful house, their only fight to get and keep their husbands. They had no thought for the unfeminine problems of the world outside the home; they wanted the men to make the major decisions. They gloried in their role as women, and wrote proudly on the census blank: 'Occupation: housewife'" (18). Of course, the ways in which postwar women understood their roles and lived their daily lives were more complicated and contradictory than this representation would suggest. As Joanne Meyerowitz maintains, there were multiple histories and constructions of gender in the 1950s, along with subcultural challenges to the feminine ideal and a wide range of experiences that did not correspond with Friedan's description of white, middle-class women's lives (1–13). However, because the feminine mystique held such powerful sway in the media and popular press as an ideal to which women should aspire, it serves here as an appropriate, if admittedly somewhat reductive, representation of postwar femininity.

Considering Auntie Mame's resolve in the novel to "prove that she could hold her own in a man's world" (48) rather than receive charity during the Depression, or her quip in the film that she is too busy being a mother to Patrick to find time to be a wife to Lindsey Woolsey, we can see the striking dissimilarity between Mame's brand of femininity and the feminine mystique. Judging from the tremendous popularity of *Auntie Mame*, we also may surmise that the feminine mystique was a troubling ideological investment for growing numbers of women who were no longer fully persuaded that homemaking and child rearing were the sole sources of personal fulfillment. Given the idealization of marriage and traditional family structures in postwar culture, it is significant that Auntie Mame sustained such a high degree of popularity. She is not only unconcerned about establishing a traditional nuclear family unit after her orphaned nephew Patrick comes to live with her, but she projects an image of fulfillment and accomplishment outside of her relationships with men.

Mame is married briefly to southern plantation owner Beauregard Burnside (before his fatal fall from an alpine glacier); therefore, she is not a single woman all throughout her life. However, she does show that an unattached woman neither lacks in achievement nor is an object of pity. Although the film version stretches her marriage to Beauregard into eight years, Russell's riveting screen presence relegates both Beauregard and her persistent suitor Lindsey Woolsey to mere ancillary figures. They may well have functioned, more or less, to secure Mame's heterosexuality, thus making her—and the middle-aged, androgynous Russell—more reassuring to audiences. Notably, Mame and Beau's eight-year marriage is condensed into less than ten minutes of screen time. Russell was able to carry the film (and the Broadway play) to great success virtually by herself.[5] Marjorie Rosen points out in *Popcorn Venus* that by the 1950s "few female stars could bear a picture on their shoulders alone" and that Hollywood was offering few productions featuring "bright and witty women who could carry a picture because their characters astounded us with style and self-importance" (246). *Auntie Mame* appears to be an anomaly in fifties film production, then, for featuring a strong, self-reliant character played by an actress whose performance alone carried the show.

One might argue that Mame's "unwomanliness" as an empowered, rich, independent female may have been recuperated through the construction of her as an eccentric aunt. Undeniably, reviews did tend to promote her character as such, describing her with phrases such as "unmitigated screwball," "lovable lunatic," "kind-hearted madwoman," and "cukey" (sic).[6] Therefore, Mame's threat to patriarchal authority may have been contained by what might be considered merely odd or whimsical behavior. Her eccentricity, however, largely generated by her social consciousness and feminism, is precisely what makes Mame a compelling and progressive cultural figure. If eccentric means, literally, off-center or located elsewhere than at the center, then, in a political sense, Auntie Mame—laughable and lovable though she may have been—registered a strong critique of mainstream values.

Given the ongoing popularity of this progressive female character at an historical moment when such representations were largely absent in the entertainment media, it is curious that *Auntie Mame*, as novel or film, has been given scant attention (other than mere passing mention) in recent scholarly investigations of popular culture. The few less recent critical remarks on the film offer polarized conceptions of its ideological effects, rather like the *Houston Press* endorsement cited at the beginning of this chapter. On the one hand, Brandon French calls the film version "a declaration of political and social revolt against human—and specifically female—oppression," and Auntie Mame "an iconoclastic woman who abhorred the emptiness and impoverishment of middle-class values" (119–20). On the other hand, film historian Marjorie Rosen presents a much different view, claiming that Hollywood had little to offer audiences of the late 1950s by way of positive female images, particularly those images of middle-aged wives and mothers. One reason for this, Rosen claims, is "the growing disdain we were nursing for Mom and marriage," which by the 1960s had become full-blown in Hollywood films.[7] Rosen grants that films depicting marital upheaval or controlling, malevolent mothers also presented a subtler message of female discontent with the lack of options and opportunities outside of their roles as mothers and wives (346). Curiously, however, Rosen fails to see the same potential message in films of the late fifties; instead, she contends: "Little on-screen related to [female audiences], and if *Auntie Mame*, *Pillow Talk*, and *Imitation of Life* lured over-forty America back to the theatre, it was for pure escapism. Nice, wasn't it, to see Rosalind Russell, middle-aged and down on her luck, fortuitously finding a genteel Southerner to lift her from the ranks of Macy's saleswomen?" (345).

That *Auntie Mame* elicited conflicting viewpoints, such as Rosen's and French's, suggests that this narrative most likely generated multiple, sometimes contradictory, messages for postwar audiences as well, which may be indicative of the growing tension between the prevailing domestic ideology and the countercultural position that women were deserving of choice and opportunity beyond the domestic sphere. However, neither of these critical viewpoints informs us as to how *Auntie Mame* specifically engaged the discourses of female gender identity in the fifties. Rosen's, in particular, ignores how narratives which appear to be fantasy or escapist fun also have the potential to alter or shape beliefs, values, and attitudes about one's social "reality" in ways that are not simply recuperations of the status quo.[8]

The aim of this chapter, then, is to furnish a more substantive investigation of how this female dynamo functioned in a cultural context that endorsed rigid, binarized gender and sexual identities, which so effectively channeled women into seeing motherhood as their primary function and life-choice. The upcoming section examines how the novel constructs Auntie Mame as a mother—the apotheosis of womanhood in the feminine mystique—in order to satirize the institutionalization of scientific motherhood, which ostensibly elevated the status of women as professional moms, but which, in fact, disguised the subordination of women by a male-dominated psycho-medical community. Following this section, I use Judith Butler's and Chris Holmlund's formulations of gender performativity and masquerade to argue that both the novel and film versions of *Auntie Mame* deconstruct the notion of gender essences. This reading posits a way that audiences may have thought beyond the regulatory claim that gender differences had ontological status, which, in turn, destined men for certain roles and women for others. The final section turns exclusively to the film version to examine how Rosalind Russell's star image inflected Auntie Mame. Russell, like her character, was a woman who did not quite "fit in" as fully "feminine" and, therefore, was associated with gender mobility and masquerade. Russell and Mame appear to be what Richard Dyer calls a "perfect fit," meaning that "the aspects of a star's image fit with all the traits of a character" (*Stars* 145). This "perfect fit" served to amplify the progressive ideas that *Auntie Mame* offered postwar audiences, who were beginning to stir beneath the seemingly placid surface of domestic suburban bliss.

"Mame-ism" and the Authority of Child Rearing "Experts"

Auntie Mame begins at the point when ten year-old Patrick Dennis is sent to live with his aunt, who is designated Patrick's legal guardian upon his father's sudden death. (His mother had died in childbirth). Patrick's father had previously arranged for his sister Mame to care for his son in case of his death, but only with great reluctance, since he disapproved of her bohemian life-style and penchant for the avant-garde. As a way of safeguarding Patrick against her "craziness," his father stipulates in his will that his son should be raised with conservative values and education and that Dwight Babcock, an officer of the Knickerbocker Trust Company, be assigned to ensure this outcome. In effect, Babcock, the "voice" of the (dead) father, represents patriarchal authority. This, of course, draws the battle lines because Mame harbors a lasting disregard for such authority ever since her father snatched her from the chorus line of *Chu Chin Chow*'s road troupe. Needless to say, when Mame becomes Patrick's guardian, she has her own ideas about family and mothering.

In a 1955 review of Dennis's novel, *Time* said of Auntie Mame: "She is a roaring Life Drive without a muffler and the most commanding prose female since Philip Wylie dreamed up 'Mom'" ("Best-seller Revisited" 74). "Mom," a pejorative label that contemporary audiences might well recognize, enjoyed widespread currency, even professional acceptance, in postwar culture. Coined by Wylie in his 1942 best-selling *Generation of Vipers*, the label applied to mothers who were supposedly over-involved with and controlling of their children. "Momism" was especially perilous to sons, who, if smothered with large amounts of maternal anxiety or encouraged to have an overly sentimental attachment to Mom, would supposedly grow up to be passive weaklings, lacking in vitality and virility (E. May 74–75). However, as Michael Rogin points out, "Momism" speaks more to male fears of "boundary invasion, loss of autonomy, and maternal power generated by domesticity" than it does to any real mothers of the late forties and fifties (242). Nonetheless, it operated as a powerful mechanism in curtailing female independence and self-confidence in mothers. While *Time*'s statement does not explicitly conflate Mame and "Mom," it implicates Mame as an imaginative descendent of the mythic and infamous meddlesome mother (after all, isn't Mame "Mom's" sister-in-law, so to speak?). Even Patrick recalls in the novel (and echoed by Lindsey Woolsey in the film) that "[Mame's] critics have said that I was simply a new lump of clay for her to shape, stretch, mold, and pummel to her heart's content, and it is true that Auntie Mame could never resist meddling with other people's lives" (25). If Mame displays some of the same qualities of which "Mom" is supposedly guilty, this does not simply reduce her to a comedic version of "Mom." Instead, Mame's unorthodox brand of parenting satirizes male authority figures who would so freely wield this label as a weapon against women.

There may indeed have been a resurgence of "Momism" at the end of the decade, as Marjorie Rosen tells us, but alongside this patent attempt to ease male insecurity, an embryonic, but insistent female rebellion was emerging against both the ideology that promoted a feminine ideal of masochistic servitude of the housewife/mother and the professional authority figures who promulgated or reinforced this ideal. As Barbara Ehrenreich and Deirdre English point out, this female rebellion often manifested itself as a malaise called "housewife syndrome" and, according to the male-dominated psychomedical establishment, as a wide-scale "pathological" rejection by women of their "femininity" (273, 281). *Auntie Mame*, however, joined this budding revolt using alternative artillery: Her "roaring Life Drive" stands as a direct rebuke to the middle-class notions of respectability as it applied to womanhood, as well as to the "suffering as pleasure" theory that psychoanalysts at mid-century proclaimed was the female lot in life (Ehrenreich and English 271). Moreover, *Auntie Mame* lampoons the "experts" who presumed to possess the cultural authority and knowledge as to what constituted healthy, adult female aspirations.

Beginning in the first few decades of the twentieth century, a whole range of professionals—physicians, psychologists, sociologists—had begun to establish themselves as indispensable figures in the culture, offering "theoretically sound" or "scientifically based" advice on a wide range of issues concerning child rearing, maternal behavior, and the female sex role. By the late 1940s and early 1950s, these experts had "define[d] women's domestic activities down to the smallest details of housework and child raising." More significantly, "the relationship between women and the experts was not unlike conventional relationships between women and men. The experts wooed their female constituency, promising the 'right' and scientific way to live, and women responded—most eagerly in the upper and middle classes, more slowly among the poor—with dependency and trust. It was never an equal relationship, for the experts' authority rested on the denial or destruction of women's autonomous sources of knowledge" (Ehrenreich and English 4). Particularly in the novel, Auntie Mame eschews this dependency on outside authority except for a brief time when she wholeheartedly embraces the advice of experts from "a splendid book on child guidance" (222) during her stint as foster-mother to six British war orphans (this episode was cut from the film). Mame adopts the practice of "permissiveness" that was endorsed by scientific child rearing theories at mid-century. Permissiveness was based on the experts' belief that "self-indulgence was healthy for the individual personality" (Ehrenreich and English 212). The mother's role in implementing permissiveness was to "engineer" parent-child interaction in order to eliminate or minimize conflict and stress for the child. Mothers were to accomplish this through "inexhaustible patience and always through indirection—showing her willingness to use endless techniques to get around rigidities and rituals and stubbornness'" (Ehrenreich and English 217-18).

Auntie Mame, thinking that "loving understanding and gentle guidance will work wonders" for the war orphans (222), sets out to become a model parent, much like the ideal advocated by the well-respected and renowned child development guru of the 1940s and 1950s, Dr. Arnold Gesell.[9] Mame is unflappable in the face of the orphans' incorrigible behavior. When Edmund introduces himself, telling her to "Call me Jack the Rippah, baby," Mame responds calmly with "How do you do, Jack?" (218). However, after several months without seeing any change in their destructive behaviors and unrelieved cynicism, she admits defeat: "If I could only see a way out of this ... this maternal situation.... I suppose it sounds unnatural and horrid of me, but much as I've tried to love those youngsters, I've failed" (228-29). Whereas Mame echoes postwar culture's readiness to blame mother, some readers might have concluded that the Gesellian notion of permissiveness allowed everyone in the family except the mother to bask in self-indulgence and that perhaps there was nothing "unnatural" after all in wanting out of her "maternal situation."

From nephew Patrick's perspective, Mame's "ideas on child raising may have been considered a trifle unorthodox—as, indeed, were all her ideas on anything," but he admits that her "unique system worked well enough in its casual way" (19). Not founded on any particular expert theory of child rearing, Mame's system was one of her own making, although she took to heart the current Freudian doctrine that too much repression was unhealthy. She bombarded Patrick with a variety of "stimulating" experiences and "liberating" ideas, including exposing him to the "exquisite mysteries" of Eastern religions and giving his libido "a good shaking up" (21). During his first summer with his aunt, Patrick reports that he was "dragged along to most of the exhibitions, the shopping forays with [Mame's] friend Vera, and to whatever function Auntie Mame thought would be Suitable, Stimulating, or Enlightening for a child of ten. That covered a wide range" (24). In addition, she gives Patrick a vocabulary pad on which he must write all the words he hears or reads—Bastille Day, Lesbian, Id, relativity, free love, Oedipus complex, stinko, and so forth—but does not understand (24).

Mame is determined to provide a corrective to Patrick's former state of parental neglect after she learns that his father's conversations with his son amounted to "pipe down, kid, the old man's hung" (23). Encouraged to mingle at all her salons and soirées, Patrick is exposed to the various intellectual streams currently circulating in the culture. "God knows you can learn more in ten minutes in my drawing room than you did in ten years with that father of yours," Mame declares. "What a criminal way to raise a child!" (23). As an adult, Patrick reflects on his early "education" with bemused pride: "My advancement that summer of 1929, if not exactly what *Every Parent's Magazine* would recommend, was remarkable. By the end of July I knew how to mix what Mr. [Alexander] Woollcott called a 'Lucullan little martini' and I had learned not to be frightened by Auntie Mame's most astonishing friends" (24).

Mame's method of parenting gives us some laughs, but her unconventional mothering works to denaturalize the culture's injunctions to be a "good" mother—versus a bad "Mom"—by submitting to "expert" advice and male authority. It also unmasks the racist and elitist underpinnings of the hegemonic order. In both the novel and the film, Mame finds herself battling with Mr. Babcock over Patrick's education. As Babcock says in the novel, Mame's desire to expose Patrick to different cultures and religions is "a lit-tle too experimental," even "dangerously radical." He objects to one school because its student body is "a pack of Jews" who would expose Patrick to "that West side element" (32).[10] Having the Law of the Father (literally) on his side, Babcock succeeds in "incarcerating" Patrick at St. Boniface Boarding School for Boys, aptly located in Apathy, Massachusetts, but not before Mame attempts to usurp his legal power over Patrick. She secretly registers him at Ralph Devine's revolutionary academy in which "all classes are held in the nude under ultraviolet ray" and "not a repression [is] left after the first semester" (21). Ralph's school has no books or traditional activities, but rather "lots of nonobjective art and eurhythmics and discussion groups" (21). "Constructive Play" consists of large group games designed to teach the students "something of Life." One such game Patrick describes is "Fish Families, which purported to give us a certain casual knowledge of reproduction in the lower orders ... Natalie and all the girls would crouch on the floor and pretend to lay fish eggs and then Ralph, followed by the boys, would skip among them, arms thrust sideways and fingers wiggling—'in a swimming motion, a swimming motion'— and fertilize the eggs. It always brought down the house" (36). In the midst of Fish Families one afternoon—just as Ralph is yelling "Spread the sperm, spread the sperm!"—Babcock collars the truant Patrick who is supposedly enrolled in the "restricted" Buckley School. To punish Mame (and ultimately Patrick, since his only "real Family" becomes a "dim whisper in an academic wilderness"), Babcock chooses an out-of-state school so that "the only time [Mame will] get [her] depraved hands on him is Christmas and summer" (37).

Babcock's horror of Mame being Patrick's "mother" reflects the ambivalence about motherhood within postwar culture. As the potential civilizers of boys and men, mothers, at least in the abstract, were held in high regard. However, in practice, motherhood was seen as a hazardous undertaking because any deviation by women from "properly" nurturing their sons could produce "uncivilized" males (juvenile delinquents, communists, or homosexuals). Helene Deutsch, a prominent psychoanalyst of the decade, theorized that "healthy" patterns of mothering were the direct result of women accepting the "feminine reality principle," meaning that female ambitions and expectations must be diminished or renounced so that a woman could nurture her children properly. Deutsch argued that motherliness "is achieved only when all masculine wishes have been given up or sublimated into other goals. If 'the old factor of lack of a penis has not yet forfeited its power,' complete motherliness remains still to be achieved." In other words, a woman must rid herself of her "masculinity complex" by "projecting [her ambitions] onto her [male] child" (qtd. in Ehrenreich and English 270). The postwar era, then, presented an interesting and unfortunate paradox: Motherhood was touted as the paragon of womanliness, but regarded with suspicion as the potential ruination of society. If challenging Babcock's patriarchal authority and refusing to diminish her own *bon vivant* attitude and intellectual pursuits were evidence of her failure to resolve her "masculinity complex," then Auntie Mame was wonderfully guilty.

Not only was motherhood surrounded by ambiguity, but also families without fathers were subject to downright attack by the psychomedical community. "Left to herself, Mom would produce emasculated males and equally Mom-ish females ... only Dad could undo the damage and guide the boys toward manliness and the girls toward true womanliness" (Ehrenreich and English 242). Such thinking emerged from the sex role theories proposed by the influential sociologist, Talcott Parsons, who, in the early 1950s, stressed that both parents within the nuclear family were essential in furnishing the "proper" sex-role models for their children. Each parent had a specific function to perform for their children, which effectively recreated the nuclear family's Oedipal drama for their children (Ehrenreich and English 248). For the most part, the experts approached the subject of the fatherless family unit with alarm and confusion.

Similarly, what distresses Dwight Babcock is the possibility that the fatherless Patrick will become engulfed in Mame's female world. By whisking him off to Massachusetts, Babcock intends to rescue Patrick from what he sees as certain psychosocial damage along with restoring his patriarchal authority. Babcock justifies this action by discrediting Mame as "crazy" and "mad," labels which historically have been applied to women who have presumed to usurp male privilege and power. Calling Mame "Jezebel" and "depraved" is similarly intended to tarnish her entire moral character. *Auntie Mame*, however, endorses neither Babcock's rhetorical posturing nor the male hegemony he represents. As a result of Patrick being removed from his "mother" and the influence of women altogether, he becomes, according to Mame, "one of the most beastly, bourgeois, babbitty little snobs on the Eastern Seaboard" (189).[11] He begins to resemble the stuffy, elitist Babcock and becomes increasingly ashamed of his aunt's free-spirited lifestyle, wishing she would "falsify" herself to be more acceptable to his fiancée's status-conscious parents. Perhaps Ralph Devine's School and its "Fish Families" seem preposterous, but *Auntie Mame* proposes that its alternative—St. Boniface—may be equally so, with its uniforms (the insignia of social difference), its exclusive old-boy network, and other trappings of elitism and white male hegemony.[12]

Mame and Masquerade

In an effort to explain how the feminine mystique became so deeply ingrained in postwar cultural practice, Betty Friedan found that it had accumulated "scientific backing, either directly or indirectly, from the theories and findings of the decade's most influential sociologists and psychologists. In general, these theories assumed women's roles were largely determined according to biological sexual function. Even among functionalists, such as sociologist Talcott Parsons, who rejected the Freudian-based notion that biology was destiny, studies of sex role functioning remained within the existing framework of sexual differentiation. Parsons examined how sex roles were learned and differentiated within the nuclear family structure, which he determined was a subsystem of society. He did not question his underlying assumptions that sex role differentiation was a given and, in fact, necessary for both healthy family functioning and for a child's later success in the social order. Parsons's functional analysis did little or nothing to address the female sex role in terms of women's social or material subordination to men; instead, sex role theory concentrated on "problems of adjustment" and the accompanying strain and conflict involved in accepting one's femininity and roles of wife and mother.[13] The end result of this approach, Friedan concludes, is that "women were being adjusted to a state inferior to their full capabilities" (135).

In the midst of these prevailing discourses on sex roles, Friedan did locate a revolutionary "vision of the infinite variety of sexual patterns and the enormous plasticity of human nature" in the work of anthropologist Margaret Mead (136). In 1935, Mead wrote in *Sex and Temperament in Three Primitive Societies*:

> If those temperamental attitudes which we have traditionally regarded as feminine—such as passivity, responsiveness, and a willingness to cherish children—can so easily be set up as the masculine pattern in one tribe, and in another be outlawed for the majority of women as well as for the majority of men, we no longer have any basis for regarding such aspects of behavior as sex-linked …. The material suggests that we may say that many, if not all, of the personality traits which we have called masculine or feminine are as lightly linked to sex, as are the clothing, the manners, and the form of head-dress that a society at a given period assigns to either sex. (qtd. in Friedan 136)

Mead's conclusions are indeed revolutionary in proclaiming that gender is not a seamless identity, but an arbitrary and socially constructed one. Her mention of clothing and manners suggests, too, that gender is linked to performance or particular effects produced on bodily surfaces. Unfortunately, Friedan notes, this liberatory vision did not translate throughout Mead's works, but became "subtly transformed into a glorification of women in the female role—as defined by their sexual biological function" (137).

Not surprisingly, this view of gender mobility and instability remained largely buried in the 1950s, and evidence to support it was systematically ignored. The result was that sex role differentiation was reinforced both within the academic community and the mass media, which reproduced and popularized the findings of social scientists. The pervasiveness of these discourses complemented the feminine mystique and provided its scientific backing. Despite its strength, however, Friedan found hundreds of women in the late 1950s and early 1960s who had begun to question the ideology of passive femininity and limited opportunities for women. It is possible that *Auntie Mame*'s magnetic attraction came out of this questioning, and it is probable that what some viewers found so appealing about Mame was the same revolutionary vision Margaret Mead had voiced twenty years earlier—that gender formation is neither a predetermined fact nor continuous with biological sex, but rather an arbitrary process.

That *Auntie Mame* foregrounds such gender instability is signaled in the opening scene of both the novel and the film. As the housekeeper Norah Muldoon and young Patrick cross the threshold of Mame's Beekman Place apartment to encounter one of her spectacular parties, their attention becomes fixed on a sight directly before them. The film, through shot/reverse-shot editing, underscores the disruptive impact this scene has on the newcomers. In the first shot, as Norah raises her eyes to take in the scene, her face registers momentary confusion, then shocked recognition. The reverse shot reveals what leaves her aghast: two cross-dressers—one male, one female—obviously sharing a joke. The shot then returns to Norah and a bug-eyed Patrick, showing Norah's now condemnatory expression and her protective gesture toward her charge.[14] This sequence is neither an endorsement of Norah's perspective because, as an unworldly observer, the joke seems to be on her, nor is it merely a gratuitous spectacle. Instead, the cross-dressers present a categorical confusion of "man" and "woman," which disrupts, if only momentarily, the appearance of a natural continuity between sex and gender, a continuity that upholds the cultural norm of binarized sexual identities. These images of drag introduce *Auntie Mame*'s profoundly radical message that gender formation involves the manipulation of signs through bodily gestures, acts, and style—that is, through performance—rather than originating as a natural consequence of anatomical sex. The presence of drag in the narratives' opening scenes reinforces the notion, in Judith Butler's words, that "gender is drag" ("Imitation" 28). By this, Butler means to emphasize that *all* gender is "a kind of impersonation and approximation" of an idealized category of identity that becomes naturalized over time through repetition ("Imitation" 21).

In *Auntie Mame*, both narratives metonymically link the man and woman in drag, the idea of gender as drag, and Auntie Mame by juxtaposing the cross-dressing scene with Mame's initial appearance, an appearance characterized by pure theatricality. In the novel, she enters in costume, "a regular Japanese doll of a woman" (13), complete with an adjustable cigarette holder, numerous rings, bracelets, bangles, sequins, and green laquered fingernails. Rosalind Russell's screen performance gives a highly stylized and staged quality to Mame's gestures as well: her body is in continuous, hurried motion; her arms reach out in wide, sweeping movements; she tilts her head back or lowers her eyelids with dramatic flair. Russell/Mame punctuates her words with her eye and hand gestures as she darts through her crowd of guests, so that the words become secondary to their delivery. Attention is displaced from what Mame says onto how she says it. This connection between Mame and performance is sustained throughout the narratives by her self-conscious use of role-playing and impersonation. The film (and Broadway play) reinforced this visually with the nearly twenty costume and five wig changes required of Russell in playing the flamboyant Mame. Mame's association with spectacle and performance is important in establishing audience recognition that her use of masquerade allows her to articulate a more unconventional representation of female sexual identity, one that takes as its strategic aim the disruption of stable and fixed gender binaries. Furthermore, in suggesting through performance or masquerade that gender is provisional, *Auntie Mame* perhaps gave postwar audiences another perspective about gender roles—one, according to Friedan, that many women longed to hear: that deviation from these roles was not a neurotic or dysfunctional response to one's "natural" state.

This reading of gender identity in *Auntie Mame* builds on Butler's theorizing of gender as "a stylized repetition of acts" that produces the *effect* of gender and "the illusion of an abiding gendered self" (*Gender* 140). That is to say, what postures as an "original" identity is merely an effect of performance or masquerade, which are regulated through the dominant discourses that rule cultural practices of male and female identities and which are repeated over time. Butler's conceptualization of repetition is useful in attributing to Auntie Mame a kind of agency and for understanding her enactments of femininity as counter-hegemonic. In other words, if repetition implies a failure to imitate the fictional ideal of femininity and therefore a compulsion to repeat this idealized identity over and over, this signals a failure to guarantee the "natural" relationship between "woman" as "feminine" and "man" as "masculine." Furthermore, if repetition is the scene of gender signification, as Butler claims, then variations on that repetition produce alternative significations or, the possibility of new configurations of gender identity. It is in the act of producing these variations that Butler locates agency.

Auntie Mame's own proliferation of gender performances allows her to use masquerade in different ways and for different purposes, including resisting male power and authority and affirming alternative patterns of female sexual identity. Chris Holmlund's work on how gender masquerades can be put to use for different purposes and within different contexts illustrates this point more clearly. Holmlund identifies several types of masquerade, including "dressing up," otherwise called embellishment; "putting on," or parody; and "stepping out," or masquerading to contest or affirm a particular identity (216). These terms are not necessarily mutually exclusive because one can "dress up to step out;" nor do they exclude the possibility of experiencing pleasure in the process of individuating one's identity through masquerade.[15]

One particular instance of Auntie Mame self-consciously "putting on," or using masquerade as a parody, in order to resist patriarchal authority is with her confrontation with Mr. Babcock over Patrick's schooling. Knowing that her bohemian life-style transgresses the boundaries of middle-class decorum, Mame attempts to conceal this fact from Mr. Babcock to avoid losing Patrick. Her plan is to pass as a "soft," "genteel," and "respectable little maiden aunt" (27) and to exhibit "appropriate" feminine qualities—charm, restraint, and passivity. Aided by the theatrical experience of best-friend Vera Charles, Mame transforms herself through manner and costume. "Clothes make the mood, the personality—everything" Vera tells her (26). It is perhaps no coincidence that Mame's closest friend is an actress who performs whether on or off stage. Born Rachel Kollinsky, "the daughter of a second-rate Jewish comedian" from Pittsburgh (207) and beginning her career in a traveling burlesque show, Vera has reinvented herself as "First Lady of the American Stage" and member of the *haut monde*. According to Patrick, Vera "spoke with such Mayfair elegance that you could barely understand a word she said" (26).

Mame's elaborately constructed camouflage nearly fails when she and Babcock square off over Patrick's schooling. In the novel, Babcock initiates their meeting by making claims to his authority and reminding Mame of their unequal status: "The boy's late father felt that it would be, uh, *wiser* if I ... were to have complete authority on that matter" (30). This all but unmasks Mame, causing her false coronet (her "halo") to rock "alarmingly." (Her coronet is designed to conceal her bobbed hair, which in the 1920s—the narrative's early setting—signified a woman who supported liberal ideas). The adversaries battle for over an hour, until Mame recognizes that a direct challenge to Babcock's authority is counterproductive. As Patrick describes it, "the argument had reached a pitch that made me fear for the complete success of Auntie Mame's genteel masquerade when a furtive, cunning look crept across her face. There was a sudden sob, then Auntie Mame buried her face in her hands and shook convulsively .... Oh, Mr. Babcock," she gasped, "how can I ever apologize for being such a foolish, headstrong thing ... a simple, single woman, unused to raising little ones—to argue with you, a father and the executor of little Patrick's estate?" (33). Her ruse of female helplessness and self-renunciation restores their equanimity; Babcock becomes solicitous and apologetic, and Mame duplicitously agrees to abide by his decision. This act of "putting on" empowers Mame, enabling her to reduce temporarily the threat she poses to male authority and thus to continue with her own plans for Patrick. Her parody of a genteel, maiden aunt—one of the few culturally acceptable positions of womanhood available to older, unmarried sisters—does more than just reduce anxiety. It recontextualizes this identity, exposing not only its constructedness, but also the power relations embedded within this construction. The maiden aunt(ie) Mame becomes a subversive imitation, then, by disclosing that such qualities as deference and fragility are part of a regulatory ideal, which women must effectively imitate in order to avoid disapproval or punishment.

Soon after, Mame masquerades again, this time as the "triumph of Southern womanhood" during her courtship and subsequent marriage to Beauregard. "Her hair was fluffier, softer; there were always a lot of camellias around the rooms; her dresses seemed to run to organdy and ruffles, and there was almost a roar of crinoline beneath her skirts" (64). Clearly, this very stylized and excessive femininity is an act of "dressing up," a kind of costuming that often accompanies courtship rituals and indicates that desire is constructed partly through surface significations of the body, but which give the illusion that desire has its origins in some interior identity. There may be an anxious quality to Mame's impersonation along with the pleasure involved in this embellishment, though, because she is aware of her marginalized status as a Yankee woman. By fictionalizing her past, inventing a "daddy" who was a colonel and herself as an accomplished equestrian, she may hope to "pass" as more acceptable to Beau's family.

The novel includes other instances of Mame's role-playing. She outdoes herself at being "Irish" when Brian O'Bannion begins to squire her around New York; she plays the "femme fatale" to Patrick's college friends and "Gracious Lady" for the Upsons of snobbish Mountebank (this latter masquerade is featured in the film as well). Patrick, as a young adult, appreciates Mame's multiple masquerades least of all. Fearing she will make a bad impression on his prospective in-laws, the Upsons, he chides her, saying, "must you always appear in a character role ... I just want you to go out there and act like a normal human being" (188–89). At this moment, though, it would be hard for audiences to miss the point that acting like a "normal" human being is just that—acting. By witnessing that when Mame acts "normal," like the maiden aunt she is purported to be, audiences see she is merely imitating or reproducing the effects of a mythical identity. Moreover, Patrick is discredited here for being a "bourgeois snob" because his idea of a "normal human being" is embedded in certain expectations of gender, as well as of class and race—expectations that reflect ruling-class values. "Normal," for him, means being "lady-like" and reserved. It means not letting the Upsons know about Mame's chorus girl days, her "queer friends on Fire Island" (189), or, as Patrick states in the film, the flaunting of "her new flames or old peccadilloes in front of Gloria."

Perhaps no character in *Auntie Mame* underscores the point about gender performativity more than Mame's secretary, the hilarious and hapless Agnes Gooch. Gooch, as even her name seems to imply, "fails" to present herself as "properly" feminine, meaning that she does not make herself sexually appealing and receptive to males. As Patrick describes her, "Miss Gooch was one of those women who could be anywhere between fifteen and fifty and nobody would care. She had colorless hair, colorless skin, and colorless eyes" (95). She wears orthopedic Oxfords and shapeless sack dresses or sweaters, mostly to conceal any suggestion of sexuality or a sexed body. In short, Gooch does not "do" her gender right. It is reasonable to suggest that Gooch's appearances are meant to draw laughter because they diverge so drastically from the collective ideal of female sexual identity, and if so, such humor belies an aggressive edge. Many women in the audience would have been bombarded with media advice such as in a 1953 *Coronet* article, advising that "the smart woman will keep herself desirable. It is her duty to herself to be feminine and desirable at all times in the eyes of the opposite sex" (qtd. in Miller and Nowak 157). But there is other significance to Gooch's "failure." As Butler makes clear, "the injunction *to be* a given gender produces necessary failures, a variety of incoherent configurations that in their multiplicity exceed and defy the injunction by which they are generated" (*Gender* 145). With regard to femininity, then, what becomes reified in a culture as "real womanhood" can be sustained neither over time nor by all women, and if this is so, then the very "natural-ness" of femininity is called into question.

That femininity has to do with bodily signification is illustrated most clearly in both novel and film by Gooch's imitation of Mame. When Mame is unable to accompany her ghostwriter Brian O'Bannion to an important party given by her book publisher, she elects to send Agnes in her place. However, in order to do so, Mame must "create a new Agnes," which, as the novel tells us, involves applying Lydia Van Rensslaer Skin-Glo, "a bit of trussing here and there," donning a tight, form-fitting Patou velvet, and instructing Agnes to "try to be soignée" and to "shave under [her] arms" so that she does not "look like King Kong" (113–14).

By putting on Mame's clothes and make-up, Agnes is not generating a mirror image of Mame; instead, she is imitating the *effects* of Mame's own masquerading. For what Agnes's transformation illustrates is how Mame sustains her own performance of idealized femininity. Moreover, the stark imagistic contrast between Mame and the "old" Agnes—acted so memorably in the film by a slouching, gawky, squint-eyed Peggy Cass—serves to highlight Mame's theatricality and emphasis on outward appearance—her basking in jewels, flashy costumes and wigs. In the film, Gooch's hunched figure, dressed in slate blues, grays, and browns, is frequently juxtaposed to Mame's, who first appears with Gooch in her stylish widow's weeds, which is slit down her back to the waist and punctuated by an oversized lavender flower. In the next scene, Mame turns up in the unforgettable shimmering, deep-burgundy gown, open in the front from waist to floor to reveal matching burgundy pants underneath. These costumes convey a certain amount of pleasure in "dressing up," but they also indicate Mame's willingness to play with the relationship between style and power by wearing pants and obviously expensive clothes. If Mame's instructions urge Gooch to "dress up" and "step out" in style in order to affirm the identity of a "real woman," this is affirming it as a provisional identity. Within this same representation of "womanhood" lies its contestation, for to be a "woman" involves enacting a particular pattern of femininity.

Agnes's parody of idealized femininity also raises questions concerning the gendering of sexuality and desire. That is to say, her gender performance also reproduces the dominant culture's notion of a "sexy" woman, one who signals sexual receptivity and objectivity. It is only after Agnes "puts on" this particular style of femininity that O'Bannion finds her desirable. This implies that desirability and sexiness within a system of compulsory heterosexuality is linked to what a culture constructs as desire and female sexuality, rather than originating from a natural, interiorized sexual essence. Thus, women are considered sexual objects for men by performing certain cultural patterns of behavior coded as "sexy." After Gooch dresses up, O'Bannion reads her new look as a sign of availability, which he assumes gives him the "right" to seduce her. Gooch's seduction, then, may be read as a parody of the power relations embedded in (hetero)sexism.

By instructing Gooch "to live, live, live," Auntie Mame unwittingly conveys a valuable lesson: If the conventional signs of gender differentiation can be masqueraded, then, so too can other configurations of gender. Mame's own proliferation of gender performances affords her a certain amount of gender mobility, allowing her to claim space in a terrain that is traditionally reserved for the male subject. Although Mame is associated with spectacle and the pleasures of dressing up, which are coded as "feminine" exhibition and to-be-looked-at-ness, she just as often reverses this situation of gendered difference. As the novel makes clear, Mame does not hesitate to control the gaze: of the naked Ralph Devine, a paragon of masculine beauty and muscularity, she remarks, "Isn't he lovely. Just like a Praxiteles" (35); of Brain O'Bannion, she murmurs, "isn't he virile" (104). In the film, Mame's obvious appreciation of O'Bannion's looks upon their first meeting is produced through shot/reverse-shot editing.

What further distinguishes Mame from conventional representations of femininity is her rejecting the sexual limitations imposed on women within a male-dominated social order. Mame sees herself as less a sexual object and more an agent of her own sexual desires (albeit still in a heterosexual world). Because more open attitudes toward sex and sexual frankness in the media and popular culture were increasingly displayed in the 1950s, middle-class, postwar audiences would likely not blanch at the representation of a "sexual" or flirtatious woman. Indeed, the idea that sexual fulfillment and satisfaction were now considered necessary to healthy adult female functioning had come into its own by mid-century. However, female sexual pleasure and satisfaction were still to be contained within the nuclear family, marriage being the only permissible arena for such expression for women. Too often, however, this meant that women had to resign themselves to the passive role of pleasing their partners.[16] Within this regulatory paradigm, women who chose to experience sexual satisfaction outside of marriage were labeled "neurotic" or "unnatural," having failed to overcome their inner masculine strivings (Ehrenreich and English 274). Worse, they were considered just plain "bad."

In *Auntie Mame*, readers and moviegoers were exposed to a positive, yet unconventional, image of female sexuality. In the novel we can infer this, since Mame is in her early thirties, yet still single and in her "heyday." Filmgoers saw an obviously older Mame played by Russell, then in her mid-forties, who for the major part of the film is unmarried and enjoying her single life. When Lindsey Woolsey proposes, apparently for the nth time, Mame laughingly refuses him, saying, "now let's not start that again." Even after Patrick arrives, she sees no urgency to establish a nuclear family unit for his (or her) sake.

The novel readers would find Mame's progressive attitudes toward female sexuality reinforced in the chapter, "Auntie Mame in the Ivy League." Unwilling to confine her relationships with men to culturally sanctioned ones, the middle-aged Mame has an affair with one of Patrick's college friends simply because she finds it rejuvenating and pleasurable. Patrick reacts badly to her affair, presumably horrified by both an "older" woman's sexuality and the sexual pairing of an older woman and a younger man. When he discovers the affair, he barrages his aunt with insults. Defending herself, Mame asserts that she is interested in Alex's mind, to which Patrick retorts, "Balls! Alex hasn't got a mind." Crudely put, however, Alex's "balls" are exactly what drives Mame's actions, and she finally concedes, "he amused me" (174). In giving Mame the last word here, the narrative seems to be endorsing her position over that of her priggish nephew. What is implied here is not that Mame is unnatural or predatory, but that male hegemony stands behind the regulation of female sexuality, determining when and with whom women can be sexual.

While both the novel and the film present Auntie Mame's nonconformity as wholly positive, it would be misleading not to suggest that the narratives' closures retreat to safer ideological ground by introducing in the final moments a model of conventional femininity in the sympathetic and pleasant Pegeen Ryan. Pegeen is "safely" middle-class, college-educated, and sensible, and she is the only female figure who is not a type or in some way exaggerated. Her marriage to Patrick not only reproduces the conventional heterosexual union at the end of a comedy, but also closes with the image of a happy, white, middle-class nuclear family. In strategically placing Pegeen and her marriage to Patrick in the final scenes, both novel and film may have tried to safeguard the status quo and the stable, binarized gender terms of postwar culture. However, given the moral force and dynamism of Auntie Mame, it is not entirely convincing that the recuperation of conventional femininity, the romantic couple, and the nuclear family unit is endorsed unproblematically. In the first place, readers of the sequel, *Around the World with Auntie Mame* would encounter in its opening pages a pointed lampoon of Patrick and Pegeen's middle-class lifestyle in suburban Verdant Greens. Furthermore, Mame's demonstration of gender as performance implies that what Pegeen's image recuperates is itself just one more type of female masquerade.

Rosalind Russell's Mame

For many Auntie Mame fans, this dynamic, irrepressible character became inseparable from what Rosalind Russell "made" of her. Richard Dyer defines this phenomenon as "audience-star identification," meaning that "the 'truth' about a character's personality and the feelings it evokes may be determined by what the reader takes to be the truth about the person of the star playing the part" (*Stars* 141). The impression that Auntie Mame in many respects *was* "Rosalind Russell" appears to have been undiminished by time. Sixteen years after Russell's performance, Lucille Ball's reincarnation of Mame in the film musical was haunted by Russell, the "real" Auntie Mame, as one reviewer called her.[17] This compels us to ask what qualities came to signify Russell's star image and, more specifically, how this persona inflected the gendering of her character role. What fostered the impression that Auntie Mame and Rosalind Russell were a "perfect fit?" What did Russell bring to Mame in terms of her former roles, other extratextual images, and her screen performance that functioned to conflate star and part, which reinforced the progressive images of both novel and film?

If we begin by considering the parts Russell played just prior to *Auntie Mame*, we would see very different "Russells" in the practical, can't-get-a-man Ruth in the Broadway production of *Wonderful Town*, or the "old maid" school teacher Rosemary in the film *Picnic*, who degrades herself by begging Howard to marry her. While these roles were far removed from the savvy and sophisticated Mame, they share in common Russell's propensity in the 1950s for playing female figures who did not quite fit in with the orthodox brand of femininity dominating the period, which, for so many white, middle-class women, translated itself into the "feminine mystique." Whether playing the sensible Ruth, the bitter spinster Rosemary, or the icono-clastic Mame, Russell portrayed women who acted "different," women who either "failed" or refused to comply with the injunction that women were subservient to and existed as sexual objects for men. Russell's two major roles preceding Mame reinforced her association with parodying or satirizing the notion that women's happiness was contingent on their snagging a husband and subordinating their own career ambitions.

Russell's star image was built up around earlier roles, as well. Beginning her film career in 1934 with Metro-Goldwyn-Mayer, Russell appeared in more than forty Hollywood films prior to *Auntie Mame*. Based on these performances, filmgoers were no doubt inclined to formulate certain expectations about Auntie Mame before stepping foot in a theatre. Middle-aged and older audiences, in particular, could recall Russell as the perennial career woman in her earlier films, such as *His Girl Friday* (1939), *Take a Letter, Darling* (1942), *What a Woman!* (1943), *Tell It to the Judge* (1949), and *A Woman of Distinction* (1950). By her own account, Russell told an audience of *Newsweek* readers in 1957 that she had played "about 23 [career girls] in a row ... doctor, college dean, head of advertising agency, crack reporter—you name it and I've done it. It got so when I picked up a script I didn't read it, I just asked: 'How many telephones on my beautiful blond desk this time—four or six.' Judging from that, I could start ordering my cos-tumes. I'd need a couple of business suits—gray flannel, one blue, and maybe one black—for the first scenes when I was ordering big hulks like Fred MacMurray and Melvyn Douglas around" (Wenning 68–69). Russell's portrayal of career women earned her an award from the National Federation of Business and Professional Women's Clubs in 1950, and the moniker "career girl" continued to define Russell in publicity articles well into the decade. Although Auntie Mame's character is not a career woman per se, Russell tells readers in her memoirs *Life Is a Banquet* that "even in all those career-women pictures I'd been Mame, so when I finally played her, it was nothing new to me, she was the same character, only a bit more exaggerated and with a little boy instead of a leading man for a foil" (Russell 200–1).

If we consider, as Molly Haskell does, that these career-women roles designated her as one of the "superwomen" of prewar Hollywood, the link between Russell and Mame becomes more apparent. In addition, it primed audiences to see Mame as an empowered woman. Haskell includes Russell, along with Katharine Hepburn, Bette Davis, Joan Crawford, Barbara Stanwyck, and Carole Lombard, in her list of superwomen, or actresses of the 1930s and 1940s who were known for their portrayals of intelligent, sophisticated, independent, career women. Significantly, one of the determining attributes of superwomen was their ability to "adopt male characteristics in order to enjoy male prerogatives, or merely to survive" (Haskell 214). Who can forget, for example, Russell in *His Girl Friday* as plucky, pinstriped journalist Hildy Johnson, whose presence in a male-dominated newsroom is distinguished by her witty repartee and verbal sparring, as well as her hard-driving work ethic and a play-to-win attitude? (Viewers may have recalled that in the original stage version of *His Girl Friday*, Hildy's part was written for a male actor). Having come to the role of Mame with this "superwoman" status fostered the impression that Russell seemed tailor-made for the buoyant, unflappable aunt that Patrick Dennis had created in print.

In addition, publicity about her personal "history"—the "real" Rosalind Russell—played up the similarities between Russell and her character roles as evidenced in the reviews of her Broadway performances in *Wonderful Town* and three years later in *Auntie Mame*. Following her explosive success as Ruth in *Wonderful Town*, for which Russell won a Tony award for best actress,[18] *Time* magazine featured her on the cover of the 30 March 1953 issue. The accompanying article credits her twenty-year success in film and stage to her "bubbling confidence," "boundless energy," and "shrewd sense of what is best for

Rosalind Russell" ("Comic Spirit" 40). It continues saying, "those who have known Ros longest and best say that her part in *Wonderful Town* is simply an enlargement of her own personality. She has always been forthright, both 'musically and noisily inclined,' and has operated under a full head of steam" ("Comic Spirit" 40). *Newsweek*'s 1957 review of Russell's stage performance of Auntie Mame made a similar comparison, stating, "the same sort of raffish spirit" that Russell attributed to her character Mame could also describe Russell herself (Wenning 70). *Cosmopolitan* spoke of "her phenomenal energy, a power source roughly comparable to a nuclear reactor" (Whitcomb 19). Such articles tended to gloss Auntie Mame through Rosalind Russell—the confident, take-charge, ebullient actress and business-woman. Interestingly, while all of these feature articles make note of Russell's marriage to Fred Brisson, a successful Broadway producer, and their only child Lance, they concentrate on her career successes and her ability, in *Time*'s words, to be the "master [sic] of her own destiny" ("Comic Spirit" 45). Indeed, columnist Earl Wilson of the *New York Post* called Russell "quite a business babe," referring to her and Brisson's successful production company, Independent Artists, which had grossed five million dollars on two movie ventures (N. pag.)

Russell proved to be equally shrewd in making *Auntie Mame* a star vehicle for herself, which is not to say that the script was written expressly for Russell, but that in casting her many of the scenes were scripted to feature her talents as a comedienne. Russell had had her eye on the story all along, having read it in galley proofs even before its publication by Vanguard Press (Whitcomb 18). When discussions were underway to turn *Auntie Mame* into a Broadway play, Russell acted quickly and bought a controlling interest of the production. She also claims to have had an active role, along with director Morton Da Costa (who she also says, was her own handpicked choice for director), in reworking Jerome Lawrence and Robert Lee's script.[19] In *Life Is a Banquet*, Russell says she "stole from everywhere," mostly to add visual gags: "People thought all these bits were straight out of the novel, but they weren't. In fact, people would come backstage and say we'd got every page of the book into the play, though, in fact, we'd left out masses of it" (191–92). Russell, likewise shrewd in augmenting her own prominence as a star, recalls, "I virtually removed myself from the second act. (This astonished theatre pros)." She and Da Costa agreed that Agnes Gooch should carry the act alone; however, said Russell, "I'll take the last scene; I'm not giving that away." Her strategy was

simple: "Let 'em say, Where is she? When's she coming back?'"
(Russell *Life* 192).

Russell recalls that she and Da Costa again teamed up to write
scenes and gags for the film version and that she had considerable
behind-the-scenes influence over the final version. Certain memorable
scenes in the film suggest that Russell's gifts as a comedienne were
being highlighted. Her particular way of doing comedy, which shifts
between a witty, sophisticated delivery and pure slapstick, altered the
novel's depiction of them; however, it furthered the impression that
Russell/Mame's identity was fluid and constructed through
performance. By and large, Russell stayed with polite comedy in
Auntie Mame, delivering her punch lines with sophisticated panache,
impeccable timing, and the arch of her eyebrow or the widening or
closing of her eyes. However, in the next moment, her humor shifts to
pure slapstick: recall the farcical hunting scene in which Russell/Mame
flops along in tiny boots that refused to go over her feet; her infamous
"seat" on the killer-horse, Meditation; her hilarious, short-lived job as a
switchboard operator in which she must answer several phone lines in
split-second, rapid succession by saying "Widdecombe, Gutterman,
Applewhite, Bibberman and Black"; or the frantic Vera and Mame
trading high-pitched insults, while Mame whirls a long twist around
her head like helicopter rotors in an attempt to make a demure
coronet. This latter scene is more in keeping with a scene right out of
The Women (1939), rather than the way Dennis had written it as two
friends sharing a secret, cozy delight in deceiving Mr. Babcock.

It is possible to read this shift to slapstick as a narrative mechanism
that contains Russell/Mame's counterhegemonic appeal. By situating
her in a position to be laughed at, rather than one of laughing with,
these several scenes may operate to recuperate this independent, strong
figure. Clearly, there appears to be a difference in the power dynamic
encoded in Russell's performance of Mame as the witty, wise,
sophisticate and in her image as the careening, female equestrian.
However, Russell's occasional shift to farce also can be read not as a
containment of this strong female, but as a sign of Russell's/Mame's
multiple and fluid identity. Moreover, her style of acting stresses the
performativity involved in identity formation. Alternating between
the screwball aunt and the drawing-room sophisticate—one minute
limbs flailing wildly, in the next, gracefully descending her grand
staircase—reveals that each identity is constructed through particular
mannerisms, facial expressions, bearing, and clothes. Thus, rather than

authorizing one pattern of female identity through her comedy, Russell dominated the film with various performances, oscillating between acting refined and reserved and less graceful and less composed.

Even if there were a tendency to see Russell's slapstick as a means of containment, the film produces its own contradiction to this position by reinvesting Russell/Mame with considerable narrative power at the end of each episode. Just before fading to black, Russell/Mame gets to deliver the final crack or knowing look, at times directed authoritatively right at the camera/audience. This is a significant departure from the novel, which privileges nephew Patrick's voice as narrator. His commentary frames the beginning and ending of each chapter, often with a humorous, but condescending assessment of his aunt's latest escapade. This strategy functions similarly to that which Patricia Mellencamp claims operated in the popular "George Burns and Gracie Allen Show." Gracie's efforts to disrupt and subvert patriarchal discourses were contained through laughter, argues Mellencamp, her resistance being recuperated by a similar framing device used by author Patrick Dennis. At the end of each weekly episode, George recovers his "benevolent" control over Gracie through his controlling look and voice-over commentary. To its credit, and perhaps, again, as a means of featuring Russell, the film *Auntie Mame* dropped the framing device of Patrick's narration, allowing Russell's/Mame's viewpoint to prevail.

In both her career-woman roles and her brand of comedy, then, Russell interrogated conventional femininity. This refusal to conform fully to the culture's firmly entrenched version of gender differences began, according to her press, as a young girl. *Time* told its reader that Russell had been a tomboy: "Ros enlisted early in the war between the sexes. In proving herself the equal of the neighborhood boys, she broke her left leg jumping out of a hayloft, her left wrist falling off a wall, her left collarbone tripping over a curb, her left arm twice—once falling off a horse, the other time when she was pushed off a chair. At summer camp, she was forever winning the cup as the best all-around athlete .... She always had the self-confidence necessary to bluff her way through tough situations" ("Comic Spirit" 41). *Time* associates this inclination toward "boyish" behavior with her later roles, particularly the character Ruth in *Wonderful Town*. One of Russell's best known songs from this play—"One Hundred Easy Ways to Lose a Man"—describes Ruth's inability to keep a man because she is too quick to upstage them: "Just throw your knowledge in his face, he'll never try for second base," Ruth warbles. Russell herself admits that this situation did not differ much from her own experiences as a young actress. Wondering why men did not flock around her as they did other young women, she asked her roommate, actress Charlotte Winters, what she did wrong. Winters replied, "Ros, you just *talk* too much" ("Comic Spirit" 41).

Russell lampooned her romantic clumsiness in a 1953 issue of the *Reader's Digest*, in which she advised single women on ways to avoid her own mistakes in scaring off prospective suitors. Her advice, however, ultimately satirized the traditional assumptions of male superiority and female passivity and dependency, which effectively made competent, intelligent women less attractive as romantic partners. With tongue-in-cheek, Russell poked fun at the masquerade of femininity that young women felt compelled to perform in order to "get a man," confessing that she, too, had tried acting helpless around men by asking them to get "poor little me a drink of water." With her characteristic gibe, she then delivered the punchline: "Sometimes I had to show them where the faucet was and get the glass" (Russell "What I've Learned" 29). Elsewhere, Russell joked about her "blunder" of being too intelligent and independent, noting that she used to insist on going home by herself on dates: "While plodding up a mountain he'd be taking home the dumb blonde who didn't even know where she lived. Those blondes still terrify me. While you're discussing Khrushchev, they're playing kneesies under the table" (H. Johnson).

In a later issue of the *Reader's Digest*, Russell again offered advice, this time in a serious vein, to single men and women about marriage. Marry later rather than younger, she urged, in order to increase the likelihood of success and happiness in the partnership. Using her own prolonged 'bachelorhood' as a positive example ("I was 29 when I said 'I do'—that's ten years later than most girls wed nowadays"), Russell urged young women to "go out and get a job" as opposed to marrying in their teens or early twenties (Russell "I'm Glad" 75). Although her counsel ultimately affirmed traditional thinking about sex roles, in that women's careers would better prepare them for their future roles as wives and managers of the household, her advice may have offered a different outlook for some young women, leading them to life-long careers and the possibility of choice. In an interview with columnist Sheilah Graham, however, Russell eschewed the idea of fixed "stages" of women's lives (first a career, then marriage and motherhood). When asked if she approved of dual-career marriages, Russell replied, "That noise about husband and wife both having careers and it can't work out is crazy" (Graham N. pag.).

Even at the outset of her film career in the 1930s, Russell made a conscious decision to go against the grain. She declined to present herself as excessively feminine and "sexy" as did other aspiring starlets, and as a result, after she had her first screen tests at Universal before signing with MGM, "no one at Universal's studio seemed to know quite what to do with Ros" ("Comic Spirit" 41). Russell was never considered a sex symbol or a glamour girl—the result of her own choice as much as Hollywood's casting decisions. In her earlier films, she was typically cast as the foil for the leading actress. In *Life Is a Banquet*, she recalls: "I was put into movies with Joan Crawford and Jean Harlow, and I was always taking their men away from them. Temporarily. It was ludicrous. There would be Jean, all alabaster skin and cleft chin, savory as a ripe peach, and I'd be saying disdainfully (and usually with an English accent) to Gable or to Bob Montgomery, 'How can you spend time with *her*? She's rahther (sic) vulgar, isn't she'?" (60). Russell admits she did not work very hard at changing her "girl who didn't get the man" status, and while this was considered unusual in an industry that equated success with romantic leading roles, she wanted to retain some balance between the demands of Hollywood and her private life. She also claims to have been "sensible enough to know [she] wasn't a sex symbol and never could be." "I was no more convincing lying on a couch," she joked in her autobiography (Russell *Life* 67). Russell says she was at MGM for five years before anyone ever asked if she had had a make-up test. Furthermore, she rejected any opportunity, in her own words, to "have my name changed or my teeth capped, or my hairline redesigned." Even after Metro's boss, Louis B. Mayer said to her, "you're a wonderful girl, but you represent yourself as a cold New England woman," Russell remained unperturbed. "If my style was off-putting, so much the better; it made my working life easier. Nobody chased me around a desk, I wasn't the type" (Russell *Life* 64–65).

If not being the "type" allowed Russell to disengage from some of the sexual politics within her profession, it also informed the way her screen image became gendered. Her performance in *The Women* (1939)—the film in which she first drew acclaim as a first-rate comedienne—illustrates this point. Russell literally stole the show, declared *Time* magazine: "Of the 135 actresses (including Joan

Crawford, Norma Shearer, and Paulette Goddard) in *The Women*, Rosalind Russell is the one usually best remembered by the millions who saw the picture. She became firmly established as the idol of a generation of less-than-beautiful movie-going girls who had to use smart clothes and bright chatter to lure men away from more luscious-looking females" ("Comic Spirit" 42). If indeed Russell became an idol for less-than-beautiful girls, a kind of "regular gal," she also illustrated that femininity was a fabrication of particular effects, in this case, clothes and bright chatter. This is interesting in light of Molly Haskell's claim that Russell "was not a favorite with men. Like Dietrich, the combination of comic intelligence (and she had the best timing in the business) and femininity was overwhelming. Men preferred ... to believe that her femininity was either absent or fake" (133). Although Haskell does not elaborate on this latter point, I think that this is what makes Russell's brand of femininity so fascinating as well as subversive: If Russell's "femininity" were absent or fake, then this calls into question any notion of female sexual identity as it essence. More precisely, femininity is *both* absent and fake, absent because exists only through its discursive production, which must then be reproduced by individual female subjects through repetition, and fake because gender has no claim to ontological status.

Russell's star persona—constituted through her images of the young tomboy, the shrewd businesswoman, the inexhaustible dynamo, the actress who played self-assured career women and who found love scenes "murder"—contributed to the expectation and image of Auntie Mame as a progressive figure. Mame's association with role-playing and masquerade in the novel, which by itself provides a reading of gender as performativity, is compounded in the film by the phenomenon of star identification. For if we read Mame through Russell as having a "masculine" edge to her femininity, then her enactment of Mame as the Southern belle highlights and heightens gender masquerading. Being a belle is most apparently created by the manipulation of signs. For instance, with a voice that had been likened to "an Ambrose Lightship calling to its mate" or "a moose's mating call,"[20] Russell managed to gush fluttery "you-alls" and "Beau, sugahs" for her pro-spective in-laws. Her flirty, delicate demeanor was further produced through various props—parasol and a frilly, white garden dress—and a blonde wig, which attempted to shave some years off Russell.

Her blondeness is important to Russell's/Mame's parody for another reason. Blondeness in the fifties, according to Dyer, was the ultimate sign of racial "purity" and sexual desirability; that is, it signified the "most womanly of women" (*Heavenly* 43–45). An important aspect of this masquerade, then, reveals the racial component ingrained in white (heterosexual) male definitions of female desirability. Interestingly, Russell does not play this role consistently, but shifts back and forth between being the belle and being the worldly New Yorker. One moment she skips across the screen, drawling about her daily romps in Central Park; in the next, she is responding to Sally Cato's "I'll hold my breath until morning" with a gravelly voiced, sarcastic "do that." The emphasis here is on the stylization and theatricality of each pattern of femininity. Oscillating between her masquerades stresses the outward appearance of femininity, not that it springs from some inner consciousness of women. Rather, it is a matter of going through the motions of social conventions or, conscientiously constructing other kinds of effects through particular mannerisms, speech, clothes, make-up, and other corporeal signs.

I have been arguing here that Rosalind Russell's star image, like Auntie Mame's character, was identified with a certain amount of gender mobility and nonconformity, which gave audiences an alternative way of imagining femininity and acting "different."[21] In a decade in which Hollywood went about standardizing the image of the desirable female, epitomized by Marilyn Monroe's vulnerability and sexual receptivity, Russell's image persisted in countering it by offering another positive identity in her plucky attitude, her purposeful and sometimes imperious stride, and a set of facial expressions that intimated wit and wisdom. (I am mindful here of the difference in ages between Monroe and Russell and, therefore, realize they may have appealed to different audiences). Not everyone may have found Russell's mixture of feminine and masculine gender cues desirable, but as evidenced by her continued popularity in postwar culture and her record-breaking success in *Auntie Mame*—the apogee of her career—we can presume that many women and men were ready and willing to intervene, once again, in the cultural conversation on the meaning of sexual and gender differences. Rosalind Russell and Auntie Mame may have been one of the power sources—"the roaring Life Drives"—that fueled this emergent discourse. It is not surprising, then, that in a tribute following Russell's death in November 1976, one writer eulogized her as "a women's libber far ahead of her time" (Sarris 57).

Both Russell's star persona and her performance in *Auntie Mame* no doubt served to reinforce how audiences also interpreted the novel as resisting dominant representations of gender and as magnifying and extending the notion that gender is an activity or a process—*always in process*—rather than a static, fixed category. In addition to her role in *Auntie Mame*, which furthered Russell's association with characters who acted "different," her performances in *Wonderful Town* and *Bell, Book and Candle* (1950) show how postwar women had to masquerade an idealized femininity in order to "pass" or find social acceptance, and in *Picnic* she calls attention to the relentless pressure on women to marry in order to be considered fully female.[22] These performances suggest that the supposedly "natural" or "normative" female gender identity is one that all women do not easily or readily assume. While Russell and Auntie Mame in the context of both the novel and film may have been read as simply an eccentric woman, an exception to the norms of the fifties, it is important to note that she also may have been viewed as the exception that shed light on the fact that the "natural" is socially constructed. As Butler points out, "only from a self-consciously denaturalized position can we see how the appearance of naturalness is itself constituted" (*Gender* 110).

In drawing on Butler's claims about gender performativity, I am not attempting to argue that fifties audiences had access to the kind of poststructuralist discourses through which Butler formulates her argument; rather, I wish to suggest that audiences could gain a sense of how femininity is fabricated and performed. Particularly through the visual representation of Mame, filmgoers watched a female figure continually manipulate gender, playing with gender, style, and power, and in the figure of Agnes Gooch, they could see how gender is fabricated through theatrical fakery, step by step, to create an effect of naturalness. By so doing, *Auntie Mame* suggests that what appears to be natural also could be stylized in different ways. Even in the novel, though, readers were continually reminded of acting and putting on different styles of femininity. One year after *Auntie Mame* captivated postwar audiences, another runaway best-seller that would shake rather than charm the literary world, presented an additional perspective on the presumed "naturalness" of female identity. Instead of Mame's comedic celebration of gender masquerading, Grace Metalious's *Peyton Place* titillated the American public with a closet full of sex scandals in small-town U.S.A.; by exposing the power dynamics embedded in the intersecting discourses of gender, sexuality, and social class, *Peyton Place* not only reinforced *Auntie Mame*'s representation of gender as socially constructed, but also implicated sexuality in masquerade as well.

6

"Damned and Banned": Female Sexuality in Grace Metalious's *Peyton Place*

When *From Here to Eternity* made the best-sellers list in 1951, it created a stir over its candid attitude toward sex and its "formidable mass of obscenities," as one review put it, but the novel was generally acclaimed for its honest portrayal of military life and its focus on defining manhood in a brutal, unyielding system. Five years later Grace Metalious's *Peyton Place* rocked the literary world with her exposé of sin and sex in a small New England town. Like James Jones's foot soldiers, Metalious's characters spoke in a vernacular, sometimes crude idiom and openly talked about or engaged in sex. Jones's novel was able to overcome these objections, but reviewers branded *Peyton Place* as "cheap," "dirty," "noxious," and "unredeemable."[1] Many readers were equally disturbed by the idea that a female writer could even imagine the vulgarities uttered by some of her characters. One reviewer remarked, "Never before in my memory has a young mother published a book in language approximately that of a longshoreman on a bellicose binge" (qtd. in Halberstam 585). Considering that *From Here to Eternity*'s "soldier talk," sex scenes, and violence were potentially neither less vulgar nor less offensive than were similar representations in *Peyton Place*, we might surmise that a particular gendering of Metalious's best-seller influenced the disparate critical reception of these two novels. The difference may be more than a generic one, more than a matter of valuing literary realism over melodrama.

The real scandal of Metalious's novel seems not to be that it was a "dirty" book, but that it was "dirty" in a particular way in that it violated the cultural norms of femininity by focusing on the sex lives—the desires, fantasies, fears, and practices—of "ordinary" women. Almost as unsettling was the fact that a female writer had produced this literary sex fest. James Jones was awarded a kind of mythic status by the press as a self-taught, self-made man and hailed as one of the promising new writers of the decade. His publicity stills, in which he looked much like a working-class tough guy, romanticized his combination of machismo and intellect. In Metalious's case, however, the press seemed to relish the "dirt" on her, emphasizing her "unfeminine" conduct and unconventional personal life, as if this somehow explained her trashy book.[2] *Cosmopolitan*, for example, reported that her neighbors in Gilmanton, New Hampshire, thought she was "a lunatic who typed stories all day long while neglecting her husband and children; who caroused till all hours of the night; who went about in dungarees; used improper language and was hardly a suitable partner for a school principal [husband George]" (Zolotow 41). Metalious, seemingly unperturbed by this kind of attention, openly admitted she rejected the accouterments of femininity. Insisting she was "just fat and happy," she refused to wear girdles, make-up, stockings, and skirts (Zolotow 38). While the media may have exploited Metalious's unconventional behavior as an aggressive marketing tool or for a feature story, the public representation of her private life unwittingly resonates with an important message of her novel: The meaning of "woman" is subject to contestation rather than originating from an apparent or natural relationship to biological sex. In other words, if Metalious dressed in drag—men's shirts, faded dungarees, and torn sneakers—perhaps so did the woman who trussed herself in girdles and hose, altered her appearance with cosmetics, and constantly dieted to maintain a culturally acceptable weight.

If Metalious's private life was singed in the popular press, *Peyton Place* itself ignited a literary firestorm so sweeping and white-hot that it polarized every level of the literary world, from publishers to vendors down to its consumers. Libraries debated whether to purchase the novel; booksellers either celebrated its astronomical sales or steadfastly refused to stock it; Canada, Rhode Island, and Allen County, Indiana, banned its sale. Nevertheless, readers purchased six million copies within a year and a half of its publication (Carbine 108).[3] Its promise of huge profits prompted Twentieth-Century Fox to release a sanitized film version in 1957, which packed the theaters and garnered nine Academy Award nominations.[4] Metalious followed this success with a hastily composed sequel, *Return to Peyton Place* (1959), written at the request of Hollywood producer Jerry Wald, who was eager for a film sequel to his production of *Peyton Place*.

That one in twenty-nine postwar Americans had purchased a book that had begun to redraw the boundaries of what constituted appropriate representations of female sexuality prompts us to ask how *Peyton Place* both challenged and reflected postwar culture. Representing the "transgressions" of middle-class women was undoubtedly a disruption of the ingrained belief that women were better suited by nature to be the standard bearers of propriety and moral stability. By weaving her narrative around incidents of pre- and extramarital sex, rape, incest, adultery, and abortion, which were still taboo subjects in the entertainment media of the 1950s, Metalious blew open the "open secret" about women and sex, naming these experiences as part of everyday life. That is to say, she talked about what everyone knew but could not, or would not, admit to knowing. More importantly, through the force of her characters' stories, she began to link this daily reality to issues of power and female oppression.

It would be mistaken, though, to think of *Peyton Place* as an anomaly of the 1950s because of its sensational impact. In several ways the novel was characteristic of the decade itself. For one, although the novel scandalized many readers, it reinforced the decade's dominant trend toward increasing sexual explicitness in popular culture (in which *From Here to Eternity* was part of the vanguard). Furthermore, just as *Peyton Place* registered a growing discontent with middle-class conformity and restriction, at the same time, it perpetuated conservative attitudes and patriarchal structures. In this case, the kind of cultural work that *Peyton Place* performed was similar to that which we have seen in *From Here to Eternity*, *Sayonara*, *Giant*, and *Auntie Mame*. By cutting across a variety of competing or contradictory discourses, these novels held significance as sites of negotiation and exchange between progressive and reactionary forces within postwar culture. As such, *Peyton Place*'s production and reception were marked in wider cultural contestations over what constituted such categories as gender, sexuality, and the literary. Therefore, the novel's designation as mass culture—the bogeyman of "taste" and "art"—did not simply relegate it to the heap of mind-numbing trash, but neither did its representation as a transgressive text mark it as wholly subversive or radical. These contradictions signal both ideological struggle over meanings and suggest that the dominant ideologies of gender and sexuality within the culture at large had begun to weaken, which then allowed for a space in which alternative identities could be imagined outside the status quo. Moreover, while *Peyton Place* tends to map out sex on a binary of licit/illicit behavior—which Michel Foucault argues is one way that sexuality functions as a site through which power is distributed—the novel at times blurs the line between the "appropriate" and "inappropriate." This blurring marks the significance of *Peyton Place* in the 1950s, indicating that sexuality is a complex and historically contested cultural category.

For postwar intellectuals and literary critics who were engaged in the ongoing debate over aesthetic standards, *Peyton Place* was hardly a liberatory text. Rather, it appeared to be a new strain of infection threatening the cultural health.[5] The novel launched a flagrant assault on the established cultural categories by flaunting its hybrid status as middlebrow and trash, refusing to be contained within either category. By venturing into the seamy territory of pulp fiction—the acme of bad taste in the 1950s—the novel adulterated the middlebrow and failed to fix high and low culture in opposition, thereby threatening to open the floodgates onto widespread cultural contamination. In his scathing review of Metalious's best-seller, publisher William Loeb clarified the stakes in safeguarding art and taste by warning Americans of the direct correlation between *Peyton Place*'s popularity and civilization's waning vitality. Refusing even to mention the book's title, Loeb concluded, "this sad situation reveals a complete debasement of taste and a fascination with the filthy, rotten side of life that are the earmarks of the collapse of a civilization" (qtd. in Toth 133). What was collapsing, however, was not civilization, as Loeb and other cultural gatekeepers feared, but a conception of civilization structured by an entrenched hierarchy of high, middle, and low culture and sustained by the authority of intellectuals to dictate what constituted each category. The distinctions between these levels of culture also were implicated in sustaining the dominant gender and sex systems of postwar society. The signifiers assigned to low or mass culture—trash, contamination, bad taste—became linked to *Peyton Place*'s female authorship, female sexuality, and the feminine. In this sense, active female subjectivity and sexuality engaging in the "filthy rotten side of life" emerged as the threatening Other of pure, contemplative, masculine art and functioned as a corrosive force on the boundaries between high, middle, and low culture.

In light of *Peyton Place*'s popular and critical reception, this chapter aims to reassess the novel's historical significance both as a transgressive text and as part of the postwar trend toward increasing sexual explicitness in popular culture. I contend that *Peyton Place* was not simply titillating trash, read by hundreds of thousands and "damned and banned" by a host of hostile critics and civic leaders.[6] The novel may well have had a more serious impact in disrupting orthodox notions of femininity and female sexuality. By presenting the difficulties that her female characters experience in taking up culturally prescribed sex roles, Metalious directed attention to the inadequacies of situating gender and sex purely in the realm of nature. The dominant discourses of gender and sex in postwar culture were largely influenced by Freudian theory, which understands sex as an innate biological drive "expressed" in accordance with a fixed notion of "male" and "female." Put simply, biological sex ("male," "female") certifies gender ("masculinity," "femininity"). Gender, in turn, determines how (hetero)sexuality is expressed. In this paradigm, female sexuality is by nature subordinate and passive compared to an active male sexuality, and its function is primarily to attract and please the male. Certain representations in *Peyton Place* refute these dichotomies, proposing instead that the "origins" of sexuality are socially constructed. In other words, the novel shows the possibility that gender and sexual identities are relational and contingent on cultural definitions of marriage, home, and family rather than on any stable or fixed notion of a female "self."

In Metalious's fictional small town, the female characters come to understand their identities by learning culturally prescribed roles, or what Stevi Jackson calls "sexual scripts." Individual women internalize sexual scripts, according to Jackson, "through the processes of learning to fit in with current institutions, ideology, and morality" that predominate in a given historical and cultural moment; "sexual dramas are scripted for actors who have different sexual vocabularies of motive and different orientations to and expectations of sexual relationships" (72). Jackson's notion of "script" suggests that women perform or masquerade particular gendered and sexual identities in relation to the dominant fictional ideal of femininity. The specific sexual script that the women of Peyton Place invest in is "having and holding," which, according to Wendy Hollway, encourages women to understand their sexuality in connection with monogamous relationships leading to marriage and motherhood. Within this script, which is clearly in accord with the Freudian-based gender ideologies of the 1950s, women see themselves as the subjects of a discourse in which men are the objects of a female desire to find and possess a husband. Female sexuality in this conceptualization is either "lacking"—a negative counterpart of the mythic male sex drive—and therefore limited to reproduction, or else it is predatory and dangerous (Hollway 86–87).

The women of Peyton Place perform the script of "having and holding" for several reasons: as a defense against social sanctions, as a way of enhancing or maintaining social status, or as a means of pleasure. Significantly, they demonstrate that investing in the have/hold ideology does not express a natural response in accordance with their biological sex; rather, their experiences suggest that this sexual script is just that—a script "written" within culture and history, which few of Peyton Place's women are able to perform successfully. Thus, an implicit question emerges from the novel: If nature were the sole or primary determinant or shaping force behind this discourse, wouldn't most of Peyton Place's women have been gloriously contented? As the novel demonstrates through its representations of female subjectivity as multiple and contradictory, the dominant discourses of gender and sexuality are never fully successful in regulating or sustaining social practice. Peyton Place's teenagers, in particular, push the boundaries of "appropriate" expressions of sexuality and critique the class bound, patriarchal investment in the sexual double standard and, therefore, offer a cogent illustration of how gendered and sexual identities are constructed within a culturally specific context.

If the novel may have raised awareness of the multiple possibilities inherent in femininity, the sanitized film version (which, ironically, capitalized on the novel's sensationalism to enhance box office draw) significantly altered the novel's complication of gender norms by reaffirming and enhancing a traditional form of femininity through heterosexual romance. While Metalious's novel leaves open the question of precisely what constitutes "womanhood," Hollywood's version constructs narrow, definitive parameters of female gender identity by following a trajectory of stripping away the various fabrications of femininity in order to get to a "real" inner, female identity behind the masquerade. Accordingly, the film's moral imperative represents "good" women in terms of authenticity and sincerity, while "bad" or confused women are characterized in terms of fabrication and hypocrisy.

To say the film is reactionary in comparison to the novel seems apropos. Even so, this assessment may be too simplistic, as I will argue in the latter part of the chapter. The film's ostensibly seamless closure featuring happy, heterosexual couplehood cannot entirely seal over the troubling issues of gender and class oppression raised earlier within its own narrative. Nor can the film's affirmation of an "authentic" female identity withstand scrutiny in light of its major star, Lana Turner (Connie MacKenzie). Turner's star text, working both with and against the film's moral imperative of defining "good" women and endorsing orthodox femininity, ultimately subverts the binary relationship of performance and authenticity. In other words, her star text and her film performance help "authenticate" Connie MacKenzie's femininity; however, at the same time, authenticity is fractured, paradoxically, by the revelation that "Lana Turner" herself is constructed in performance and theatrical fakery. The "true" Connie/Lana is authorized by representation (and is clearly overdetermined within it). Gender authenticity is finally an illusion, and representation is all there can be known of true womanhood.

Sex in the Fifties Goes Public

In an interview promoting *Peyton Place*, Grace Metalious made the following comment about small New England communities: "To a tourist these towns look peaceful as a postcard picture, but if you go beneath that picture it's like turning over a rock with your foot. All kinds of strange things crawl out" (Zolotow 38). In postwar America "strange things" could encompass any number of social practices that blasted the image of the happy, middle-class, nuclear family—a key signifier of national identity. Particularly, when problems with the institutions of marriage or family were acknowledged, the solutions offered in the popular press rarely threatened the status quo. More often, people were given advice and instruction on how to live best within the parameters of the breadwinner ethic and monogamous marriage. A case in point is *Life*'s article, "Modern Marriage," which disclosed that divorce rates and female discontent with domesticity were rising. While the article offered some social and historical explanations for the diminishing investment in traditional marriage, which in itself suggests that gender roles were not predicated solely on biological difference, it nonetheless avoided suggesting alternative configurations of these roles. The article's one concession to female discontent was to "permit" part-time work "as long as [women's] primary focus of interest and activity is the home" (Coughlin 115). Likewise, an August 1955 article in *Parents Magazine* never questioned the fixed notion of female gender roles when it asked, "Which are you first of all, wife or mother?" or when it prescribed "Rexalls for a happy marriage" in its June 1956 issue.[7] *Better Homes and Gardens* (April 1955) offered advice on how wives could help their husbands succeed,[8] while a *Life* article stated more bluntly: "If a woman can do a man's job better than he, and if she lets him know it, she is no true woman"

(Skinner 73). *Peyton Place*, however, pierced these images with its depiction of family and marriage as a minefield rather than a road with some occasional ruts and bumps.

Glorifying and sanctioning motherhood and homemaking was an effective means of regulating female sexuality within the postwar climate of anti-communist hysteria and the purported "crisis" of masculinity. As a means of making domesticity appear more enticing to women, the ideal of the companionate marriage was exalted on the grounds that both men and women would be full partners in the relationship and presumably achieve emotional compatibility and mutual sexual satisfaction.[9] The significance of sexual satisfaction cannot be underestimated in the postwar era; sex, social historian Benita Eisler claims, became "the cornerstone of a happy marriage" (143). Accordingly, female sexuality enjoyed a new "permissiveness," meaning that sexual satisfaction—the elusive vaginal orgasm, that is—was now open to married women. This "permissiveness," ironically, was entirely consistent with regulating female sexuality within Cold War ideology because, in order to claim the "right" to sexual satisfaction, a woman had to be married. One of the many popular marriage manuals of the decade, *Sex: Methods and Manners*, made clear the connection between sex within marriage and national interest by situating its stated purpose—instructing couples on achieving sexual compatibility—in the context of political and moral stability: "In a world of chaos and in an era in which national and international integrity have fallen to a low level, there remains only the solid structure of the home to form the basis for the re-establishment of the ancient standards of virtue." What, according to the manual, was "one of the major threats to the stability of the home?" Answer: "Sexual incompatibility" (Eisler 143–44).[10]

The impulse to regulate sexual behavior during this period and to confine it to heterosexual marriage does not mean that sex was either unmentionable or fully repressive, however. According to Barbara Klinger, "the 1950s saw an explosion of discussions and representations of explicit sexuality that made sex an aggressively integral part of public life" (51). There was greater freedom of sexual display in films, particularly in melodramas that featured adult themes, psychological dysfunction, sexual excess, or identity crises. Paperbacks with racy covers and lurid passages garnered big profits and galvanized a congressional investigation on the paperback industry in 1952. "Sex and sin" magazines, like *Confidential*, flourished, and Marilyn Monroe and *Playboy* introduced a new emphasis on a specifically female sexual explicitness. Marginalized expressions of love and sex in gay subcultures gained some limited currency, while the Beats' philosophy of free love derided both monogamy and marriage (Klinger 51–57). Plus, a burgeoning youth culture thrived on rock and roll with its coded sexual meanings in its pulsing rhythm and in its seemingly innocent lyrics of love. Along with these emerging trends in popular culture, Alfred Kinsey's *Sexual Behavior in the Human Female* (1953) rocked the nation with its revelations about the frequency and normalcy of previously unmentionable female sexual activities, such as pre- and extramarital sex, masturbation, and nocturnal sex dreams. In dry, straightforward prose Kinsey revealed the disparity between what women were reportedly doing sexually and what society believed they were doing. This landmark best-seller also subtly suggested that just about any sexual practice—social or solitary—was an acceptable form of sexual outlet.[11]

While media images of monogamous marriages and happy homes may have prevailed, these were being challenged by an explosion of cultural representations—*Peyton Place* among these—that situated sex outside these institutions or the accepted ideas about sex. However, Klinger cautions, this proliferation of sexual discourses and display did not function to condone all kinds of sexual freedom. For the most part, these discourses still existed within a dominant cultural climate which "tended to associate sex with traditional patriarchal pleasures and a domestic ideology that saw women as avid consumers of conflicted romantic narratives in the style of *True Confessions*" (56). Nonetheless, these competing images and discourses indicate that the boundary between "licit" and "illicit" sex was becoming an openly contested space in mainstream culture.

In light of the proliferation of sexual discourses and re-presentations, it is safe to suggest that *Peyton Place* was not a postwar anomaly because of its focus on sex; rather, it gathered some of its transgressive status—as Klinger says is true of postwar film melodramas—because it was part of a growing trend of representing sex in all forms of popular culture (56). Some of its important cultural work lay in reflecting the tension between Cold War domestic containment and the explosion of public discourses and representations of sexuality, some of which did not simply reconfirm the dominant ideology. Even within the milieu of openness, however, *Peyton Place* pushed the limits of acceptability in its blending of pulp fiction and middlebrow melodrama. Metalious went beyond lurid innuendo, which had to suffice in film and magazines, to lurid description—lurid, that is, by 1950s standards.

To Have and to Hold: Marriage, Sex, and Female Empowerment

Despite its scandalous reputation, *Peyton Place* is in some ways a rather conventional melodrama, propelled forward by the interlocking stories of Constance (Connie) MacKenzie, a thirty-five-year-old single mother, her teenage daughter Allison, and Allison's friend Selena Cross. Each woman confronts an emotionally devastating crisis: Connie is forced to confront her secret past; Allison discovers that she is "illegitimate"; Selena stands trial for killing her abusive stepfather. Metalious frames the narrative around the changing seasons, which coincide with the vicissitudes of life in her Depression-era mill town, suggesting there is a natural order of things both human and nonhuman. In the opening sentence, Indian summer—"like a woman ... ripe, hotly passionate, but fickle"[12]—makes false promises, but spring returns in the closing pages of the novel, bringing closure to life's travails: Connie finds love anew with a handsome newcomer, Allison blossoms into adulthood after a turbulent adolescence, and Selena is acquitted of murder. The "good" are rewarded and the "bad" receive their "comeuppances." The social structure remains unchanged. An elite group of professional men continues to run the town, and, except for Leslie Harrington, a power-driven, ruthless mill owner, this small coterie practices a kind of benevolent paternalism: They "provided jobs for Peyton Place. They took care of its aches and pains, straightened out its legal affairs, formed its thinking and spent its money" (21). Matthew Swain, the town's elder physician, "a good and upright man, and a lover of life and humanity ... [who] always spoke the truth" (42–43), is given a privileged voice in the narrative.

While Metalious establishes this patriarchal structure, she focuses primarily on the town's female figures, showing how the codes governing gender and sex have a repressive impact on their lives. Metalious aptly used the home as the site in which women experience contradictory messages about identity and empowerment. The home is not a sanctuary of security, but a dysfunctional, restrictive trap in which women and children either accommodate themselves or subtly resist. Therefore, while the novel never suggests that patriarchy should be dismantled, it clearly decenters the exclusive authorization of male interests and values, and more explicitly, undermines the postwar ideal of home and family with its relentless parade of frustrated women and disappointed men. The coherence of life is shown to be illusory in *Peyton Place*, which subtly calls into question the novel's closure on a happy family reunion. Furthermore, readers are able to see that, in order for life to retain a semblance of coherence, women must perform or masquerade a brand of femininity authorized by the dominant discourses of gender or else face public ridicule or ostracism.

Connie MacKenzie constructs the most elaborate masquerade, posing as a widow to conceal her daughter's illegitimacy. As a young woman fully invested in the have/hold ideology and the breadwinner ethic, Connie moved to New York City with "the idea of meeting, going to work for, and finally marrying a man of wealth and position (15). Her youthful expectations of happily-ever-after are deflated when she becomes pregnant by her employer and lover, the already married Allison MacKenzie. Connie is held hostage to his promise to support her and the baby, knowing that, but for the fact that he was a "good man in his fashion" (16), MacKenzie could abandon her, forcing her into poverty or to return home in shame. When baby Allison is three, MacKenzie suddenly dies, prompting Connie to return to Peyton Place where she operates a dress shop purchased with money MacKenzie discreetly leaves her. Connie presents herself as a widow, taking MacKenzie's name and prominently displaying a photograph of her deceased "husband" in the living room. As Allison grows up, she clings to an idealized notion of her father as the kindest, handsomest man in the world. Connie, however, is inwardly consumed by the fear that her secret will be discovered. "In her worst nightmares she heard the voices of Peyton Place .... That whore Constance Standish and her dirty little bastard" (16).

The disjuncture between Connie's youthful expectations of a secure marriage and the reality of getting "knocked up," to use Peyton Place vernacular, uncovers an alternative discourse about the pitfalls of female dependency. Her circumstances clearly suggest that women who rely solely on men for emotional and economic well-being live precariously. Connie's status in Peyton Place also raises questions about a punitive double standard. As a "widow," Connie remains celibate not simply to avoid scandal, but to maximize control over her life. "Men," she maintains, "were not necessary, for they were unreliable at best, and nothing but creators of trouble" (17). Avoiding romance and sex and being "cold" and "practical" help her effect a masquerade as a respectable, middle-class mother. "If at times she felt a vague restlessness within herself, she told herself sharply that this was *not* sex, but perhaps a touch of indigestion" (17). Thus, when Tomas Makris,[13] the new school principal, attempts to court her, Connie responds by drinking tall glasses of bicarbonate of soda.

Readers may have understood Connie's predicament as a warning about "illicit" sex: If you play, you must pay, so it is best to confine your sexuality to monogamous marriage. Independent, self-sufficient women like Connie are constrained to choose asexual "respectability" over sexual pleasure. As an unattached female who is unable to have-and-hold her lover, Connie's sexuality becomes potentially threatening to the existing social order. In effect, she polices herself by repressing her sexual desire and presenting herself as a self-sufficient widow rather than a suspect or pitiable one. In other words, she abides by the cultural constraints to be a "good" widow, not a "bad" one. Even so, her masquerade does not afford Connie full acceptance in the community; she has no friends, which her daughter attributes to there being no father in the home. They were "a different kind of family from most, and therefore other people did not care to be involved with them" (12).

While this message of warning to "loose women" is certainly plausible, it is undercut by Metalious's satiric treatment of sexual hypocrisy and repression throughout the novel. The narrative does not treat Connie's affair or her having a child out of wedlock as morally objectionable. Rather, Connie's predicament suggests that, within a heterosexual economy organized around the breadwinner ethic, women experience undue social repercussions for being sexual outside the culture's accepted boundaries. If she is chastised at all, it is for her complicity with this noxious discourse in the first place, which motivates her defensive masquerade and, later on, her obsessive desire to monitor Allison's sexuality. Consumed by fear that what happened to her will also befall Allison, Connie resolves to "tell her daughter how dangerous it is to be a girl" (51). Her vigilance gives way to explosive anger when she mistakenly believes Allison has had sex with Norman Page while the two have been picnicking. When Allison returns home, Connie blurts out that she is "the bastard daughter of the biggest bastard of all," cruelly revealing her illegitimacy (237). Devastated, Allison vows to leave home after high school and sever all ties with her mother.

In contrast to the feminine mystique that glorified domesticity, *Peyton Place* implies that when women perceive life as a prescripted role, they sacrifice personal fulfillment and integrity. As Barbara Ehrenreich points out in her study of postwar gender ideologies, *The Hearts of Men*, such self-sacrifice results in "instability" and "indignity" for women (182). Aside from Connie, Metalious's novel features several female figures that have sacrificed their dignity and stability in order to have and to hold. Marion Partridge is Peyton Place's smug, self-appointed guardian of middle-class morality, who, like so many actual women in the 1950s, was "Mrs. Someone" by virtue of her husband's earning power and social status.[14] As the wife of the town's leading attorney, Marion has a vested interest in having and holding and preserving the status quo because it gives her considerable power to dictate social mores. Connie is one of Marion's prime targets because she is single and self-reliant. "Don't tell me [Connie] doesn't do a lot of running around that no one has heard about," Marion fumes. "Don't tell me she hasn't got an eye on every man in town" (44). Behind Marion's acrimony lies her fear of the mythical, sexually voracious widow who indulges her carnal lust with "innocent" husbands, while callously leaving broken homes in her wake. We can surmise, too, that Marion is compelled to protect her own vulnerable status as a dependent, because she—like other wives who are not self-supporting—has no sure claim on her husband's wages, and, therefore, she may fear the possibility of becoming "a loser in a sexual free marketplace" (Ehrenreich and English 320).[15]

Marion's need to maintain respect and prestige in Peyton Place is also linked to her ability to have-and-hold her spouse. During Selena's murder trial, Marion experiences a jolting fear that her husband Charles may be infatuated with his beautiful young defendant, which prompts Marion to admit "she would rather have Charles slobbering at the mouth and wetting the bed than to have him infatuated with Selena. Folks could feel sorry for a woman with a sick husband, but a woman with a husband who ran after young girls automatically became a laughing stock" (346). In this view, women are to blame for failing to have-and-hold, again indicating how tenuous their hold on dignity is within this social order.

Metalious continues to show through Hester Goodale's story that traditional sex roles did not serve the interests of all women nor guarantee them a position of respect and dignity in the community. The elderly Hester has lived in seclusion ever since her youthful courtship went awry, the result of her domineering father chasing her suitor away. The townspeople call her "loony," but Hester has merely taken up a socially prescribed role—the eccentric spinster—that is open to women who fail (or choose not) to find a mate and who cannot imagine or realize self-fulfillment outside of heterosexual couplehood. Like Connie, Hester follows the social injunction to be nonsexual, but she also seems to resist this in ways that would shock the town matrons. By positioning her rocker on the back porch so that she can see through her hedge, Hester secretly watches her neighbors having oral sex. She rocks away in her chair (we cannot miss the implications of this) while her mewling tomcat rubs against her legs!

By withdrawing from community life, Hester reduces the threat she poses to the breadwinner arrangement as an "unattached" woman, and, therefore, the town tolerates her eccentricity. However, the narrative withholds any such sympathy for unmarried women, like the Page sisters, who go about in twos. Unlike Hester, Caroline and Charlotte Page are neither lovelorn nor reclusive, but simply reject male companionship altogether. The novel, however, implies that when women remain outside of direct male control, they are troublesome and unfeminine. Indeed the sisters are depicted as malevolent and sharp-tongued, the tongue not only signifying a female "weapon"—an appropriation of phallic power—but also a sexual organ, which implicates the inseparable Page sisters in homosexuality. When newcomer Tom Makris first sees the Pages, he concludes: "They looked like a pair who had worked too long at the same girls' school ... maybe they're the town's two Lizzies" (101). Literally and figuratively "sisters," the Pages are much more threatening to the social order than Hester, who is allotted some sympathy for having missed her chance to have-and-hold. Even while the novel puts forth a critique of fixed sex roles, then, it clearly situates homosexuality outside the limits of acceptable sexual practice.

Highlighting further the links between marriage, sex, and power, Metalious "reveals" one of Peyton Place's most delicious secrets: Harmon and Roberta Carter's courtship. As a young woman, Roberta marries the elderly Doc Quimby solely to secure his money. Roberta virtually imprisons Quimby at home so that he becomes the town's laughing stock. He soon commits suicide, after which Roberta claims his inheritance and marries her boyfriend Harmon. Unquestionably, the narrative does not condone Roberta's actions, but it does imply that within traditional marital arrangements, the line between marriage and a form of prostitution can easily become blurred. Roberta and Quimby's union parodies marriage insofar as she performs wifely duties for him in exchange for his economic support. She mimics the female role in traditional marriage, which is structured by a division of labor dependent upon her unpaid (domestic) work and maintaining a well-run home.

While the notion of romantic love, or what Ehrenreich and English call "sexual romanticism" (314), functions to legitimate uncompensated women's work, this arrangement also binds women to men under the threat of financial hardship or even poverty. For Roberta, who sees her working-class existence as a dead end, obtaining economic security depends on her unpaid labor, or "housework"—her bargaining chip in securing Quimby. Without the obfuscation of romantic love, her charade reproduces the material arrangements of marriage, laying bare the relationship between power and money and marriage. Roberta's mercenary aims are not admirable, but her motives do not differ in kind from young Connie's or Marion's, both of whom considered marriage a means of financial security and social mobility. However, for Connie and Marion the hope of a loving marriage justifies its pragmatic aspects. Because Roberta's marriage lacks any such love, she has no compunctions about "jailing" Quimby and rewriting the have/hold discourse to ensure that she does not become one of the losers in the sexual free marketplace.

Metalious's satiric treatment of Roberta Carter and Marion Partridge is harsh, considering that she punishes them instead of critiquing an oppressive social order that curtails female independence and opportunities outside of marriage. While these female figures bear the brunt of Metalious's condemnation of bourgeois hypocrisy and pretension, they may demonstrate something other than rapacious or nasty female behavior. Readers may have considered how female subjectivities are shaped and limited by the dominant discourses of class, gender, and sexuality within a patriarchal social order. Furthermore, these characters' behaviors illustrate how women seek empowerment within their particular subject positions, even though these means do not always benefit other women or foster social arrangements in which women are able to retain their dignity. For Roberta, empowerment means literally holding her husband hostage; for Marion, it involves controlling "dangerous" women with her spiteful, yet powerful tongue. Through these examples, Metalious presents a fairly cogent critique of how relations of money, status, and power are firmly entrenched in marriage and male breadwinning. The intersection of economic factors and culturally determined gender roles functions to define and regulate female behavior and sexuality. By critiquing the means by which women attempt to obtain financial stability and security within the ideological imperatives of the breadwinner ethic and the discourses of having-and-holding, Metalious's novel may have laid some groundwork for theorizing female oppression.

Peyton Place does not thoroughly vilify the have-hold ideal, however. By the close of the novel, Connie and Tom Makris resecure the representation of happy couplehood, which underscores my point that the novel both challenges and reflects postwar gender norms. As Jackie Byars notes in her research on postwar melodrama, Metalious draws on the conventions of melodrama by using a patriarchal, "intruder-redeemer" figure—Makris—to restore the heterosexual social order within an all-female community or household (147–49). College-educated, yet "street smart" by virtue of his urban, working-class background, Makris represents "progressive" change for this backwater village. A conventional romantic hero, he is swarthy, virile, sexy, and fully masculine. Even though Connie represses her own initial desire for him, she remarks, "*anyone* would be impressed with a man that size" (106), size implying Makris also is sexually well-endowed.

Eventually breaking down her resistance, Makris begins to date Connie, but unlike traditional melodrama, which ultimately gives the female protagonist the option to reintegrate into the heterosexual order, the novel denies Connie this choice. Impatient with her refusing sex, Makris turns Connie's sexual "awakening" into sexual assault. During an evening swim, he rips off her top, saying harshly, "I want to feel your breasts against me when I kiss you." He abruptly drives her home and demands, "Which room is yours?" When Connie protests, "Get out of my house ... I'll have you arrested ... for breaking and entering and rape," Makris slaps her with "a stunning blow across the mouth," ordering, "don't open your mouth again ... just keep your mouth shut." Connie then hears "the sound of his zipper opening as he took off his trunks." A year later when she recalls this incident, Makris dismisses it: "Don't think about it. That part is all over with now" (149–50).

Meant to be Connie's reinitiation into romance and sex, this scenario blurs the difference between sexual fantasy and practice. As a description of fantasy, readers may well have found this scene titillating simply because it follows the conventions of romance novels, which alert readers that Connie belongs with this "redeemer" lover and is therefore in no serious danger. In other words, Connie is in control of being controlled. However, within the diegetic world, readers may have recognized that this is not fantasy, but Connie's "reality." Instead of critiquing the male "sex drive" and the violent subordination of female sexuality within compulsory heterosexuality (presented here as sexual "liberation"), the text implies that "no" means "yes." Accordingly, while women are required to contain their sexuality (saying "no"), they do not necessarily have to be taken seriously, which then justifies forced sex. This, in turn, appears to pose a solution for female sexuality when it does not serve male sexual interests.

Furthermore, by using similar words to describe Connie's date rape as she uses to describe Selena's rape by her stepfather, Metalious creates an unsettling resemblance between the two incidents. Like Makris, Lucas Cross "slapped his stepdaughter a stunning blow on the side of the head" and proceeds to rip her blouse off. However, the narrative absolves the charming, charismatic Makris of any wrongdoing. After all, he stands for reason and morality in Peyton Place, signified by his declaration that he "[hadn't] met ten people ... in this goddamn town who don't need to douche out their souls" (151). Thus, it seems that men—men like Makris, at least—really are the best judges of what women want or need sexually, and if charm and tenderness do not arouse them, then sexual violation and violence can. Once Makris thaws Connie's "frigidity," he sets out to remake this cold, practical woman into a tender and passionate lover, and indeed she hires Selena to manage her dress shop in order to give more attention to her man. Becoming a successful businesswoman for Connie appears to have been an unfortunate and temporary necessity, whereas the real key to her happiness and fulfillment is sex, love, and marriage, just like the prescription for women in 1950s America indicated.

Connie's sexual "awakening" has the potential to generate multiple interpretations for readers. Clearly, this incident makes less legible the boundary between rape and a certain kind of female sexual "pleasure." However, when this scenario is contextualized in fifties discourses of sexuality, we can see how Makris's actions may not have been viewed as entirely offensive or unusual. Recall that postwar marriage manuals designated men to "instruct" their sexual partners, to teach the female how to enjoy mutually satisfying sex. Furthermore, Connie's "obstinacy" about sex could be seen as a repudiation of the new "permission" women were given to enjoy sex within monogamous marriage. (Although Connie and Tom are not married, conventional wisdom tells readers they soon will be). According to the Freudian-driven discourses of sexuality, female surrender to the male sex drive was supposedly part of the pleasure for women; conversely, any explicitly active female sexuality was considered predatory or neurotic. Indeed, although Connie recalls that this incident "was like a nightmare from which she could not wake," she did eventually respond to Makris's force that night, experiencing "the first red gush of shamed pleasure, that lifted her, lifted her, lifted her and then dropped her down into unconsciousness" (150).

Present-day readers who have benefited from feminist ideas produced in the intervening years since the novel's publication will most likely find the male-generated violence of Connie's sexual "awakening" disturbing and outrageous. Even so, the disparate interpretations that this scene may elicit suggest that female sexuality is constituted by "gender appropriate" behaviors, which are themselves constructed in historically and culturally specific discourses and relations of power. In other words, reading Connie's sexuality on a continuum of rape (Selena) and a more active female sexuality (Allison) allows us to understand better how sexuality is neither a fixed nor a natural category. Rather, we are able to see how the meaning and practice of sexuality shift in relation to how sex is defined in a given historical moment within the discourses of gender and its intersecting categories of class, race, ethnicity, and so forth.

Teen Culture: Sexual Confusion and Resistance

While Connie is forever caught somewhere between dependence and independence, her daughter Allison rebels against the sex roles of her mother's generation. At the outset of the narrative Allison is on the threshold of adolescence, a time in which she feels lonely, gawky, and unattractive. Except for Selena, a poor "shack dweller," Allison is virtually friendless. Dreading puberty and its gender-specific script instructing girls to be crazy about clothes, lipstick, and boys, Allison tries to forestall the inevitable. She revels in the "delights of childhood" and dreams of becoming a writer, thoughts which make her miserable when she thinks how "the other girls in her class would laugh to let her know that [her] kind of joy was wrong ... babyish" (11). Fearing her schoolmates will discover her secret pleasures, Allison learns to act "normal," window shopping with Selena and spending money on junk jewelry, movie magazines, and "Blue Plum" lipstick. Often the two pretend to be grown-ups, rich housewives out for a stroll with their sleeping infants (34). Allison knows, however, that her career aspirations conflict with this prefabricated notion of womanhood. Because a career is more important to her than marriage and babies, she alleges that she is "going to have affairs instead" (191). Her friend Norman, citing from a marriage manual he secretly ordered by mail, warns her that she will be "maladjusted." Scoffing, Allison insists that she will be "very particular" about her lovers, and once she becomes a famous writer, there will be no time for children (192–93). Always outspoken, Allison chastises her friend Kathy Ellsworth for wanting to marry her high school sweetheart and have lots of babies instead of becoming a writer. "Marriage is for clods," Allison sneers, "and if you go and get married the way you plan, Kathy, that will be the end of your artistic career. Marriage is stultifying" (212).

Allison's proclamations offer an alternative to the have/hold discourse and a passive female sexuality, especially for *Peyton Place*'s teen readers, who in the 1950s were beginning to question their parents' routinized, conformist lifestyles within corporate America and planned suburban communities. For the first time in history, teens were following a different set of values and standard of conduct apart from those of their elders. The media and the marketplace, quick to recognize young people as a new and profitable consumer group, helped construct this new peer culture in the form of rock and roll, culture icons, and a variety of consumer goods—cosmetics, movies, magazines, clothes—specifically designed for teen consumption. Sex was also an integral part of teen culture: having sex appeal, sexy "wheels," sexy music, sexy stars. Several cultural historians argue that sex signaled teen rebellion.[16] Metalious's biographer Emily Toth, for one, claims that in 1956 rebellion and sex were mutually reinforced by the best-selling *Peyton Place* and by Elvis Presley, who had just made his television debut with his number one song, "Don't Be Cruel." Because *Peyton Place* was forbidden reading for teens, it not only fueled their desire to read it, but signaled rebellion when they did; Elvis Presley, who signified a kind of dangerous, but riveting working-class sexuality associated with black males, became a leading symbol of nonconformity and rebellion for white, middle-class teens (139).

However, sex for postwar teens was a social terrain marked by mixed signals and intersections with race and class. In this respect, Peyton Place's teen culture reflected fifties U.S.A. in that middle-class white girls ("nice girls") like Allison MacKenzie were judged by a higher standard of conduct than were either black girls or lower-class white girls. "Nice" girls could "go to the brink" but never all the way with a boy, although sexual intercourse was tacitly accepted if, and only if, a young woman was going steady or "pinned" to a young man she planned to marry. For all Allison's radical talk of future lovers, she knows what teens could not do in Peyton Place. She and her friends play "Postman" at her birthday party, and she practices kissing and talks about female erogenous zones with Norman, but it is only when Allison becomes swallowed up in the anonymity of New York City that she dares to have her first full-blown affair. While intercourse was off-limits to small-town, middle-class girls, lower-class girls were less stigmatized for having sex. Thus, Rodney Harrington, the spoiled mill-owner's son, knows he can get Betty Anderson, the mill-worker's daughter, to "put out" for him, but he knows to act the perfect gentleman as Allison's prom date. Betty is considered a "slut," but because no middle-class boy would ever date her seriously, she is little threat to middle-class hegemony. In fact, Betty's status as a "slut" helps establish the boundaries of middle-class respectability for comfortable, smug Peyton Placers.

The postwar emphasis on virginity and the double standard for girls, however, was beginning to come under pressure, primarily because the media began to present dramatically different cues for female behavior. As Wini Breines notes, oppositions, such as "domesticity and glamour, virginity and sexuality, romance and sexual negotiation," were present in advertisements, popular magazines, and movies aimed at women (125). These oppositions created both passive and active images for girls, "a kind of double bind and cultural incoherence," which fueled discontent and sexual confusion (Breines 87). Teenage girls learned to cope with this incoherence by keeping up appearances of being "nice" while secretly engaging in a wide range of sexual behaviors with boys. Such contradictory codes of behavior prompted an *Atlantic Monthly* contributor to conclude that a female teen "tries to be a sexual demon and Miss Priss at tea at the same time; she tries not to see what strange companions love and propriety are" (N. Johnson 59). *Peyton Place*'s Allison gave voice to the discontent or anxiety young women may have experienced in masquerading as respectable while trying to be sexy and popular, while trying to fit in or risk being laughed at. Teens may have identified with Allison's humiliation when Rodney, preferring to neck with Betty, abandons Allison at the prom. They may have felt her "embarrassment to tears" when Connie scolds her for purchasing a rubber-padded bra, insisting that it makes Allison look like "an inflated balloon" (109). They may have understood her vexation at Norman's reluctance to kiss her passionately.[17]

While Allison typified teens' sexual confusion, she also conveyed the message that "nice girls" could go all the way and not be punished for it. After moving to New York City, she loses her virginity during a weekend tryst with her literary agent. Because he is married with children, Allison seems to be repeating her mother's past, but she is different from Connie in that her goal is not to find, have, and hold a husband. Her foremost aim is her career. Although initially heartbroken by the affair, she discovers that women do not need to get caught up in "the business of confusing love and sex" (368). Allison prefigures by a half-dozen years the phenomenon of the "single girl," described in Helen Gurley Brown's *Sex and the Single Girl*, a manifesto of career success and glamour for unmarried young women. Brown endeavored to take the scandal out of premarital sex, boldly announcing that "theoretically a 'nice' single woman has no sex life. What nonsense! She has better sex than most of her married friends" (196). Allison was already thinking and doing what was to become more commonplace in the early sixties: the young single woman with a career, her choice of lovers, her own apartment, and no guilt. Brown's single-girl credo does not necessarily constitute a feminist position because being sexy could mean being what men found sexy, and marriage was still the (deferred) goal.[18] However, Allison promoted an emergent discourse in the 1950s that competed with the dominant ideology, which stipulated that mutually satisfying sex was for married women only. At the very least, Allison's (and later Helen Gurley Brown's) linking sex and single women posed an alternative to the masquerade of sexual innocence that young women were compelled to construct, all the while actively engaging in a variety of sexual practices.

Even though "nice" middle-class girls who read *Peyton Place* might distinguish themselves as socially and sexually different from working-class teens like Betty and Helen who "did the dirty deed" (a popular fifties euphemism), they may have responded vicariously and pleasurably to its juicy passages. Both young women revel in sex with Rodney Harrington: "'Look at that,' [Helen] said, cupping the breast of her hand, 'no bra. I've got the hardest breasts you ever played with'" (314). Likewise, "[Betty's] nipples were always rigid and exciting and the full, firm flesh around them always hot and throbbing." While sex for Betty has a masochistic quality—"Come on, honey; come on, honey. Hard. Do it hard, honey. Bite me a little. Hurt me a little" (203)—her expertise with the inept and fumbling Rodney is clearly erotic. Betty's sexuality is transgressive by fifties standards, but, at the same time, she exposes middle-class readers to an alternative "reality" by critiquing the double standard and class difference. Satirizing the "male sex drive," Metalious portrays Rodney as arrogant, insensitive, and fixated on sexual conquest. When Rodney asks the respectable Allison to the prom instead of Betty, Betty gets revenge by luring him outside to a parked car during the prom, teasing him into a sexual frenzy, then asking, "Is it up, Rod? Is it up good and hard?" When Rodney whispers "Oh, yes," Betty lurches away, screaming "Now go shove it into Allison MacKenzie" (124). Betty, of course, uses sex as a weapon to punish Rodney (deservedly) and Allison (undeservedly), but in her crass manner she is actively fighting back, resisting both her class oppression and societal punishment for her sexuality.

When Betty becomes pregnant by Rodney, his wealthy father tries to buy Betty off with a $500 check (presumably for an abortion). She refuses it, insisting that Rodney marry her or else face charges of "bastardy." Leslie then threatens her with prostitution charges, insisting he will get his mill-workers to testify (falsely) against her. Knowing who will be believed in court—the mill owner, not the mill hand's daughter—Betty backs down, now with only $250 and a warning that if she returns the amount will become $125. The Harringtons get their "comeuppances" for their classism, however. In a moment of poetic, if rather harsh justice, Rodney is killed in a head-on collision because Helen fondling her breasts mesmerizes him while he is driving. The Harrington dynasty ends with a bang, but not the kind Rodney had hoped for.

Rather than foregrounding teenage sexual confusion, Selena's story involves rape and abortion. Determined to escape her brutal, "white trash" existence, she sees her steady boyfriend, Ted Carter, as a passage to the middle class. She adopts middle-class values and standards of propriety, delaying gratification, saving her money, and deciding to remain a virgin until their marriage after Ted finishes law school. When her stepfather Lucas rapes and impregnates her, her dreams are shattered. Terrified that Ted will abandon her and that the town will stigmatize her (she remembers Betty's unmarried pregnant sister who had to move away because she could not even get a job), Selena asks the trusted Doc Swain for an abortion. He consents only after she reveals who the father is. Although torn by the legal and moral prohibitions against abortion, Swain overrules these on the grounds that an unwanted pregnancy resulting from incest will ruin her life: "She is only sixteen years old. She has the beginnings of a pretty good life mapped out for herself. This would ruin her" (144). He reasons that he is "protecting life, *this* life, the one already being lived by Selena Cross" (145).

Selena's abortion raises one of the most important women's issues in *Peyton Place*, that abortion may be a question of a woman's right to have control over her body and reproduction. Up until the 1973 landmark Supreme Court decision, *Roe v. Wade*, women obtained abortions through a secret underground world. Information about abortions was passed by word of mouth, making the process even more fearful and uncertain. Many women, particularly those without recourse to ready cash, information, or a sympathetic family doctor, were more apt to face hazardous, unsanitary conditions, and inept abortionists. Despite the terror of serious health risks, death, discovery, and possible legal prosecution, women persisted in seeking abortions throughout the 1950s. The national director of Planned Parenthood estimated that, "roughly 2,000 [abortions] a day, every day are performed in the U.S."; according to criminal analysts, by the early sixties abortion constituted "the third largest criminal activity in the country, surpassed only by narcotics and gambling" (d'Emilio and Freedman 253). Unlike millions of women in postwar America, Selena was fortunate to have a sympathetic Doc Swain. Still, Selena is haunted by fear and shame even after Swain forces Lucas to sign a confession and then leave town permanently. (Selena's mother, Nellie, another casualty of the rape, commits suicide after she overhears Lucas's confession to Doc). When Lucas returns a year later and tries to rape her again, Selena fights back, killing him with a poker. Fearing no one will believe a poor shack-dweller, she buries Lucas in their sheep pen, but when neighbors find her half-burned, bloody bathrobe, she is tried for murder. Knowing that Ted will never accept her secret horror, Selena refuses to supply a motive for the murder and swears Swain to secrecy about her rape and abortion. Doc breaks his promise, however, and testifies about Lucas's sexual violence in order to get her an acquittal.

While the sordid details of Selena's story perhaps offended the William Loebs of the nation, this incident sends a serious message about the relationship between sex, power, and violence and the fact that rape is not simply a private incident, but a public affair, affecting men and women collectively. Furthermore, the narrative castigates Peyton Placers for stigmatizing Selena and, by extension, all rape victims. By making Selena an extremely sympathetic figure, the novel clearly endorses a woman's decision to fight back, choosing empowerment over victimization. Seeing Selena as a liability to his legal career, Ted Carter drops Selena at the outset of the trial. She courageously faces life alone after her acquittal, managing Connie's dress shop, and providing a home for her orphaned brother.

Although *Peyton Place* may have been contraband reading for many teens, it contained numerous points of identification for young readers by reflecting the culture's contradictory messages about gender and sex. By breaking apart the dichotomy of good/bad girls, by empowering a female victim of sexual violence, by representing female teens enjoying erotic pleasures and sexual experiences, Metalious's novel contributed to the breakdown of Cold War discourses of female sexual containment. Teen readers very possibly found substance for speculation or analysis even while they enjoyed the titillating parts of the novel. However, when these same readers saw the movie, they found a town populated with a whole different set of teens, created by a thoroughly charming and refreshing group of young actors, each of whom provided a strong identification figure for filmgoers. Along with this likable young cast came the erasure of the novel's problematizing of gender, sex, and class within teen culture.

Peyton Place Hollywood-Style, or Douching Out the Filthy, Rotten Side of Life

When Jerry Wald's production crew went scouting for a New England town in which to replicate "Peyton Place," it was unprepared for the repeated rejection from towns unwilling to be associated with the scandalous novel. Hoping to shoot in Woodstock, Vermont, Wald settled for Camden, Maine—the only town willing to welcome the film crew (Thompson 1). Mid-fifties Camden was a rural idyll, surrounded by beautiful countryside with covered bridges, rolling hayfields, and a spectacular rocky coastline. The village featured oak-lined streets with neat, white clapboard houses, a quaint business district, and village green—clearly a far cry from Metalious's drab mill town riddled with class and labor tensions. Such old-fashioned charm reinforced visually the ideological differences between the film and novel, lending the proper ambiance for Hollywood's nostalgic portrait of Americana and its idealistic vision of communal harmony.[19]

In transposing novel to film, Metalious's lengthy book had to be condensed and altered, necessitated, in part, by the Production Code. The screenplay whittled the novel down to its basic storylines of Connie (Lana Turner), Allison (Diane Varsi) and Selena (Hope Lange), but, in terms of ideological significance, expanded Betty Anderson's (Terry Moore) story. Along with the novel's cynicism, the film purged several important events that had been crucial in multiplying the novel's positions of gender identification. Hollywood's *Peyton Place* reaffirmed the postwar ideal of femininity, defining womanhood in terms of monogamous heterosexual relationships that presumably end in marriage. By the film's end, social class differences were erased and female sexual "problems" were resolved. Women who had been too flashy (Betty), frigid (Connie), or vulnerable (Selena) were safely tamed, thawed out, or ritually cleansed in order to make them "proper" marriage material. The mystical ingredient effecting these changes was, of course, romantic love. However, the film's pat ending and its narrower concerns put a false spin on the narrative.

In its determination to reform its "bad" women, Hollywood softened the edges of Metalious's callous working-class "tramp," Betty Anderson, who in the film becomes a respectable, middle-class wife. No longer the self-absorbed creep, Rodney Harrington (Barry Coe) appears as Betty's high school sweetheart, who rejects his father's disapproval of Betty as not a "girl of quality." Betty is determined to marry Rodney and takes aggressive steps to land her man, beginning with the most basic prescription of having-and-holding: making one's self sexually attractive. While her girlfriends watch her try on a low-cut, tight red dress from Connie's store, Betty wises them up when they suggest the dress is too old for her: "Men can see much better than they can think .... Believe me, a low neckline dress does more for a girl's future than the entire Encyclopedia Britannica." Betty voices what young women watching the movie already knew—an education does not lead the way to the altar, but being sexy and attractive does, a doctrine that Betty Friedan claims in *The Feminine Mystique* was accepted even by college women. Betty Anderson may be calculating and manipulative, but the film shows her strategy to have-and-hold to be quite successful.

First, though, Betty must groom Rodney to be a good bread-winner—to be responsible, mature, and to listen to her, not his father. Unlike the novel, in which Rod and Leslie are pals, the film locks father and son in a classic Oedipal conflict in which Rodney struggles to escape his father's autocratic rule. In the film's steamiest love scene in which Rodney tries to seduce Betty after they go skinny dipping, Betty suggests they get married first. He hedges, saying his father won't like it, but Betty retorts: "Are you going all through your life only doing what your father lets you do?" Provoked, he declares his independence: "What good is life if I go through it knowin' I didn't have the guts to live it my way!" Several scenes later the couple visit Leslie after having eloped. Betty now wears a conservative blue traveling suit and a prim hat (no more sexy outfits for her!). When Leslie barks, "What about Harvard?" Rodney declares he is not going because he has a wife to support. His transformation to breadwinner is complete.

Despite Leslie's disapproval of his son's new wife, after Rodney dies (heroically) in World War II, Leslie approaches Betty after church to ask if she needs anything. When Betty snubs him, he admits, "Rodney was a better boy for having married you," which then prompts her to justify her former image: "I was a kind of flashy girl, I know, but Rodney liked flashy girls, so that's the way I was going to be." Seeing that Betty is changed, in other words, that she has ceased to *act* flashy, or to put on her trampiness, Leslie pleads, "Let's keep what's left of the family together." In altering the Betty/Rodney story, the film effectively erases Metalious's critique of the male sex drive, the have/hold discourses, and social class difference. Social class difference becomes a matter of Betty's choosing to act trampy. In other words, the material realities of social stratification and class-based discrimination are reduced to personal choices involving taste and style. Rodney is reincarnated in the film as both responsible breadwinner and patriot—the epitome of ideal Cold War masculinity— rather than a sensation seeking, hormonally charged juvenile delinquent who is obliterated in a hot car with a hot girl. Handsome, charismatic Barry Coe adds to Rodney's appeal, supplying some on-screen beefcake with his muscular, tanned torso featured prominently in the beach scene.

The film also alters Selena's story, which effectively produces another erasure of social class difference and celebrates heterosexual couplehood. Casting the young, blond, Hollywood ingenue Hope Lange as Selena transformed Metalious's dark-haired, voluptuous, cynical teen into a sweet, gentle, wistful, young woman, which makes explicit how both Metalious and Hollywood made certain assumptions about the coding of sex and class within these two ethnic body types. Lange is clearly less convincing as Metalious's shack dweller, who in the novel must endure the sordid squalor of her one-room house in which she witnesses Lucas's physical and sexual violence against her mother. Given Hollywood's rose-colored vision of Peyton Place, however, Lange is "right" for the film, which also sustains her relationship with squeaky clean Ted Carter (David Nelson). No longer a self-serving, opportunistic law student, Ted stands by Selena, even wearing his military uniform throughout her murder trial. Thus, Selena is spared the stigma associated with her rape and pregnancy, unlike in the novel in which losing Ted further victimizes her. In the film, Selena is "cleansed" by a dramatic communal ritual in a moment of collective forgiveness after Doc Swain (Lloyd Nolan) delivers a rousing jeremiad in the courtroom—again, not in the novel—against gossip and divisiveness in Peyton Place. As Selena exits the courthouse, the town, seemingly forgiving her lower-class origins, surrounds her in a gesture of sympathy and welcomes her into their fold. Moreover, because Hollywood's Production Code forbade mentioning abortion, Selena's pregnancy terminates in a miscarriage caused by a fall when Lucas (Arthur Kennedy) is chasing her through the woods. The miscarriage effectively eliminates any discussion of female reproductive rights raised in the novel.

While the film preserved Allison's and Connie's stories for the most part, several alterations worked to endorse traditional female gender roles. For one, Allison's affair with her literary agent is dropped and replaced with the hint of a romance with sweet, awkward Norman (Russ Tamblyn), a "sissy" and Mama's boy who manages to escape the clutches of his neurotic overbearing mother by joining the paratroopers and becoming all confidence![20] Allison's venture to New York is couched as a temporary rebellion against Connie, rather than being motivated by a desire to test her mettle as a writer. Aside from dropping Connie's date rape scene and other steamy sexual encounters between her and Makris (Mike Rossi in the film), the film follows the novel's trajectory where Connie goes from masquerading as a respectable widow to finding happiness in love. The film's major change for Connie was her appearance as a witness at Selena's trial, which provided the moment in which she "confesses" to Allison that she has failed as a mother. Motherhood is redeemed here publicly and later privately through Allison and Connie's reconciliation, two scenes that authorize traditional female sex roles.

If the film narrative itself worked to endorse orthodox female identity, Lana Turner as Allison's sexually repressed mother introduced the element of instability into the representation of gender. Turner was not only the film's only major star, but she was also the one star whose image was associated with glamorous, smoldering sex *and* scandal. Given that the film had purified a novel whose very name signified illicit sex, Turner supplied a link back to the original narrative. More importantly, her star image complicates the notion that gender is a stable category of identity. True, on the one hand, Turner's persona helped to authorize the truth of her character, Connie. On the other hand, it exposed the fact that "real" or "authentic" identity is based on performance and theatricality. Because Turner, more than any other star in *Peyton Place*, troubles the binary relationship between authenticity and performance, I follow here with a somewhat lengthy discussion of Turner's star text.

According to Richard Dyer, there was a "high degree of interpenetration between [Turner's] publicly available private life and film," ("Lana" 409). As such, her film roles often worked to authenticate "Lana Turner," and, in turn, Turner gave a particular inflection to her film characters, ostensibly lending "truth" to them. The reverberations between her personal life and characters were a phenomenon sustained throughout Turner's film career, beginning with her first film, *They Won't Forget* (1937), in which Lana, just fifteen, had a bit part requiring her to walk from a soda fountain to her school where she would be raped and murdered off screen. Two things were significant about this role: first, Lana's studio publicity, alleging she was discovered at a soda fountain while skipping school, echoed her appearance in the film; second, her two-minute walk down the street in a tight sweater—breasts and buttocks made to jiggle in sync with the music—launched her as MGM's new sex symbol (Morella and Epstein 24). "The Sweater Girl" was born.

Turner's transformation from Sweater Girl to Glamorous Star

came with her first major part in *Ziegfeld Girl* (1941), in which Turner played an elevator girl turned Follies star, again echoing her own rise from ordinary girl to major star. Dazzled by the wealth and glitter of being a Ziegfeld girl, Sheila Regan literally parties herself to death. Off screen, Turner, then only nineteen, acquired the title "Queen of the Night Club" for her frequent partying at well-known night spots (Morella and Epstein 27). Also at this time Turner's four-month marriage to band leader Artie Shaw, after a one-night courtship, marked her as impulsive, immature, and easily taken in by men. This, along with her desire for expensive entertainment, clothes, and jewelry was featured in *Ziegfeld Girl*. Sheila Regan is somewhat redeemed at the end of this film by a death bed reunion with a loyal boyfriend and her famous walk-down scene. Expelled from the Follies, Sheila decides to see one last show before she dies, but feeling ill, she leaves the theater by way of a grand staircase. When she hears "her" song, she pauses, then descends the stairs in a statuesque, show-girl style, reaffirming her dedication to her career. This mixture of "badness" and "goodness" became a staple of Turner's film roles. "This ambiguity, the 'bad' woman who suffers for her badness and thus becomes an identification/sympathy figure, is the emotional timbre that is caught in all her subsequent films" (Dyer, "Lana" 413).

Between *Ziegfeld Girl* and *Peyton Place*, Turner married four more times, but each marriage was marked by scandal or embarrassing legal problems. Again, reinforcing her off-screen image as emotional and impulsive, she married Stephen Crane after knowing him only nine days, but two months into the marriage, she discovered that he was not fully divorced from his first wife (Basinger 103–4). Their marriage had to be annulled, but this left Lana with an image problem: She was pregnant and having a baby out of wedlock was unthinkable for a major Hollywood star. Turner reluctantly agreed to remarry Crane once he was legally free, but they promptly divorced when baby Cheryl Crane was six months old.

Shortly after her divorce, Lana acquired her playgirl reputation. Between subsequent marriages and divorces she was paired with a seemingly endless string of celebrities and Hollywood leading men, including Victor Mature, Robert Stack, Buddy Rich, Rory Calhoun, Howard Hughes, Fernando Lamas, and Tyrone Power. Accused of being a home wrecker several times, she was once named co-respondent in divorce proceedings. Her romantic venture with businessman Bob Topping also proved humiliating when Turner's plan to announce their engagement with a $40,000 party was abruptly halted after Topping's wife told the press that he was not yet divorced from her. In 1948 Turner and Topping did marry, but their union got off to a rocky start when the press reported it was not legitimate, since the Presbyterian minister who performed the ceremony was bound by church canon not to marry anyone whose divorce had not been legal for at least one year; Topping's was two months old. MGM took this bad press seriously enough to begin grooming Ava Gardner for Turner's roles (Morella and Epstein 119–20).

Lana was also chastised in the press for her "flaunting of morality ... without benefit of clergy" when she toured Europe with Lex Barker of Tarzan fame (Morella and Epstein 146). Turner and Barker eventually married, but nasty rumors about Lana's infidelity plagued the marriage.[21] Lana's "badness" inevitably spilled over into her film roles, which, in turn, flowed back into her personal life. In *The Postman Always Rings Twice* (1946) and *The Three Musketeers* (1948), she played alluring, sexually dangerous women; in *The Flame and the Flesh* (1954), she was a lustful, but self-sacrificing prostitute; *The Prodigal* (1955) cast her as a pagan sex goddess who dies in a flaming cauldron in retribution for neglecting her kingdom.

If Turner was supposedly immoral, impulsive, and stupid about men, she also seemed to suffer for her "badness." Her tumultuous engagements ended in bitter divorces, invariably costing her money; she suffered three heartbreaking miscarriages, and the man she called the love of her life, Tyrone Power, publicly ended their affair, as did *Latin Lovers* (1953) co-star Fernando Lamas. This "punishment" was reflected in her screen roles. John Updike, reflecting on her image and acting legacy, maintained, "Turner, in most of her roles, lives for love and takes her lumps. Erotic high points of her film career include being knocked unconscious by Robert Taylor [*Johnny Eager* (1942)], offering to drown herself for John Garfield [*The Postman Always Rings Twice*], being rolled from a moving car in *Cass Timberlane* (1947), and going to the scaffold in *The Three Musketeers* (1948)" (72). Incidents from Turner's films and her personal life became mutually reinforcing, supposedly authenticating the "real" Lana by "revealing" her personality or her type of person. Conversely, Turner brought to her roles a subtext not written into the script. *Peyton Place* was no exception.

Peyton Place was Turner's comeback film for which she received her first Oscar nomination for Best Actress. Her film career had been in a steady downward spiral in the mid-fifties, and her film just prior to *Peyton Place, The Rains of Ranchipur* (1955), was universally panned. MGM, her home studio for eighteen years, terminated her contract, leaving the thirty-six-year-old Turner out on her own. When Wald offered her the part of Connie, Turner's friends advised her against taking it because playing a teenager's mother might alter her sex symbol image (Morella and Epstein 171). *Peyton Place* was a boon for Turner, however, reestablishing her as a major box office draw.

Turner's star image had strong resonance with Connie MacKenzie. Despite her hesitation to play a mother of a troubled teen, Turner herself was the mother of troubled thirteen-year-old Cheryl Crane, who was having difficulty coping with Turner's career and her revolving door of boyfriends. Several months before *Peyton Place*'s release, newspapers nationwide reported that Cheryl had run away from boarding school and was found wandering alone at midnight in a Los Angeles skid row. Cheryl reportedly told police she ran away because she had a fight with her mother and her home was breaking up, referring to Barker and Turner's impending divorce (Morella and Epstein 172–73). As if imitating life, Connie and Allison MacKenzie would "replay" the Turners' mother-daughter discord: Allison leaves home after feeling betrayed by her mother. Like Lana, Connie is a woman with a past, who in a vulnerable, lonely moment takes up with the wrong guy, a married man no less; such "illicit" behavior causes her to take her lumps, just as Lana always seemed to.

However, in playing Connie, Turner had to rein in her on-screen sexuality, in order to portray a cold, practical woman. Rather than creating the impression that Turner was miscast, however, this contrast between star and character fostered the film's ideological work that requires Connie to drop her masquerade and "become" the woman she really is meant to be—a warm, but sexual woman who really just wants to be loved. "Lana Turner"—or what audiences believed they knew about her—continually directed attention to what was behind Connie's plain wrapper, which was something more akin to "Lana Turner." Again, ripples of Turner's private life mingled with her character, authenticating Connie's motives for masquerading. When Connie rebuffs Mike Rossi (Lee Philips) after the school prom, he verbally attacks her: "It's not sex you're afraid of. You can say yes or no to that. It's love that you're afraid of." Given that Turner's marriage to Barker just ended in divorce, Rossi's words rang "true" for both star and character, for it was unlikely that anyone would believe the Sweater Girl was afraid of sex, but they might well believe she was wary of love. However, Turner would risk losing love again, precisely what the film requires of Connie to ensure its "happy" ending.

Although Connie is a bundle of nerves about sex, especially where Allison is concerned, Turner's association with sex and badness helped to falsify Connie's diatribes against sex. We don't really believe Connie when she says to Allison: "I don't like the way [Betty] talks about sex and men." Later, when she reprimands Allison for allowing her friends to neck at her birthday party, the exchange between mother and daughter is fraught with double meaning. Allison insists she "just wants to be like everyone else," but Connie retorts, "Well, I don't want you to be like everyone in this town. I want you to rise above this place ... its standards are low." Allison then responds, "I don't want to be perfect like you, Mother. I don't want to live in a test tube." Filtered through Turner's image, Connie's words seem to turn back on themselves, negating their intended meaning. When Connie decides to let her guard down, she shows up at Rossi's door in a bright red dress—similar to the dress Betty tries on in her store, the one she uses to capture Rodney. The red dress, a departure from her otherwise chic, yet severe wardrobe of blues, blacks, and beiges, signals her pursuit of love and sex as Turner had so many times in "real" life and on screen. As Updike puts it, Turner believed in "love as a divine force, a magic potion, a doom that survives betrayals and double crosses and angry blows" (72).

Connie's transformation to the "real" warm-blooded woman beneath her cold widow masquerade, though, is not complete until her breakdown at Selena's trial. She is ready to be Mike's lover, but she still is locked in conflict with Allison. When Connie is called as a witness, she attempts to explain why Selena may have killed Lucas Cross; instead, she looks pleadingly at Allison and snuffles out a veiled apology about mothers not listening to their daughters' problems. Unable to bear Allison's cold expression, Connie collapses, hysterical, necessitating a recess so that Doc Swain can sedate her. This public outpouring of emotion, which significantly takes place on a witness stand in front of a town willing to hear one's most private confessions, signifies Connie's moment of "truth," revealing what lies at her inner core. Interestingly, Turner's clothing style was altered for this scene to complement this revelation. Previously, she appears in stiff dresses or suits—all angles, lines, and belts. For the courtroom she wears a pale blue knit suit with white trim. The loose, soft material refuses to cinch her in, barricade her emotions, or cage her "interiority." Even her gestures change. Instead of her crisp movements and rigid poses, Connie is hesitant and uncertain, finally collapsing into a crumpled, limp heap. Connie's hysteria convinces Allison of her sincerity and willingness to be a "proper" mother, one who no longer fabricates a life, then hides behind it in neurotic self-absorption. In the final scene, Allison runs toward Connie's waiting embrace. Happy at last, Connie has all a woman apparently needs—motherhood, marriage, and home.

Incredibly, this courtroom collapse would prove to be still another echo of Turner's life. Less than four months after *Peyton Place*'s release, Cheryl stabbed and killed Lana's boyfriend, small-time gangster Johnny Stompanato, in her bedroom when he apparently threatened to cripple Lana and cut her face.[22] *Peyton Place* was still playing strong around the nation when, one week after the murder, Turner took the stand at Cheryl's inquest, and, as if repeating Connie's tearful testimony, Turner sobbed her way through the hearing. The similarities continue: Connie is in court because a teenage girl has killed her stepfather; Turner is in court because her teenager has killed her mother's boyfriend. Moreover, just as Connie had to reveal the truth of her sordid past, first to Mike Rossi and then to Allison, Turner had to endure an astounding degree of media coverage, which laid bare every detail of the Stompanato murder, including the contents of her love letters to him. Compounding these reverberations, *Life* ran a photo layout juxtaposing Turner on the witness stand next to three films in which she also testified in a courtroom: *The Postman Always Rings Twice, Cass Timberlane,* and *Peyton Place* (Morella and Epstein 203). Furthermore, after the Stompanato incident, the novel's steamy sex and sexual violence between Connie and Makris that had been cut from the film may have been reintroduced by the highly publicized relationship between Lana and her gangster lover. Audiences did not need to see Connie getting roughed up by Mike Rossi on screen; it was already there in Lana Turner.

While Connie and Lana's courtroom testimonies may have produced a mutually reinforcing effect, "authenticating" star and character, some of the press coverage of Turner at the inquest may have functioned in precisely the opposite way: that is, indicating what anyone could know of the "real" Lana was illusion. For example, a typical headline of her testimony read, "Lana Turner, battling to save her teenage daughter, played the most dramatic and effective role of her long screen career. The coroner's jury awarded her the Oscar"

(Morella and Epstein 201). Although it seems unfair, even cruel, to suggest a parent would merely act a role in such circumstances, the press was intrigued by the possibility that "Lana Turner" was the effects of performance and fabrication.

This very possibility, which followed Turner throughout her career, is precisely what introduces ambiguity into the film's project of affirming a "true" female identity. While star and character seemingly reflected each other's "true" self, what can never be fully or finally erased was the obvious manufacture of Turner's gender identity, foregrounded in her star image, her former film roles, and in *Peyton Place*. The construction of "Lana Turner," according to Dyer, is emphasized, even celebrated, in *The Bad and the Beautiful* (1953), a film about an actress whose star rises purely on the merits of her screen presence as opposed to her acting ability. Audiences watch Georgia/Lana transformed before their eyes from ordinary woman to glamorous star, her glamour patently constructed on theatrical fakery. Dyer aptly notes: "The film is giddy with reflection images, reflections, moreover, of a woman preparing her appearance at a dressing table"; however, paradoxically, the illusion of beauty and the star image itself are not demystified in this film. Rather, Dyer argues, "it is the techniques of illusion that stimulate the 'real magic' of the star, the 'truth' of her 'performance'" ("Lana" 419). Nonetheless, the "truth" of Georgia/Lana is predicated on fabrication and acting. Truth is merely the reality of illusion.

Both on- and off-screen Turner's femininity was built around a series of performative gestures that called attention to its manufacture and masquerade. For example, while she managed to reconcile such contradictory elements as "ordinary" and "sexy," these components of Turner's image alluded to the necessary acting required to transcend the conflicting demands of each (Dyer "Lana" 410). Her love of clothes, jewelry, and her changes in hair color contributed to audiences' fascination with her image as well. Turner admitted that "when [she] hit [her] stride, [she] spent money faster than it came in, mostly buying jewels" (Morella and Epstein 29). She smoldered in strapless, black evening gowns or radiated expensive sex in white mink, satin, and diamonds. Her hair changed from red to blond to brown and back again (although by the mid-fifties, Turner was "permanently" blond). A variety of clothing styles was always part of her image, featured in such costume dramas as *The Great Garrick* (1937), *The Adventures of Marco Polo* (1938), *Dr. Jekyl and Mr. Hyde* (1941), *Green*

Dolphin Street (1947), *The Three Musketeers* (1948), *Diane* (1955). In *Ziegfeld Girl* (1941), Turner appeared in outlandish outfits of tulle, sequins, and rhinestones, looking much like a "human chandelier," to use Jeanine Basinger's phrase (44). In *The Postman Always Rings Twice*, her white shorts and halter made an indelible impression on America's cinematic memory; in *The Prodigal*, Turner played a priestess of Damascus, clothed in beaded hot pants and a top held together by a few stitches.

MGM never invested much time or energy in teaching Turner to act, since her function in many films was to present "pure image or screen presence," not to attempt to interpret a character (Updike 70). In *Peyton Place*, her presentation of pure image was made more explicit in the context of Diane Varsi's "driving intensity" (Laitin 140), which aligned her with the talent and "naturalness" of the new crop of fifties Method actors.[23] Varsi, one of Hollywood's rising young stars, was not "discovered" while sipping soda at the corner drugstore; instead she stumbled into film almost by accident, but took her acting very seriously and rejected the Hollywood glamour scene. While the popular press characterized Varsi as an introvert, non-conformist, and a bohemian, they also called her "a pure talent" ("Girl Who Walks" 93); conversely, Turner's early studio publicity had proudly proclaimed that "Lana Turner ... brought *It* back to the screen" (Morella and Epstein 37). "It," of course, did not translate into serious acting talent.

Audiences were captivated not simply with Turner's glamorous image, but were fascinated with the fabrication of this image, hardly a "natural" femininity since Turner was perennially and commercially processed through costume, jewelry, make up, and hair style. While Turner had to suppress "It" in *Peyton Place*, her performance foregrounded acting and artifice (perhaps the ironic result of MGM never teaching her to act in order to mask acting) to the point where acting and artifice pressured any stable representation of femininity, a stability produced through a resistance to performance. Whereas her star text works to authenticate the "truth" of her character, Turner's construction of Connie through gestures, clothes, and social differences indicates that femininity is pure representation, not natural essence. Stanley Kauffmann, whose 1958 film review of *Peyton Place* indicates an awareness in this decade of the relation between Turner and artifice, put it succinctly: "Lana Turner has at least one gift: she can walk into a real scene (much of this picture was shot in New England) and make it seem synthetic" (22).

Certainly, compared with her co-stars Lange and Varsi who appear refreshingly sincere and innocent, Turner/Connie's on-screen presence had an inflexible, highly mannered, poised quality. In Turner's first scene, her presence contrasts sharply with Varsi, who is all bright chatter and energy. Lana/Connie looks stiff and restrained in a stylish, blue dress and tightly wound French twist. With few exceptions, Lana/Connie appears in smart suits or chic dresses appropriate for her line of work as a retail clothier, which seeks to create images of femininity through clothing and style. However, none of her outfits makes Connie look "natural"; she invariably seems uncomfortable, constrained. Her gestures complement her armored appearance: She repeatedly smooths her hands over her skirts, plucks at her sleeves, and crosses her arms in a protective gesture. Although this outward discomfort supposedly signifies inner anxiety and repressed sexuality, at the same time, it foregrounds the way clothes and gestures help to construct image.

In addition, Connie's clothes and mannerisms advance the idea that gender is constructed through social differences. Her *haute couture*—the film capitalizes on Turner's association with clothes and glamour even in the context of motherhood—stands out from poor Nellie Cross's shapeless sacks and the down-home, cotton shirtwaists of the mill hands' wives. Likewise, her brittle, blonde French twist contrasts with their drab brown pin-curled look. At the school prom, Lana/Connie, a chaperone, is featured in a salmon evening gown, made elegant by its simplicity. In several wide-angle shots of the dance floor, she vividly stands out from the school marms and teens, all in pale gowns with girlish ruffles; even flashy Betty wears a demure pastel. Prom night clearly belongs to Lana (and Connie).

Perhaps the most obvious way that Turner focuses audience attention on performance and artifice is in her acting style, her ability to bring a synthetic quality to a scene. Turner was noted for acting with her eyes as opposed to delivering her lines or using other bodily movements. Hurt, anger, fear, confusion, and happiness are expressed from one moment to the next by minute changes in her eye muscles, all while her body remains rigidly posed. While these fleeting looks may suggest interiority, this expression of a "real" Lana/Connie continually points to an *enactment* of emotion. There are moments, too, where Turner's acting actually overshadows the "intent" of the scene. When Allison informs her mother she is leaving home for good,

Connie exits her bedroom, then pauses on the stair landing. She then makes a dramatic walk-down (reminiscent of *Ziegfeld Girl*), slow, hesitant, stiffly poised, until she collapses in tears at the bottom. The purpose of course is to "express" her distress, but our attention is drawn to her performance of emotion. *Peyton Place* contains numerous scenes as well, in which Turner is simply required to pose in front of the camera, using only her eyes to reveal a thought or feeling. This posing begins to eclipse the narrative; the "real" becomes overruled by performance, raising the question of what exactly is real.

To summarize, Turner's casting in *Peyton Place* complicates any simple conflation of her star text and character that would reveal the "truth" of both. The obvious manufacture of Turner's gendered identity and her acting style, which always calls attention to itself, undermine the collapse of performance and authenticity, ironically, in a film about the need to stop performing and "act" real. In other words, the complexity that Turner's image brings to the film involves slippages in this binary relationship. I am reminded here of Judith Butler's distinction between gender mimesis and gender performance: Gender mimesis refers to an imitation that promises to authenticate identity, in the way that Turner's star image—produced by a series of gendered effects—served to authenticate Connie MacKenzie. In contrast, gender performance refers to an imitation that exposes identity as fabricated, as Turner's mannered acting style signified pure artifice rather than interiority and truth of character.[24] In this case, the film's representation of a "real" womanhood can never be fully successful.

Even so, the pressure "Lana Turner" brings to bear on the film's representations of gender identity does not measure up to Metalious's more radical troubling of traditional conceptualizations of gender and sexuality. While her star text reintroduced some of what the novel was doing, Turner, by comparison, was "trashy" and tame, as opposed to being "damned and banned." The disruptive elements that Turner introduced were still contained within Hollywood's feel-good production, which reified couplehood and a kind of 1950s "true womanhood."

Interestingly, film critics considered Hollywood's alterations of the novel an aesthetic improvement, although it was clear from the book's astronomical sales that readers were much less concerned with questions of art. Reviewers, in fact, praised the film by comparing it to the novel: Elspeth Hart of *Films in Review* proclaimed, "*Peyton Place* will long be cited as an example of how a fine motion picture can be made out of a cheap and dirty book" (26); Stanley Kauffmann called the film "an overlong exercise in sentimentality," but conceded "the film's better than the book," mainly because Hollywood was forced to eliminate the "excesses" Metalious was "unable to control" (21). *Newsweek* assured readers, "The screenplay has no trace of bad taste" ("Best-Seller on Film" 76). Not only did these critics represent the film as an improvement rather than seeing its condensation as a kind of literary emasculation, but they reiterated the initial hostility of the novel's critics, who, as we recall, felt compelled to preserve the sanctity of art by denouncing the novel as unadulterated trash. However, precisely what was the film an improvement over? A novel that was rude and crude, seamy and steamy? Middlebrow dressed in black fishnet stockings and red stiletto heels? "Excess" that presumed to be "literary"?

The real threat of Metalious's *Peyton Place*, it seems, was a brazen female sexuality that flounced into the living rooms of respectable American families and plopped itself on the coffee table right next to Alfred Kinsey's *Sexual Behavior in the Human Female*. *Peyton Place* perhaps gave rise to a creeping fear that the sexual revelations unleashed by the Kinsey report were indeed true. In an ironical twist, Metalious's imaginative portrayal of social "reality" authenticated the scientist's findings. If the film version "improved" anything, it was the condition of patriarchy's denial of social transformation. By contrast, as indicated by the novel's critique of "having-and-holding" and the sexual double standard, Metalious was making a significant gesture toward a more open discussion about the politics of gender and sex. For only when women are able to address sexuality and their bodies, and how these relate to power and oppression, in a public, critical way, are they able to assert significant control over their discursive constructions and material practices. We have to wonder, then, if *Peyton Place*'s emphasis on the values, attitudes, and practices that were vital and important to women's lives and female empowerment was the very thing William Loeb considered "the filthy, rotten side of life." The lofty claim of preserving "art" and "taste" seems, in part, to have been a ruse in suppressing an "errant" female sexuality. What Loeb and others sought to expunge from the literary, however, was precisely that which women needed (and still need) to confront candidly and collectively.

Metalious's *Peyton Place* most likely fostered increasingly open representations of female sexuality in postwar popular culture. Following this momentous best-seller, the American public consumed a variety of narratives dealing with issues of female or marginalized sexualities, such as *A Summer Place*, *Baby Doll*, *Butterfield Eight*, *Suddenly Last Summer*, and *The Chapman Report*—all of which were produced as films. Titillating the public with voyeuristic fantasies, sexual women, or frank "scientific" discussions about female sexuality did not necessarily guarantee progressive messages or liberatory images. Representations of more open sex could function under the sign of power as a regulatory strategy to define "appropriate" and "inappropriate" subject positions and sexual practices. However, bringing such representations into the public domain provided opportunities to contest the meanings attached to them and to allow alternative discourses of sexuality to emerge and gain cultural legitimacy.

7

Conclusion

In a 1957 issue of the *Hudson Review*, literary critic Herbert Gold not only chastised mainstream America for its "close squeezing to belong, to conform, to adjust, to sing praise to what-is in America," but also criticized popular novelists for falling short of an avant-garde idealism. All too many writers were churning out "upper-middle soap operas," Gold insisted, in which life is not writ large, but reduced to "a world of contracting freedom and organized satisfactions" (587–88). In his assessment of things, social protest had become an anachronism in the middlebrow novel, its moral message consisting of "faithful submission ... to the way things are." "If you are still troubled," Gold advised, "be patient" .... "The path of righteousness will be made abundantly clear in the VistaVision version" (591). Gold's incisive remarks encapsulate the position of cultural élites who feared that popular novels did little more than reflect a massified, conformist culture whose new and only frontier was "Adjustment." The Hollywood film version, as Gold implies, merely served up leftovers, obscuring its predecessor's and its own mediocrity with the spice of visuals, color, and the garnish of stardom.

Situating the postwar debates about culture in dichotomous terms of high culture's proclivity for social protest and avant-garde innovation versus middle and low culture's vapidity and complacency had several implications for conceptualizing the ideological function of literature within that culture. The attempts by the guardians of culture to reassert agreement on aesthetic standards and to make causal links between art and the quality of civilization, even "freedom" itself, tended to divert attention away from the increasing visibility of diversity within postwar culture and the potential for popular culture to reflect this diversity. Furthermore, by focusing on formal properties of literature, locating its supposed universal and timeless themes or making claims on how the literary contributed to the mythic definition of America, literary critics and scholars effectively marginalized writers who were developing alternative styles, narrative forms, and cultural traditions apart from a modernist ideal. Neither did widely accepted New Critical methods of explicating the literary object account for the multiple discursive histories embedded in its production; nor did this methodology account for the variance among consumers, hence the multiple interpretive strategies brought to bear in making meanings. The literary critic who sought to mediate between the reader and the text by posing the "correct" interpretation or meaning of the work was unable to value the specific knowledges and multiple experiences that shaped readers' understandings.

Moreover, despite the claims to its avant-garde protest, what counted as high culture did not necessarily promote a dismantling of power hierarchies built on such categories as class, gender, race, ethnicity, and sexual preference. The aesthetic object, as we know, is inevitably produced and interpreted within particular ideological and historical matrices. However, the politics of representation embedded within that text are not necessarily made explicit. Instead, the very textuality of the high art object may be obscured or denied under the guise of neutrality or universality. Therefore, if what is designated as high culture is viewed as the only kind of culture that is capable of significant social or individual protest—as was true of the 1950s—then this is to overlook its own potential for complicity with systematic forms of oppression. This interpretation, of course, is not to suggest that popular or mass culture, by contrast, had certain politically transformative powers, which were overlooked by cultural critics in their attempt to safeguard Art and reduce popular culture to mass-marketed pabulum. Rather, the discursive frameworks that gave shape to and sustained distinct categories of culture eclipsed the contradictions inherent in the high/low binary, which stagnated the entire debate over aesthetic value in a reductive "either/or" skirmish. The cultural gatekeepers, it seems, urged readers to choose between "good" and "bad" literature or art and to understand that the ultimate stake in such a choice was preserving western civilization itself. In an attempt to move beyond this critical impasse, this book has taken as its point of departure and its underlying assumption the historicity of the literary as a category.

One of the overarching concerns throughout this book has been to examine the dichotomy of high/low culture by focusing specifically on best-selling novels, which has enabled me to illuminate the critical gaps that emerged from the struggle to maintain categorical divisions of culture. This study offers a more nuanced account of the relationship between literary and filmic texts and ideology than was otherwise made explicitly available to postwar readers and filmgoers by serious literary critics and intellectuals. More specifically, I have attempted to reassess the best-seller and its film version not solely in terms of whether it reproduced a "faithful submission to the way things are," and hence a stagnant or conformist image of nation, but in terms of how these narratives engaged in a dynamic contest over what constituted America's self-definition. In exploring how these popular texts entered into the cultural conversation over national identity, the previous chapters have sought to identify and analyze specific symbolic components that comprised images of nationhood in the decade following World War II, namely gender and its intersections with race, class, sexuality, and ethnicity. The historical analysis, which has been central to this work, indicates ways to read gender as multiply constituted yet contained within dominant, systematic power hierarchies. Within the logic of Cold War ideologies, then, it follows that if gender is shown to be multiple and fluid, then any understanding of nation as monolithic or coherent becomes problematic as well.

Gender is at the center of each narrative included in this book. However, collectively, these novels and films do not all tell the same story about gender identity and its symbolic resonance with national identity. James Jones's *From Here to Eternity* and James Michener's *Sayonara*—both preoccupied with male codes of behavior and definitions of manhood—offer models of masculinity that ultimately reaffirm the culture's alignment of strong nation with strong men. Edna Ferber's *Giant*, however, dissects this model of white hegemonic masculinity from a feminist perspective by exposing its racist and sexist underpinnings. The novels *Auntie Mame* and *Peyton Place* consider the issue of national identity from the perspective of femininity—masculinity's subordinated "Other." These narratives offer insight as to how the mutually reinforcing images of masculinity and nation also depended upon a particular fictional ideal of womanhood. As it turns out, the female figures in these texts demonstrate how gender is constructed within oppressive power hierarchies and how imposing a feminine ideal on all women ultimately serves to denaturalize femininity.

Because these five narratives do not rehearse the same story about gender and nation, they do not portray a coherent picture of this categorical relationship. Nor do they provide a monolithic view of the interaction between texts, history, and contexts. Together, however, they do tell us something about the powerful investment during the first decade of the Cold War in perpetuating certain configurations of masculinity and femininity and about the difficulty in challenging this investment. At times, these texts make clear the impossibility of performing one's assigned gender identity and expose the anxiety, frustration, and the defensive masquerading of individual subjects who felt compelled to comply with the dominant gender ideologies. In short, these popular texts brought to the fore the ideological crises grounded in representation.

As this study shows, popular narratives perhaps functioned in a compensatory way for fifties audiences, making cultural diversity and "otherness" more palatable and less threatening. For example, *From Here to Eternity* reconciles the hegemonic and rebellious, nonhegemonic males through a "middle management" figure—an enlisted first sergeant who appears to straddle social class and other differences to solidify an all-male community. The film version of *Giant* smoothes over the white Texas rancher's race and class oppres-sion through sentimentality—specifically in scenes of the dynastic family mourning for a Mexican-American war hero or the white patriarch's brown and white grandchildren sharing a playpen. Both novel and film version of *Sayonara* re-present "Japan" as an amalgam of feminine beauty, exoticism, and time-honored traditions, all purportedly signifying a nation amenable and receptive to the cultural penetration of western ideological and economic objectives, which were requisite to the success of American global hegemony. However, the images of harmony, reconciliation, and sentimentality in these several narratives do little to dislodge systematic gender, class, and racial inequities. Conversely, *Auntie Mame* and Grace Metalious's *Peyton Place* refrain from wholesale attempts to compensate for cultural discord and conflict. Instead, they dispel the myth of coherence by bringing to the fore the discursive heterogeneity that was obscured or subordinated by the national preoccupation with Cold War domestic containment.

One would be hard pressed to argue that social protest is made explicit or consistently hard-hitting in postwar best-sellers and films. Their overall tendency, to be sure, is to weave somewhat simple solutions out of complex social threads in their closing pages or scenes. Perhaps the most striking example of this is Michener's *Sayonara*, which attempts to purge white America of its racism, only to retreat from its own test case—miscegenation—by relegating interracial union to the safety of contemplation and memory. Hollywood's version of *Peyton Place* leads viewers to think that if people did forgo gossiping and if mothers listened to their daughters' problems, then the conflicts and inequities of being female in a patriarchal culture would melt away as sure as the spring thaw and apple blossoms will arrive in idyllic Camden, Maine.

However, if the popular novel and film perhaps fell short of being something other than obedient to or complicit with dominant ideologies, this investigation has sought to argue that popular narratives require a closer inspection of their internal fissures and contradictions in terms of the representations of gender. By paying close attention to the historical and cultural contexts in which each of these texts was produced, I have been able to illuminate the multiple network of signifying practices and representational strategies that gives evidence of postwar culture's plurality and conflict. Rather than generating narratives of open protest or explicit politics, these texts tended to offer more oblique signs of difference and counterhegemonic discourses. In the case of Hollywood films, this difference was often made legible in star images, particularly in the gendering of these images.

Pairing the novel with its film version has given this study some critical advantages over previous investigations that have taken either written or visual texts as their objects of study. For one, "reading" the novel through the film and vice versa, as I suggest fifties audiences did, broadens the field of literary inquiry and cultural critique. It allows for an understanding of how reading and viewing audiences could register both the discernible and subtle shifts in how intersections of gender, race, class, and sexuality constructed individual subjectivities as well as images of nation. The similarities and differences made visible by two versions of one basic storyline provides some valuable insights on a variety of representational issues: generic limitations and possibilities, changes in political, social, and historical circumstances, the significance of stardom, censorship, and marketing strategies. Furthermore, the analysis of these paired versions directs attention to the competing and contradictory discourses circulating within postwar culture itself: a single plot alteration—the different conclusions of the novel and film of *Sayonara*, for example—readily accentuates the competing strains within the discourses of gender, race, and class. Michener's Major Gruver illustrates the reluctance of hegemonic males to relinquish their symbolic and material dominance at the apex of the Red Scare, whereas Hollywood's version indicates that Major Gruver feels less obligated to maintain institutional ties between hegemonic males. Regarding the production of gendered subjectivities, being able·

to see the visual representations of gender performances in the films along with the powerful inflections of star personas make all the more discernible the fact that performance and masquerade call into question the authenticity of the thing being represented, namely masculinity or femininity. Structuring each chapter in this comparative approach illustrates more clearly what was privileged, silenced, marginalized, or struggled over in representations produced within 1950s USA. Furthermore, it heightens the sense that what was read and watched everyday—popular culture—contained something more than mere entertainment or escapist value. Without question, popular culture held a central place in constructing social "realities" for its consumers.

This book lays suggestive groundwork for further work in cultural studies through its historically grounded investigation of some of the material conditions and dominant discourses that allowed particular gender ideologies to flourish within a socially contested, representational field. In this sense, more research and analysis needs to be devoted to the reception of the best-seller and film by extending the archival research begun here in this study. This would need to include inquiry into nonmainstream audiences as much as possible. Because best-sellers were largely produced for and consumed by white, middle-class audiences (which very likely functioned either to silence or appropriate the voices of others), my investigation has had little to say about the possible interpretive strategies of nonwhite, lower-class, or gay and lesbian readers and viewers, all of whom were active consumers of popular culture in the 1950s. While I recognize such limitations here, I have tried to be careful about pointing out sites in these narratives that demonstrate how reading is layered, multiple, and unpredictable.

Finally, what I hope to have accomplished in these chapters is to provide some understanding about how popular culture can foster social transformation by calling our attention to larger core issues of textuality and representation. Images of masculinity and femininity were relentlessly reproduced in novels and films of the 1950s as a means of organizing an array of other social coordinates—class, race, ethnicity, sexuality—which, in turn, fed into systematic formulations of family, corporate culture, national security, and foreign policy. The insistence on using gender in such an ideologically precarious manner—as a stabilizing force in an unstable, multifarious social field—made its representation all the more impossible to present as natural and fixed. As these novels and films have shown, gender, while always central to these narratives' ideological and thematic concerns, is inevitably depicted as complex and multiple, as well as manufactured and performed both in compliance and resistance to the cultural ideals of "manliness" and "womanliness."

Notes

1. The Fifties Best-Seller: Texts, Contexts, and Gender Identity in the Postwar Era

1. In 1951 President Eisenhower's economic adviser, Arthur Burns, remarked that "the transformation in the distribution of our national income ... may already be counted as one of the great social revolutions in history." At the end of the decade, sociologist Seymour Lipset declared this transformation had been accomplished: "The fundamental problems of the industrial revolution have been resolved ... [with the] triumph of the democratic social revolution in the West." See Wittner 78.

2. See Rogin's full discussion on communism, motherhood, and Cold War films in *Ronald Reagan: The Movie and Other Episodes in Political Demonology* (Berkeley: U of California P, 1987), 236–71.

3. According to Charles Lee in *The Hidden Public: The Story of the Book of the Month Club*, 44–59, the fact that book clubs positively affected retail stores was sharply contested by book traders and sellers when book clubs started to become highly successful in the late 1920s. Trade store owners claimed that book clubs threatened their livelihood and that they were given preferential treatment by publishing houses. John McCrae, president of E. P. Dutton, led an early crusade against book clubs until he was sued by Book of the Month Club for libel. There was never any concrete financial evidence that book sellers suffered from book clubs; in fact, the book business experienced steady gains in sales and profits, right along with the success of book clubs.

4. In the decades following World War I, book reviews became a regular feature of newspapers and radio programs. Under the editorship of Stuart Pratt Sherman, and later Irita Van Doren, readers could check the *New York Tribune's Books* section for guidance in selecting reading material. Or they could listen to William Lyon Phelps and Alexander Woolcot, two book reviewers achieving near-celebrity status in the thirties, through their regular radio appearances on the "Swift Hour" and "Town Crier," respectively. See Shelley, especially chapters 2 and 6.

5. The phrase "The Group" appeared in a 1958 *Look* magazine article, "The American Male: Why Is He Afraid to Be Different?" which critiqued the decade's organization ethic and the pressure to conform. Conformity and groupism were targeted as the cause of feelings of emasculation, psychic confusion, and anxiety that males of the 1950s seemed to experience. See Leonard 95–104.

6. The Frankfurt School was originally formed in 1923 in Germany as part of the Institute of Social Research at the University of Frankfurt, but it relocated to New York City in 1933 when Hitler came to power. Its most influential members were Theodor Adorno, Max Horkheimer, Leo Löwenthal, Walter Benjamin, and Herbert Marcuse.

7. The following essays published in Rosenberg and White's *Mass Culture in America* summarize the principal concerns of the postwar argument against popular culture: Dwight MacDonald's "A Theory of Mass Culture," 59–73; Clement Greenberg's "Avant-Garde and Kitsch," 98–107; and Irving Howe's "Notes on Mass Culture," 496–503. See also MacDonald's "Masscult and Midcult" in *Against the American Grain*.

8. According to Shelley, the term "middlebrow" was coined most likely by Van Wyck Brooks, who in 1915 called for a "genial middle ground" that would democratize literature by rescuing it from both the elite custodians of highbrow culture and the pragmatic, materialistic lowbrows, who rejected aesthetic productions (xii). The etymology of the "brows" derives from nineteenth-century phrenology, which determined the height of the brow to be a sign of intelligence, an assessment that was implicated in racial differentiation as well. In this context, then, both the creator and consumer of highbrow culture were considered educated, intelligent and Anglo-European. Likewise, during the twenties and thirties, consumers of middlebrow were believed to be fairly discerning and intelligent members of a middle class eager to broaden their knowledge and improve themselves socially (xii).

9. For a fuller discussion of the Gathings Committee, House Select Committee on Current Pornographic Materials, see Davis pp. 218–36. Interestingly, Davis notes none of the paperback books cited at the Committee's hearings had been criticized when they were released in hardback; it was only the paperback editions that brought loud protests (218).

10. Ross uses the word "health" intentionally. In his research on the discourses of mass culture in the 1950s Ross found that much of this discourse was cast in the rhetoric of disease; words like rot, pox, contamination and spreading ooze were common descriptors of popular culture (45–47).

11. The number of films based on best-selling novels increased dramatically in the 1950s, in part, because filmed novels were more likely to be financially successful at a time when film studios experienced declining profits and because they were consistently Oscar contenders. The increase in filmed novels generated scholarly interest in the aesthetic and technical aspects of adapting films. George Bluestone produced one of the earlier full-length studies on film adaptations, *Novels into Film* (1957), in which he examined an array of differences and similarities between literary and film narratives in terms of modes of consciousness, time, space, and what was lost or changed in the process of transforming novel to film. Prior to Bluestone's study, Lester Ashiem produced a doctoral dissertation in 1949 also investigating the transformation from novel to film; one of his findings revealed that filmmakers, motivated by profit margins, tended to increase the love emphasis and use the happy ending, even if it meant rewriting the original story to do so, in order to capture a wider audience. Other scholarship has followed Bluestone's study, including Robert Richardson's *Literature and Film* (1969), Fred Marcus's *Film and Literature: Contrasts in Media* (1971), and John Harrington's *The Rhetoric of Film* (1973). My own interests in the transformation from novel to film overlap some of the concerns of these earlier studies; however, one of the components that distinguishes my study is the focus on how star texts inform and mediate the filmic incarnations of the novel.

12. The Hayes Production Code (named after Will H. Hayes, the first head of the Motion Picture Producers and Distributors of America) was devised in the 1930s as a strategy for fending off state and local governments' censorship of films. Public indignation became increasingly provoked by a looser morality in films and a series of scandals in the film industry itself throughout the 1920s. In response, the Production Code provided a system of self-regulation whereby severe restrictions were placed on what could be seen and heard in film. Prohibitions were in place against such things as nudity, the use of vulgarity, obscenity, or profanity, repellent subjects, brutality, sexual

acts, sexual perversion, miscegenation, white slavery, and drug use. The Production Code remained influential until the mid-1950s when the Supreme Court ruled against studio-owned theaters in an anti-trust suit, which effectively weakened the Production Code Administration's (PCA) power over films. Otto Preminger also challenged the Production Code in 1955 with the release of *The Moon Is Blue* through United Artists without PCA approval. The film's financial success proved that producers could make money without Code approval.

2. Masculinity and Male Power in James Jones's *From Here to Eternity*

1. The film won Oscars for best picture, best screenplay, best director (Fred Zinnemann), best supporting actor (Frank Sinatra), best supporting actress (Donna Reed), sound recording, black and white cinemaphotography, and editing. Deborah Kerr, Burt Lancaster, and Montgomery Clift were nominated for best actress and actors.

2. The phrase "organization man" gained widespread currency in the 1950s with William H. Whyte's description of this collective ideal in *The Organization Man* (1955), an ideal fostered by the shift in postwar America's predominant social ethos from one of individualism and competition, which had shaped national self-image in prewar decades, to an ethos promoting belongingness, conformity, and group life. Sloan Wilson readily captures this postwar ideal in his best-seller, *The Man in the Gray Flannel Suit* (1955), which was made into film in 1956 starring Gregory Peck. Handsome, smartly tailored, white, and upwardly mobile, Peck supplied a visual icon for this hegemonic ideal, what Douglas Brode calls in *Films of the Fifties* "a clearly representational image of modern man of the fifties" (178).

3. The surge of enthusiasm for do-it-yourself projects was the subject of Dwight MacDonald's 1954 essay, "Howtoism," in which he disparages the skyrocketing production and consumption of self-help and how-to books, like the cooking and gardening best-sellers of 1951. Although MacDonald calls these books part of the "great gray mass" of middlebrow fare, he attributes their popularity to a cultural need "to be a good person—in Americanese, a happy and successful person" (*Against* 385). This explanation is in keeping with the organization ethos documented by William H. Whyte and David Riesman's corresponding argument in *The Lonely Crowd* (1950), in which he claims postwar society as a whole was becoming "other-directed" with people's tendency to be sensitive to the expectations and needs of others. Anxiety in the fifties, Riesman argues, arises from worry about popularity. How-to books, in part, may have been a direct response to this anxiety: They were marketed on the basis of their ability to supply answers to almost any social, personal, familial, or technical problem imaginable, which, in turn, fostered outer-directedness and a dependency on or a faith in the soundness of mass-produced advice and communal common sense. MacDonald wryly notes in "Howtoism" that "one sometimes wonders ... whether a number of these problems would perhaps never have arisen to bother us if books had not been written telling us how to solve them" (*Against* 362). The implications of these social trends—organization life, outer-directedness, and how-toism—fueled the "crisis" of masculinity in postwar culture because these trends were believed to be

partly responsible for emasculating the American male.

4. Screenwriter Daniel Taradash's adaptation managed to condense Jones's 861-page novel into two hours by eliminating numerous subplots, characters, explicit sex scenes, and its liberal use of obscenities—shocking even to many novel readers. Taradash also altered the film so that Columbia Pictures could obtain permission from the U.S. Army to shoot on location at Schofield Barracks. Jones's novel presents a scathing attack on military corruption and brutality, practiced or condoned by officers. The film eliminates this critique, including the inhuman, barbarous conditions of the Stockade and Captain Holmes's promotion, despite his inept command of G Company. Angered by these cuts, Jones scoffed: "Columbia Pictures ass-kissed the army so they could shoot the exterior of the film at Schofield Barracks ... without being bothered" (see Bosworth 253). Interestingly, Jones dedicated his best-seller to the United States Army despite his criticism of its practices.

5. Typically, Hollywood's *Eternity* codes "bad" males with physical or personality traits that disqualify them as rightful leaders: the opportunistic Captain Holmes neglects his command and wife; Galovitch's broken English connotes limited intelligence and foreignness; "Fatso" Judson is oafish and overweight. While Company Clerk Leva (Mickey Shaughnessy) is not associated with undemocratic males, he, too, is fat, a sign of his laziness and inefficiency, which serves as a contrast to Warden. Leva, candy bar in hand, is inevitably paired in scenes with Burt Lancaster, whose chiseled physique and alert, brisk manner speaks to the self-control and discipline necessary to lead others. By contrast, the "democratic" males, Warden, Prewitt, and Maggio, form bonds of mutual respect and friendship, have a strong sense of fair play, and possess intense courage in moments of adversity. Notably, too, Lancaster, Clift, and Sinatra do not sport regulation army crewcuts like the "bad" guys but wear their hair slightly longer in keeping with their star images.

6. This and all subsequent references to the novel are from James Jones, *From Here to Eternity* (New York: Charles Scribner and Sons, 1951).

7. *Life* magazine's promotion of the film *From Here to Eternity* features two scenes with Lancaster, which add an extratextual dimension to managing the possibility of his signifying as sexual difference. One shows him in the beach scene, kneeling, his torso erect and knees spread apart over Deborah Kerr's supine body. The other shot prominently foregrounds him in uniform—clenched fists and feral expression—rallying his scattering troops during the attack on Pearl Harbor. Both scenes emphasize his power and superiority: In the first, through his muscular body and visual domination of Karen, the second, in his ability to lead others and bring order to chaos. Again, though, I would argue that the beach shot produces an unstable subject of Lancaster's body, which oscillates between being the subject of sexual activity and object of erotic contemplation. See "Soldier Versus System," *Life* (31 Aug. 1953): 81–83.

8. Laura Mulvey points out that the very (male) act of investigating or interrogating the female "Other" in films is activated as a means of circumventing and compensating for the original trauma of castration, represented by the female body. At the same time, then, this act of investigating exposes both the anxiety produced by this original trauma and the instability of phallic superiority, which is meant to smooth over the trauma. See Mulvey 21.

9. The novel's array of diversity is striking in comparison with the film version, which

leaves only Angelo Maggio as the marker of racial and ethnic differences. Gone from the film are the Jewish soldiers, Bloom, Rosenberry and Ross, whom Warden disparages as "the Jewish problem"; the Native American, "Chief" Choate; the Italian-Americans, Leva and Mazzioli; the callow, gentle "boy," Friday Clark; and the quiet Indiana farm boy, who cracks up under the pressure of prison life. Maylon Stark appears only momentarily in the film as the urbane, friendly adviser warning Warden about Karen Holmes's bad reputation, while in the novel he is a racist, Southern sharecropper's son, whose grim naturalistic view of the world helps to authorize Prewitt's belief in the integrity of the self. Gone are Honolulu's civilian, homosexual males and the socially radical, ex-Wobblie Jack Malloy, who is a kind of guru for Prewitt in the Stockade. Gone is the sharp contrast between the social positions of officers and enlisted men, which effectively eliminates the novel's gesture toward a materialist critique of class difference. Even Jones's underdog "hero," Prewitt, the son of a poor Kentucky coalminer, forced by poverty to go out-on-the-bum, is socially elevated, mainly by the level of sophistication and intensity Montgomery Clift's screen performance and star image brings to his character.

10. No doubt Sinatra's 1952 film, *Meet Danny Wilson*, portraying a nightclub singer's rise to fame through underworld connections, helped to authenticate the negative publicity concerning Sinatra's alleged Mafia connections.

11. Maggio being beaten in the film version of *Eternity* produced an interesting effect other than simply reflecting the vulnerable side of Sinatra's star image. "Maggio" may have helped to revive Sinatra's waning career. Sinatra's popularity had plummeted in the early fifties, in part, because he had severely alienated the press, who apparently violated his "right" to privacy once too often. His display of temper and his physical threats toward reporters were well documented, apparently competing with his romantic, crooner image. Not only did Sinatra alienate reporters, whose refusal to give him press coverage damaged his career, but he alienated fans as well when he left his wife for Ava Gardner. According to Mitch Miller, "By getting stomped to death in that movie, [it was like] he did a public penance for all [the wrongs he had done]. You can chart it. From the day that movie came out, his records began to sell." See Friedwald 219.

12. See Theweliet's full discussion of gender and the formation of the *Freikorps* in *Male Fantasies*. Vol. 2. (Minneapolis: U of Minnesota P, 1989).

13. Cohan's discussion of Montgomery Clift's performance in *Red River* is in *Masked Men: Masculinity and the Movies in the Fifties* 201–20.

3. "Madame Butterfly with a Social Conscience": Gender, Race, and National Identity in James Michener's *Sayonara*

1. Michener's magazine publications on Japan include "Kabuki is a Must for America," *Theatre Arts* (March 1954): 74–75; an article on interracial marriages in *Life* (21 Feb. 1955): 124–41; "Why I Like Japan," *Reader's Digest* (Aug. 1956): 182–86; "Madame Butterfly in Bobby Sox," *Reader's Digest* (Oct. 1956): 21–27; "The Facts about the GI Babies," *Reader's Digest* (March 1954): 5–10; and a book review of Jiro Osaragi's *Homecoming* in *The Saturday Review* (22 Jan. 1955): 26. Between 1955 and 1962,

Michener published four books on Japanese art, including *The Floating World*, featuring Japanese woodblock prints, and *Japanese Prints: From the Early Masters to the Moderns*. In addition to his interest in Japan, he wrote two articles on Korea and one on Thailand for the *Reader's Digest*, "The Way It Is in Korea" (Jan. 1953): 1–6+, and "One Must Respect Korean Culture" (Apr. 1954): 15–19, and "Thailand: Jewel of Asia," (Dec. 1954): 57–66. In "The Sea of the Talented Traveler," *The Saturday Review* (23 Oct. 1954): 47–48, Michener asks, "Why has the Pacific Ocean consistently called forth great writing?" His own answer, which exoticizes and sexualizes the East in language consistent with orientalist and colonialist discourses, suggests the Pacific is a "mysterious and wonderful" place that ignites the imagination of writers and affords them a "sexual holiday" from the stuffy western morality that deeply influenced attitudes toward their writing.

2. *Newsweek*'s review of *Sayonara* was subtitled "Again, the Warm Voice of Asia."

3. The prohibition on U.S. military personnel marrying Japanese women was lifted three times during the occupation but covered only 19 out of the total of 88 months that the ban was in effect. See Michener, "The Facts" 7.

4. *Sayonara* was a top moneymaker for Warner Bros., in addition to garnering nine Academy Award nominations for best picture, director (Joshua Logan), best actor (Marlon Brando), best supporting actor (Red Buttons), best supporting actress (Miyoshi Umeki), best screenplay, cinematography, art/set direction, and sound recording. The film won four Oscars for best supporting actor and actress, art/set direction, and sound recording.

5. Qtd. in Goldman 250.

6. In "Pacific Rim Discourse: The U.S. Global Imaginary in the Late Cold War Years," Christopher Connery describes in further detail the orientalist and binary thinking of the postwar geo-imaginary, which gave shape to economists' and U.S. policy makers' symbolic constructions of Asia, Europe, and North America in the early years of the Cold War. By the mid-1970s, a late capitalist geo-imaginary emerged that was fueled by multinational capitalism and therefore required a nonothering discourse and a "centeredness with no central power" (34).

7. According to McCormick, the Korean War was a boon for Truman, who faced an uphill battle with a fiscally conservative Congress for authorization of funds for NSC-68. Secretary of State Dean Acheson supposedly remarked that "Korea came along and saved us" (98). Not only did the Korean War serve the political purposes of intimidating the USSR and reassuring Japan of military protection, but economically it would benefit the Japanese industry through military expenditures on auto and truck production, subcontracts from high-tech industries, and sale of goods and services to U.S. armed forces stationed in Japan (105).

8. Kelly's reasons for seeking a Japanese wife are rooted in his lower-class status, which precludes him from accessing certain patriarchal privileges and exercising the same degree of power accorded to hegemonic males. By marrying the obliging, submissive Katsumi, Kelly may find both solace from the psychological injury of his own subjugation and empowerment through dominating his wife.

9. This and all subsequent references to the novel are from James A. Michener, *Sayonara* (New York: Random House, 1953).

10. *Sayonara*'s demonizing Anglo-American women is not a separate, but a related practice to the novel's other formulations of "otherness," in terms of gender and race. The

cultural value placed on femininity is contingent upon historical circumstances and how these circumstances intersect with patriarchal interests. As racial others, nonwhite females present a threat to Anglo "purity," but can serve as romantic and/or sexual outlets for white males who fear the "power" of American mothers and their daughters. However, Anglo-American females insure the continuance of "whiteness." The cultural stock in one brand of femininity fluctuates in relation to which category of identity—race or gender—is more privileged at the moment.

11. Although the terms "tolerant, humane, and correct" imply softer, feminine qualities, these qualities can just as easily be considered paternalistic and, therefore, not necessarily feminizing Gruver or the American image. In other words, patriarchy can preserve its gender hierarchy by reforming or transforming itself in response to demands for social, political, or economic changes.

12. Arthur Schlesinger, Jr.'s, *The Vital Center*, became one of the definitive political texts in postwar America advocating centrism and consensus formation as the most viable means of responding to the exigencies of the Cold War. Stating that "compromise is the strategy of democracy" (174), he argues that "the non-Communist left and the non-fascist right must collaborate to keep free society truly free" (209).

13. Although *The Bridges of Toko-Ri* was published in July 1953, six months before the release of *Sayonara*, Michener had actually begun *Sayonara* in 1952 and set it aside to write *Toko-Ri* for *Life* magazine. The intertextuality of the two novels is made apparent in the themes of personal sacrifice and commitment.

14. America's reform agenda for Japan, according to John W. Dower, "rested on the assumption that, virtually without exception, Western culture and its values were superior to those of 'the Orient'" .... "The occupation was in this sense but a new manifestation of the old racial paternalism that historically accompanied the global expansion of the Western powers" (211).

15. For a full discussion on the process of creating Japan's new constitution, see chapter 13, "Japanizing the American Draft," in John W. Dower's *Embracing Defeat*.

16. See "MacArthur: Father and Leader of Postwar Japan," *Catholic World* (July 1951): 246–51; "Japan's Still Under Our Wing," *Business Week* (15 Sept. 1951): 73; "Free Japan: A U.S. Headache," *U.S. News and World Report* (12 Sept. 1952): 29–31; "Japan: Free World Responsibility," *America* (20 Nov. 1954): 203–5.

17. This Department of State report was compiled by John D. Rockefeller, 3rd, who accompanied Ambassador John Foster Dulles to Japan in January 1951 for the conclusion of the Peace Treaty. Rockefeller was asked to devise ways to promote cultural cooperation between Japan and the United States.

18. A. Grove Day, Michener's colleague, friend, and biographer, states that Michener was driven by the underlying belief that "Asia must inevitably become more important to the U.S. than Europe" so that a greater understanding of Asian culture was needed (70). In addition to being Michener's "love letter" to Japan, Day calls the novel "a warm exemplum on Michener's perennial theme of universal equality, of love as the catalyst of interracial tranquillity" (79, 82).

19. Paul Lyons, in "Pacific Scholarship, Literary Criticism, and Touristic Desire: The Specter of A. Grove Day," provides an insightful discussion of how western travel and exploration writing of the Pacific not only authenticate a certain "history" of the Pacific for touristic consumption, but also "encode and legitimate the aspirations of economic expansion and empire" (58). Writers, such as A. Grove Day and James

Michener, cast a "one-way gaze" on the East in their scholarship and touristic writing, which was perhaps a well-meaning effort to use reading and writing to unify East and West, but, at the same time, functioned as "a way of taking possession without subjugation and violence" (50).

20. The Madame Butterfly tale has circulated in various genres in western art and culture since the late nineteenth century. Perhaps best known through Puccini's *Madama Butterfly*, it has been authorized as having "truth" value by virtue of its status as high cultural humanism. The basic story involves a love affair between a white male and an Asian female, whom he eventually abandons to return home and marry a white woman. Meanwhile, his nonwhite wife, now the mother to his child, pines for her western lover until she realizes he is never returning; she then commits suicide, leaving her child to be adopted by her lover and his white wife. Gina Marchetti argues that the components of the Butterfly tale manifest themselves in the symbolic representation of gender and nationality: The Butterfly character's suicide "represents the necessary sacrifice of all people of color to assure Western domination. In addition she provides a model for all women, white and nonwhite ... [in that] romantic love promises compensation for the loss of themselves" (79).

21. Although Hana-ogi does not commit suicide, Michener's incarnation adds the double suicide of Joe Kelly and Katsumi. When Kelly receives orders to return to the States, he and Katsumi commit suicide. However, because Kelly is aware that the process of amending the laws is under way, their suicides seem unaccounted for in the narrative. By displacing personal tragedy onto the secondary characters, *Sayonara* purportedly allows the main protagonists to represent a positive turn in East-West relations, and, at the same time, gives the upper classes the credit for seeing the consequences of their "illicit" love through.

22. See Smith, J. and Worden 26–27 +, and Worden 38–39 +.

23. Takarazuka actresses remained celibate and lived in dormitories owned by the theater company; their fans were almost exclusively female admirers.

24. While *Sayonara* presented the fictional containment of Japanese female "voices," illustrated by Gruver's defusing the political impact of *Swing Butterfly*, what readers could not know, given the Japanese government's secrecy, was the material reality of many Japanese women, who were doubly silenced during the occupation. As a 27 October 1995 newspaper article makes painfully clear, thousands of U.S. servicemen dispatched to Japan after the surrender caused widespread fears of rape and sexual abuse of Japanese women by G.I.s. In order to establish a "sexual dike to protect the chastity of Japanese women" the Japanese government asked "patriotic women" to sacrifice themselves as "comfort women" for "sex-starved" American soldiers. More often than not, these women—some 55,000—were those without means or other options, being war widows, homeless, or too poor to feed their families. Clearly, patriarchal attitudes of the Japanese allowed, indeed insisted upon, the exploitation of these "comfort women," as much as the assumptions by U.S. military personnel that they were entitled to the "spoils" of war. See Albany, NY, *Times Union*, "Japan Set Up Brothels" 27 Oct. 1995: A4. See also John W. Dower's *Embracing Defeat*, 122–39.

25. Even Marlon Brando, so intent on *Sayonara* making "some points about racial intolerance," was not exempt from Hollywood's practice of role segregation. In *Teahouse of the August Moon* (1956), Brando was transformed into the Okinawan interpreter Sakini through a racist cosmetology, which involved creating an epithantic

eyefold; giving him a cheesy, slick, black wig; and darkening his skin. Brando produced racial difference through noncosmetic effects as well by using pidgin English and stylizing gestures and body movements to approximate Asian mannerisms. Placing Brando in this role was consistent with the casting of white males in roles that were either sympathetic to Asians or that place them in positions of gaining "fame, fortune, heroism, and pride" (Wong 47). Accordingly, Brando's Sakini is shrewd, wily, and sympathetic in his efforts to foil American plans to westernize Okinawa. Paradoxically, while the film purports to critique cultural imperialism, its representations of Okinawans are condescending, and while Brando's Sakini is roguish and likable, his impersonation resonates with a long lineage of blackface performers.

26. Marlon Brando was not the only one to object to the novel's ending. In 1954, Michener was introduced to Mari Yoriko Sabusawa, a Japanese-American who had been in an internment camp during WWII. One of Sabusawa's initial remarks to him was that she did not care for the ending of *Sayonara* because interracial marriage need not always spell tragedy for the lovers—prophetic words, because Sabusawa was to become Michener's second wife within the next year. See Day 25.

27. "Variation on the Puccini Caper," *The New Yorker* 89.

28. The press later claimed Anna Kashfi was not Indian at all, but was Joan O'Callaghan, born to English parents and raised in Calcutta. Kashfi insisted that her parents were Indian and that after her father Devi Kashfi died, her mother married William O'Callaghan. Brando, stunned by these reports, said, "I never doubted she was a Hindu" (Thomas 140–41).

29. As Barthes describes, Bunraku puppets are three to five feet high, each moved in the performance by three visible men, who surround it, support it, and accompany it. Musicians and speakers are set behind the puppets, again visible. The art and the labor are exhibited to the audience, which divides the spectacle between speech, gesture, and music, and the illusion of totality originating in the body—which is offered in western theater—is dispelled (*Empire* 54).

30. For Cohan's discussion on Brando's performativity in *Streetcar*, see *Masked Men* 243–49.

31. See *Saturday Review*, Rev. of *Viva Zapata!* 9 Feb. 1952: 25; and *New Republic*, Rev. of *Viva Zapata!* 25 Feb. 1952: 21.

4. "Slipping from under Me Like a Loose Saddle": The Degeneration of Dynasty in Edna Ferber's *Giant*

1. Christopher P. Wilson maintains that Ferber's own career signified in a manner similar to her fictional heroines, in that her literary trademark became narratives of women "battling the odds in a man's world" (57).

2. *Giant* won an Academy Award for best director (George Stevens). The film was nominated for best picture, best screenplay, best actor (Rock Hudson and James Dean, posthumously), best supporting actress (Mercedes McCambridge), art and set direction, music, costuming, and editing.

3. A few Texans continued to hold a grudge. During on-location filming near Marfa, Texas, some cast members received threatening letters, saying things like, "Get out of

Texas. Get out or you'll be shot." A security guard was posted at the production site, but nothing ever came of the threats. See Parker 104.

4. See Biskind 285–95.

5. In Simon Watney's discussion of Rock Hudson, whom he calls a "gentle giant," he argues that Hudson's brand of masculinity did not coincide with orthodox male identity in fifties films; rather he signified sensitivity and a softer masculinity, despite his large stature (88).

6. This and all subsequent references to the novel are from Edna Ferber's *Giant* (Garden City, NY: Doubleday & Co., Inc., 1952).

7. In his review of *Giant*, John Barkham refers to the new "species" of wealthy Texans as *Texacanus vulgaris* (4).

8. Spindletop was the first major oil gusher discovered in 1901 near Beaumont, Texas. No minor discovery, Spindletop flowed at 75,000 barrels per day, inaugurating the Texas oil boom and a riotous period of investment and wildcatting. See Yergin 82–85.

9. Ferber set the Lynnton home in Virginia perhaps to draw comparisons between the ingrained racism of Southerners, which does not seem to exist in the liberal Lynnton family, and racial injustice toward Mexican Americans. Hollywood moved the Lynnton home to Maryland, one state from the Confederacy, perhaps saving Elizabeth Taylor from having to effect a heavier southern accent. The film prominently features the Lynntons' black servants, especially the dignified Jefferson, who appears attached to the family and is seen sharing snapshots of the Benedicts with the Lynnton parents. This is in obvious contrast to Reata's furtive, silent Mexican American servants, obscured in distant camera shots. Race and class differences are muted in the Lynnton house by giving servants dignity of place and inclusion in the family. Leslie takes this attitude with her to Texas in the film, but the effect is that she does not work to level class differences, which fall out along racial lines, but to eliminate extreme poverty.

10. See Ehrenreich 30–41.

11. Inexplicably, the film reduces Reata's two and a half million acres to a "mere" 595,000 acres. In actuality, one of the largest working ranches in Texas at this time was the King ranch of about one million acres—an area larger than Rhode Island.

12. Qtd. Pierre and Renée Gosset, "Life in America—As Seen by Visiting Europeans," *U.S. News and World Report* (1 Jan. 1954): 104.

13. Ferber's novel introduces an alternative historical perspective about vaqueros, not included in the film, which corresponds to historian J. Frank Dobie's 1931 account of vaquero life on Texan ranches (289–93). Dobie recorded what Ferber recreates fictionally, that a feudal order structured ranch life and inscribed the vaqueros' positions within it: They bought their supplies from a ranch commissary, they voted as the ranch owner advised them, and very often regarded the ranch as a unit of citizenship, much like one would consider himself a part of a town.

14. Ferber may have modeled the circumstances of Angel's death after a real-life incident involving Mexican-American Felix Longoria, who was killed in action in the Philippines but refused funeral services in Texas because he was nonwhite. On hearing this, Senator Lyndon B. Johnson notified Mrs. Longoria that he would arrange burial for Felix in Arlington National Cemetery. See "Texas Tackles the Race Problem" (23).

15. My point that *Giant*'s critique of race prejudice against Mexican Americans referenced

the national problem of race relations between blacks and whites has an ironic aspect to it. According to Carloz Munoz, Jr., many middle-class Mexican American activists in the 1950s were unwilling to identify themselves as nonwhite or to promote a nonwhite racial identity for their people, but instead advanced an identity of Mexican Americans as a white ethnic group. This distancing from black Americans and, for some, from their own African-American backgrounds, was a move to avoid being categorized as people of color, thus experiencing even harsher forms of discrimination. By presenting themselves as nonracial, Mexican Americans hoped to deflect further anti-Mexican sentiment. See Munoz 47–51. By the same token, John Rechy reports that lower-class Mexican Americans living in the barrios had "no greater object of contempt than a Mexican American who 'passes for' or claims to be 'Spanish,'" (212).

16. *Pachucos* often were considered troublemakers within their own communities for giving their people a bad name. However, when a group of *pachucos* were attacked in a Los Angeles movie theater by white sailors and marines on leave during World War II, many older Mexican Americans began to take "greaser stomping" more seriously. Although the servicemen started the violence, the *pachucos* were arrested for inciting a riot—called the "zoot suit riot," because *pachucos'* zoot suits (the signature style of certain Mexican-American youths) were ripped off in the attack. Only after the Mexican government protested the discrimination against the *pachucos* and the leniency toward the servicemen did U.S. officials address the situation more equitably, mainly because U.S. officials worried that Mexico, in protest, might not renew agreements to allow temporary field workers into California at harvest time. See Machado 83.

17. The collective efforts of nonwhite minorities after World War II were largely due to race and ethnic mixing in the armed services and demographic changes brought on by postwar industrial expansion, which brought minorities en masse to urban centers where they encountered mainstream culture for the first time. Mexican Americans formed social and political organizations soon after the war's end, including the Veterans' American G.I. Forum, the Mexican American Political Association, and the Political Association of Spanish Speaking Peoples. The League of United Latin American Citizens worked for good education, housing, and social services. See Munoz 35–50. The more radical Asociacion Nacional Mexico-Americana, which stressed Popular Front tactics and labor union activities, was also formed during the Cold War. See Garcia 199–227.

18. The manner in which Jett acquires "Little Reata" underscores Bick's brutality. Jett claims his father mysteriously disappeared on Reata while hunting for food to feed his eight, poverty-stricken, motherless children. Soon after, Bick presented Jett with a small piece of hard scrabble land to compensate for the family's loss. Jett implies, however, that the land may have been to prevent Jett from asking questions about his father's disappearance.

19. My argument here is indebted to Steven Cohan's reading of *Red River*, in which he details how gender meanings of the cowboys who worked on ranches like Tom Dunson's were organized on the basis of the ranch hierarchy. Cowboys not only occupied a different economic position, but they occupied an ambiguous gender position—"not properly male"—because they were socially and economically powerless. Significantly, the gendering of an economic category of identity, according to Cohan, tends to displace any homoerotic component of the cowboy/cattleman

dyad. A similar dynamic appears to emerge in the first half of the film *Giant* between Bick and Jett: Bick's masculinity, like cattleman Tom Dunson's, depends on maintaining his authority over subordinate males like Jett Rink through a particular economic structure that produces a gender distinction between boy and man. See *Masked Men* 208–20.

20. It is possible to imagine that Bick may find Jett's status as "adult boy" enviable. Despite his financial deprivation, Jett has not had the burden of responsibilities that have been placed on Bick; nor has Jett's life been foreordained since birth, like Bick's. Bick has had to forgo his youth and the opportunity to have dreams and adventures by virtue of his being a Benedict. Jett has been able to have the impulsive, unrestrained, and reckless life of a boy.

21. Alexander 269–70.

22. See for example, Roth 62–65, and Scullin 120–24+.

23. Richard Meyer argues that Rock Hudson functioned in an analogous way to his female counterparts, particularly in Douglas Sirk's melodramas. Referring to *Written on the Wind*, Meyer states, "As in *Magnificent Obsession*, the dysfunction and desire of the female character are here opposed to the immobile, immaculate masculinity of Rock Hudson" .... "It was Rock Hudson's very 'immovability' which fractured his female companion into sickness and desire, which, in effect, 'split' her into the subject of melodrama" (271).

5. Contesting the Feminine Mystique: Gender Performance and Female Identity in Patrick Dennis's *Auntie Mame*

1. This quote was reprinted on the inside cover page of the 1956 Popular Library paperback edition of *Auntie Mame*. Despite its hyperbole, the either-or consequence (total revolution or escapism through laughter) suggests that a culture's ideologies are embedded in what it finds humorous and that the novel itself contains a range of potential meanings for its readers.

2. This and all other references to the novel are from Patrick Dennis, *Auntie Mame* (New York: Vanguard Press, 1955).

3. *Auntie Mame* received six Academy Award nominations: Best actress (Rosalind Russell), best supporting actress (Peggy Cass), best picture, art direction, editing, and cinematography.

4. Patrick Dennis was a pseudonym for Edward Everett Tanner III, who, at the time of *Auntie Mame*'s publication, was a promotions manager for *Foreign Relations* magazine, living in Manhattan with his wife and children. In a *Time* interview he said he regarded writing as an "after-hours prank" ("Best-seller Revisited" 74), but he eventually left his full-time job to write. Before his success with *Auntie Mame*, Tanner published two other books—*House Party* and *Oh, What a Wonderful Wedding*—under the pseudonym Virginia Rowans. He also collaborated as Patrick Dennis with two other writers on *The Pink Hotel* with Dorothy Erskine and *Guestward Ho!* With Barbara Hooton. Reviewers of *Auntie Mame* were intent on finding some biographical connection between Patrick Dennis and "Patrick Dennis." They found that Tanner had a fairly traditional background, but, like his fictional "Patrick Dennis," he had grown up in

Chicago, the son of a stockbroker and, like Auntie Mame, was billed as a "socialite." A subsequent issue of *Time* likened Tanner to Britain's P. G. Wodehouse, saying "his Mame-brained characters with their vestigial memories of wealth and lineage are certainly kin to those of the great master of total piffle" ("Hairy" 106).

5. Rosalind Russell was the only member of the film cast who had leading star status. She was joined by Forrest Tucker (Beauregard Burnside), Fred Clark (Mr. Babcock), Coral Browne (Vera Charles), Roger Smith (Patrick Dennis) and Hollywood newcomer Peggy Cass (Agnes Gooch). While Clark and Tucker were well known character actors, neither was considered a leading man.

6. These phrases appeared in the *Columbus Citizen* (cited on the inside cover of the 1956 Popular Library edition of *Auntie Mame*); *Time*, "New Plays" 71; and *Look* "Wonderful Wizardry" 68, respectively.

7. According to Marjorie Rosen, the following 1960s films revived "Mom": "the malevolent, controlling, fascistic mother and wife, Angela Lansbury, in *The Manchurian Candidate* (1962). Selfish and irritable Shelley Winters, responsible for causing daughter Elizabeth Hartman's blindness in *A Patch of Blue* (1965); Shelley, again a whining windbag in *Wild in the Streets* (1970). Ruth Gordon protecting sonny boy from Tuesday Weld in *Lord Love a Duck* (1966), grandiosely observing, 'In our family we don't divorce our men—we bury them.' Bette Davis as Mum in *The Anniversary* (1968) verbally dueling with her cheeky son's fiancée for the boy's obedience" (346).

8. Theater critic Ethan Mordden also read *Auntie Mame* as an escapist narrative, calling the stage production "the Peter Pan of the post-war era" (220).

9. Arnold Gesell, a pioneer in the scientific investigations of child development in the 1930s, was well respected by psychologists, parents, and teachers through the 1950s. Founder of the Gesell Institute, he is largely responsible for the establishment of norms of behavior for children at each successive stage of their development. He also promoted the ideology of "permissiveness" in child rearing, popularized by the renowned Dr. Benjamin Spock.

10. Interestingly, the 1956 Popular Library paperback edition changed "pack of Jews" to "pack of Latins."

11. In the sequel *Around the World with Auntie Mame*, Patrick is a paragon of 1950s hegemonic masculinity: the man-in-the-gray-flannel-suit. He and wife Pegeen live in a suburban development, lampooned as "Verdant Greens, a community of two hundred houses in four styles." Patrick commutes daily to his job, as an ad man, no less, a purveyor of marketable, consumable images. His life has become as predictable and staid as the *Reader's Digest*, which everyone in Verdant Greens "swears by." Recalling his aunt's dictum, "Live, live, live. Life Is a Banquet and most poor suckers are starving to death," this is clearly not what Mame would have envisioned for her nephew.

12. I am aware of the contradiction in comparing Mame's "liberatory" methods of parenting with Mr. Babcock's. Mame's notions of child rearing have an affinity with pop-Freudian psychology, which reinforced patriarchal thinking. However, I take Mame's position to be one that also threatens and subverts the normative thinking of the fifties and one that seeks to expose Patrick to difference rather than elitist strictures. Furthermore, Ralph Devine's emphasis on Freudian sexual development and repression is also satirized in the novel.

13. See, for example, Talcott Parsons and Robert F. Bales, *Family, Socialization and Interaction Process* (New York: The Free Press, 1955).

14. In the novel, the description of the cross-dressers is as follows: "The man looked like a woman, and the woman, except for her tweed skirt, was almost a perfect Ramon Navarro" (13). Present-day readers cannot miss the implications here for recognizing that sexual identities are constructed through performance: the image of a double impersonation in a woman masquerading as a (gay) man, who had masqueraded as a straight, romantic male lead in silent screen performances.

15. Holmlund does not limit the application of these terms to any one particular theoretical view of masquerade. For example, "putting on" can apply to a Lacanian model of masquerade as an anxiety-ridden attempt to hide the lack of the phallus; or it can refer to Joan Riviere's notion that "masculine" females masquerade to hide the possession of the phallus; Holmlund also uses it to explain a politically motivated use of disguise, as with Algerian women's veils (217–19). My use of Holmlund's terms is in keeping with Judith Butler's theory of gender as a series of corporeal significations. Therefore, while "putting on," "stepping out," or "dressing up" gloss different contexts and links to power, I also mean them to refer to the variations of bodily enactments.

16. Accounts of female sexuality in the 1950s were based on Freudian, which held sway in the psycho-medical community, particularly in influential accounts such as Marynia Farnham and Ferdinand Lundberg's *Modern Woman: The Lost Sex*, and Helene Deutsch's *The Psychology of Women*. According to these theorists, the vaginal orgasm was evidence of mature or "normal" sexuality in women, while clitoral orgasm signaled a woman's rejection of her femininity. The result of such thinking, according to Ehrenreich and English in *For Her Own Good*, was to provide women with another experience of powerlessness and masochism because vaginal sexuality was simply another way to subjugate women to the penis (272). See also Miller and Nowak 157–59.

17. In *Films in Review*, Page Cook opens his review of Lucille Ball's *Mame* with a paean to Russell's acting in the 1958 film, later calling Russell "the *real*, one and only Auntie Mame" ("The Sound Track" 296). Of Angela Lansbury, he writes, "in playing Mame [she] never posed a serious threat of eradicating the memory of Rosalind Russell"; of Ball, Cook says, "the filmization of *Mame* was foredoomed by the casting of Lucille MacGillicuddy Ricardo (Ball)" (295). Pauline Kael's review of Ball's *Mame* in *The New Yorker* was equally damning; like Cook, Kael evokes the memory of Rosalind Russell, finding Ball solely wanting in Russell's sophistication, energy, youth, and flair (122).

18. *Wonderful Town* was a remake of the 1942 film *My Sister Eileen*, for which Russell received her first Oscar nomination for best actress.

19. In Richard T. Jordan's chronical of the Auntie Mame phenomenon, *But Darling, I'm Your Auntie Mame*, he states that Director Morton Da Costa flatly denies Russell's claim that she and Da Costa made extensive revisions to Lawrence and Lee's script and that Da Costa was Russell's own hand-picked choice for director (32, 64).

20. See "Comic Spirit" 40; and Hyams 20, respectively.

21. Arthur Bell, Michael Bronski, and Eric Myers have offered another perspective on audience identification in their noting the importance of Russell's performance for gay audience members. Theatre critic Bell, in his eulogy after Russell's death, points out "there was both strength and vulnerability, both masculinity and femininity in almost

every part Roz played. Unwittingly, she represented liberation: not only women's liberation, but, in some strange, odd way, gay liberation before there was such a thing" (119). Bronski, claims that "*Auntie Mame* may have been the last extreme in placing a hidden gay sensibility upon the Broadway stage. (It was *very* extreme ... Rosalind Russell in her Travis Banton outfits looked more like a drag queen than an eccentric woman)" (122). The narrative itself appealed to gay audiences because it emphasized "acting different and acting out." Bronski rightly states that audiences were diverse and brought a variety of perspectives and readings to a performance. Furthermore, since few, if any, positive images of homosexuality existed in mainstream culture in the 1950s, Bronski's calling attention to how and where gay audience members located such images adds to an understanding of how marginalized groups used popular culture in counterhegemonic ways to meet their own needs. In Eric Myers's recent biography on author Patrick Dennis, he claims, "Homosexuals immediately warmed to the character of Auntie Mame, and for good reason: she was the essence of camp, and this was that first time that elusive component was successfully distilled and introduced into mainstream American literature. While British wits ... had already camped up their work, no American novelist had bothered or dared to until Pat [Dennis]" (106–7).

22. Rosalind Russell toured with the Broadway production of *Bell, Book and Candle* in 1950, a play about three witches, which Michael Bronski also notes contained an obvious homosexual subtext: "If it was impossible for gay people to write openly about themselves, they would find other ways to express their experiences on stage" (119).

6. "Damned and Banned": Female Sexuality in Grace Metalious's *Peyton Place*

1. Noted Hemingway scholar Carlos Baker did find merit in *Peyton Place*, casting Metalious as a "sister-in-arms," along with renowned small-town chroniclers Sherwood Anderson, Edmund Wilson, John O'Hara, and Sinclair Lewis, against the "false fronts and bourgeois pretensions of allegedly respectable communities" (Baker 4). More often, though, reviewers dissuaded the public from reading the novel. The *Library Journal* pronounced it "rampant with general disagreeableness" (Rev. of *Peyton Place*, 15 Sept. 1956): 1993. The *New York Herald Tribune* said it read like "a tabloid version of life" (Feld 8), and the *Christian Herald*, declaring it "quite beyond redemption," maintained "a novel so obscene should neither have been written nor published" (Zolotow 38). The *Catholic World* stated, "This novel is one of the cheapest, most blatant attempts in years to present the most noxiously commonplace in ideas and behavior in the loose and ill-worn guise of realistic art" (Rev. of *Peyton Place*, Nov. 1956: 152).

2. For a full discussion of Grace Metalious's literary career, her relationships with family, New Hampshire neighbors, the publishing world, and Hollywood, and treatment of her life and work in the press, see Emily Toth's informative biography, *Inside Peyton Place: The Life of Grace Metalious* (Garden City, NY: Doubleday and Co., Inc., 1981).

3. Best-seller chronicler Alice Payne Hackett reports by the mid-1960s *Peyton Place* ranked

as the top best-selling fictional work and, if nonfiction titles were counted, as the fourth all-time best-seller (12).

4. *Peyton Place* received Academy Award nominations for best picture, best director (Mark Robson), best actress (Lana Turner), best supporting actress (Diane Varsi and Hope Lange), best supporting actor (Arthur Kennedy and Russ Tamblyn), best screenplay (John Michael Hayes), and cinematography (William Mellor).

5. Andrew Ross's research on the postwar discourse of mass culture shows that the cultural gatekeepers often couched the effects of mass culture on art and civilization in the rhetoric of disease. This rhetoric was part of the "hysterical discourses that contributed to the Cold War culture of germaphobia" (45). Intellectuals, who were invested in containing the "threat" of mass culture, took on a new public role as self-appointed "inspectors of the national cultural health" (51).

6. The phrase "damned and banned" appeared on the cover of the 1957 Dell paperback edition of *Peyton Place*.

7. See M. C. Boyle, "Which Are You First of All, Wife or Mother?" *Parents Magazine* Aug. 1955: 34–35+, and C. Foster, "Rexalls for a Happy Marriage." *Parents Magazine* June 1956: 32–33+, respectively.

8. See D. Carnegie, "How to Help Your Husband Succeed." *Better Homes and Gardens* Apr. 1955: 24+.

9. As early as 1928, sociologist Ernest Groves posited that the ideal of companionate marriage was concomitant with the fear that the institution of marriage was falling apart. The availability of birth control and increasing independence for women in the 1920s appeared to threaten the stronghold marriage had over containing women sexually and economically; thus, in order to make marriage more attractive to women, sex became a much more important aspect of the husband-wife relationship. See d'Emilio and Freedman 266–67.

10. The goal of achieving sexual compatibility was, for women, perhaps one of the most oppressive notions that came out of the postwar marriage manuals. As Benita Eisler points out, the "burden" of achieving mutual pleasure, paradoxically, fell on the husband. Marriage manuals, which flourished in the 1950s, were "addressed almost exclusively to men," who were advised to assume the role of "teacher" in "educat[ing] his wife one step at a time, in the art of joyous mating" (143). Male initiative and direction, then, circumscribed sexual "permissiveness" for women, more or less. Furthermore, the sign of sexual compatibility was the simultaneous orgasm, meaning vaginal orgasm for women. Derived from Freudian psychoanalysis, "mature" or "adult" female sexuality was defined as a woman's relinquishing clitoral orgasm in favor of obtaining satisfaction through the mythic vaginal orgasm. What was purportedly a liberatory idea of female entitlement to sexual satisfaction could easily become for many women an imprisonment in frustration and denial of pleasure.

11. One of the most important findings of Alfred Kinsey's 1953 report on female sexuality was his discrediting Freudian theory by asserting the importance of the clitoris rather than the centrality of the vagina in achieving orgasm. Not only is the vaginal orgasm a "biological impossibility," said Kinsey, due to the insensitivity of the vaginal wall, but "this question is one of considerable importance because much of the literature and many of the clinicians ... have expended considerable effort trying to teach their patients to transfer 'clitoral responses' into 'vaginal responses'"; these efforts have led to thousands of women feeling "much disturbed" by their failure to

do so (584).

12. This and all subsequent references to the novel are from Grace Metalious, *Peyton Place* (New York: Julian Messner, Inc., 1956).

13. In subsequent printings of the novel, the name "Tomas Makris" was changed to "Mike Rossi" after an acquaintance of Metalious—Thomas Makris—filed a law suit for $100,000, charging the author's use of his name had caused him mental pain, suffering, and anguish. Metalious insisted the name Makris was a common Greek surname, one she had borrowed from the name of a diner. The case was eventually settled out of court.

14. "Mrs. Someone" is a phrase Brett Harvey uses in her oral history of women in the 1950s to describe the investment women had in marriage and motherhood as opposed to their pursuit of careers or other forms of self-fulfillment (68).

15. In *For Her Own Good*, Barbara Ehrenreich and Deirdre English maintain that women who presently support a conservative, neoromanticist ideology do so in part because they view the alternatives to the breadwinner ethic as threatening. A "sexual free marketplace" threatens them with the loss of husbands and incomes. Without the means to be self-supporting or enter the job market and without being able to depend upon husbands' incomes, many women will find themselves much worse off financially. These fears were very likely present in the 1950s, as well, when the ideology of male breadwinning prevailed (319–20).

16. I use the word "rebellion" cautiously in thinking about postwar teens' rejection of mainstream values regarding sexuality. Sex was being produced by and for market capitalism, which makes problematic any bold claims that teens either had full control over the terms of this "rebellion" or were, in fact, producing any significant opposition to hegemonic structures. The commodification of sex in teen culture did not necessarily guarantee that sex was more liberatory, given the fact that in a market economy, the production of sex for consumption may have resulted in an alternative kind of disciplining of sexuality, particularly female sexuality.

17. Adult readers, conversely, could identify with Connie's anxieties about raising a teenage girl. Parents were turning to a cadre of media "experts" who offered advise on coping with teenagers in articles such as "How to Handle Your Teenage Daughter," *Cosmopolitan* (Sept. 1955): 112–17; "The Fearful Aspect of Too-Early Dating," *Good Housekeeping* (April 1956): 60–61+; and "Counsel and Comfort for Troubled Parents," *Parents Magazine* (Feb. 1956): 40–41+.

18. In her analysis of the television series, *Peyton Place*, and the single girl phenomenon of the 1960s, Mary Beth Haralovich offers an intriguing perspective on the single girl, arguing that this figure may have produced a different economy of desire, specifically, a female homosociality. Images of the "single girl" as professionally savvy, successful, sexy, and beautiful offered female consumers a sense of female agency and a form of self-validation and expectation of femininity through the approval of other women, apart from male opinion.

19. Film promoters did not hesitate to capitalize on the novel's sensational impact in order to draw moviegoers to the theater. As if hinting the film had something to hide, the movie trailer plastered large, bold-lettered messages over scenes from the film: "AT LAST IT'S ON THE SCREEN," "THE TOWN EVERYONE IS TALKING ABOUT," "IT'S ALL HERE FOR EVERYONE TO SEE." This sales pitch not only misrepresented the film's laundering of the novel, but it also recirculated the novel's

"badness." What filmgoers actually saw on the screen was suitable enough to earn an 'A' rating by the Catholic Church's Legion of Decency. See Rev. of *Peyton Place*, dir. Mark Robson, *Variety* 18 Dec. 1957: 6.

20. Norman Page and his mother are two characters that appear to be drawn from an intersection of fifties pop Freudianism and Philip Wylie's stereotypical "Mom," whose overbearing treatment and emotional and sexual possessiveness toward her son "creates" his homosexuality. Evelyn Page's frequent administering of enemas to Norman—partly her own sexual pleasure, according to Doc Swain—seems to be at the crux of Norman's being a "sissy," who has difficulty even fantasizing about sex with Allison; his budding "perversion" is seemingly confirmed when he strangles Hester Goodale's cat in a moment of hysteria and horror at witnessing a married couple having oral sex. When Norman is drafted during WW II, he purposely shoots himself in the foot—a symbolic castration?—to obtain a discharge, at which time he returns home to his mother, who insists he use a crutch and wear fake medals to present himself as a hero. His relationship with Allison ceases to exist after high school. Notably, in Hollywood's version, Norman is transformed into the sweet boy next door, who becomes a heroic paratrooper in the war.

21. According to one tabloid smear, when Lex Barker was away filming on location, Lana allegedly "had an affair with a French actor, George Sorel, and that Monsieur Sorel had been locked in her bedroom for three weeks. Barely given enough nourishment, they said, he could put up no fight when Barker returned and threw him bodily out of the house" (qtd. in Morella and Epstein 162).

22. According to media accounts of 4 April 1958, Turner and Stompanato were quarreling violently while Cheryl was in the house. Lana refused to continue paying his gambling debts, and Stompanato was angry because she wanted to break off their relationship and to avoid being seen with him in public. Because Stompanato presumably had Mob connections, Turner, conscious of her star reputation, was reluctant to be linked with him. See Morella and Epstein 167–206.

23. The publicity Varsi received in conjunction with the filming of *Peyton Place* and afterward described her in terms similar to the young Marlon Brando and Montgomery Clift: Called the "new promising talent," she defied Hollywood tradition, refusing glamour parties and nightclub hopping—precisely the opposite of Turner's entrance into stardom. The twenty-year-old Varsi was intensely private, refusing to speak publicly about her two marriages and her two-year-old son. When not working, she dressed in bag dresses and heavy stockings or blue jeans and tee-shirts. "It's pretty obvious what kind of girl I am," she said of herself. "I don't go to parties, I don't wear make-up or fancy clothes, I don't have dates because there's nobody I really like" ("Girl Who Walks" 91). See also Laitin and "Star with a Strange Horizon."

24. Butler discusses the subtle, but highly significant, difference between gender mimesis and gender performance in "Lana's Imitation," a complex, insightful investigation of Turner's subversive performativity in *Imitation of Life* (1959), her next film after *Peyton Place*.

Works Cited

Primary Works

Novels:

Dennis, Patrick. *Auntie Mame*. New York: Vanguard Press, 1955.

Ferber, Edna. *Giant*. Garden City, NY: Doubleday and Co., Inc., 1952.

Jones, James. *From Here to Eternity*. New York: Charles Scribner and Sons, 1951.

Metalious, Grace. *Peyton Place*. New York: Julian Messner, Inc., 1956.

Michener, James. *Sayonara*. New York: Random House, 1953.

Films:

Auntie Mame. Dir. Morton Da Costa. Perf. Rosalind Russell, Forrest Tucker, Coral Browne, Peggy Cass. Warner Bros., 1958.

From Here to Eternity. Dir. Fred Zinnemann. Perf. Burt Lancaster, Frank Sinatra, Montgomery Clift, Deborah Kerr. Columbia, 1953.

Giant. Dir. George Stevens. Perf. Rock Hudson, Elizabeth Taylor, James Dean. Warner Bros., 1956.

Peyton Place. Dir. Mark Robson. Perf. Lana Turner, Lee Philips, Diane Varsi, Hope Lange. 20th Century–Fox, 1957.

Sayonara. Dir. Joshua Logan. Perf. Marlon Brando, Miyoshi Umeki, Miiko Taka, Red Buttons. Goetz Pictures–Pennebaker, 1957.

Secondary Works

The Adventures of Marco Polo. Dir. Archie Mayo. Perf. Gary Cooper, Sigrid Gurie, Basil Rathbone. MGM, 1938.

"Again, the Warm Voice of Asia." *Newsweek*, 25 Jan. 1954: 92–95.

Ager, Cecelia. "Brando in Search of Himself." *New York Times Magazine*, 25 July 1954: 24, 33.

Aldridge, John. *After the Lost Generation: A Critical Study of the Writers of Two Wars*. New York: McGraw-Hill, 1951.

Alexander, Paul. *Boulevard of Broken Dreams: The Life, Times, and Legend of James Dean*. New York: Viking, 1994.

All That Heaven Allows. Dir. Douglas Sirk. Perf. Jane Wyman, Rock Hudson, Agnes Moorehead. Universal, 1955.

Alpert, Hollis. "It's Dean, Dean, Dean." Rev. of *Giant*, dir. George Stevens. *The Saturday Review*, 13 Oct. 1956: 28–29.

The Anniversary. Dir. Roy Ward Baker. Perf. Bette Davis, Jack Hedley, James Cossins. Warner Bros., 1968.

"Anti-American Line ... It 'Pays.'" *U.S. News and World Report*, 26 June 1953: 76, 78–79.

Ardomore, Jane Kesner. "Brando: Why 'Dolls' Love the 'Guy.'" *Woman's Home Companion*, Nov. 1955: 22–26, 35.

Around the World in Eighty Days. Dir. Michael Anderson. Perf. David Niven, Robert Newton, Shirley MacLaine. United Artists, 1956.

The Bad and the Beautiful. Dir. Vincente Minnelli. Perf. Kirk Douglas, Lana Turner. MGM, 1952.

Baker, Carlos. "Small Town Peep Show." *New York Times Magazine*, 23 Sept. 1956, 7: 4.

Bakhtin, Mikhail M. *The Dialogic Imagination: Four Essays by M. M. Bakhtin.* Ed. Michael Holquist. Austin: U of Texas P, 1981.

Barkham, John. Review of *Giant. New York Times Magazine*, 28 Sept. 1952: 4–5.

Barthes, Roland. *Empire of Signs.* New York: Hill and Wang, 1982.

Basinger, Jeanine. *Lana Turner.* New York: Pyramid Communications, Inc., 1976.

Baudrillard, Jean. *America.* Trans. Chris Turner. London: Verso, 1986.

Becker, George J. *James A. Michener.* New York: F. Ungar Publishing Co., 1983.

Bell, Arthur. "A Fan's Notes." *The Village Voice*, 13 Dec. 1976: 119.

Belsey, Catherine. *Critical Practice.* London: Methuen, 1980.

Bérubé, Allan. *Coming Out Under Fire: The History of Gay Men and Women in World War Two.* New York: The Free Press, 1990.

"Best-Seller on Film." Rev. of *Peyton Place*, dir. Mark Robson. *Newsweek*, 23 Dec. 1957: 76.

"Best-Seller Revisited." *Time*, 4 July 1955: 74.

Biskind, Peter. *Seeing Is Believing: How Hollywood Taught Us to Stop Worrying and Love the Fifties.* New York: Pantheon Books, 1983.

Blue Sky. Dir. Tony Richardson. Perf. Jessica Lange, Tommy Lee Jones. Orion, 1994.

Bosworth, Patricia. *Montgomery Clift.* New York: Bantam Books, 1979.

Bowman, James. "Presumed Innocence." *The American Spectator*, Nov. 1994: 68–70. *InfoTrac: Magazine Index Plus.* CDROM Information Access. 10 Aug. 2000.

Boyle, M.C. "Which Are You First of All, Wife or Mother?" *Parents Magazine*, Aug. 1955: 34–35+.

"Brando as Rogue." Rev. of *The Teahouse of the August Moon*, dir. Daniel Mann. *Newsweek*, 3 Dec. 1956: 98–99.

Breines, Wini. *Young. White, and Miserable: Growing Up Female in the Fifties*. Boston: Beacon Press, 1992.

Brod, Harry. "Masculinity as Masquerade." *The Masculine Masquerade: Masculinity and Representation*. Eds. Andrew Perchuk and Helaine Posner. Cambridge, MA: MIT Press, 1995. 13–19.

Brode, Douglas. *Films of the Fifties: Sunset Boulevard to On the Beach*. Secaucus, NJ: Citadel Press, 1976.

Bronski, Michael. *Culture Clash: The Making of Gay Sensibility*. Boston: South End Press, 1984.

Brossard, Chandler. "From Here to Nowhere." *American Mercury*, July 1951: 117–21.

Brown, Helen Gurley. *Sex and the Single Girl*. New York: Bernard Geis Associates, 1962.

Brown v. Board of Education. 347 US 483. U.S. Supreme Court. 1954.

Brute Force. Dir. Jules Dassin. Perf. Burt Lancaster, Charles Bickford, Hume Cronyn. Universal, 1947.

Butler, Judith. *Gender Trouble: Feminism and the Subversion of Identity*. New York: Routledge, 1990.

———. "Imitation and Gender Insubordination." *Inside/Out: Lesbian Theories, Gay Theories*. Ed. Diana Fuss. New York: Routledge, 1981. 13–31.

———. "Lana's 'Imitation': Melodramatic Repetition and the Gender Performative." *Genders* (fall 1990): 1–18.

Byars, Jackie. *All That Hollywood Allows: Rereading Gender in 1950s Melodrama*. Chapel Hill: U of North Carolina P, 1991.

Capote, Truman. "The Duke in His Domain." *New Yorker*, 9 Nov. 1957: 53–100.

Carbine, Patricia. "Peyton Place." *Look*, 18 Mar. 1958: 108–10.

Carnegie, D. "How to Help Your Husband Succeed." *Better Homes and Gardens*, Apr. 1955: 24+.

Carrigan, Tim, Bob Connell, and John Lee. "Hard and Heavy: Toward a New Sociology of Masculinity." *Beyond Patriarchy: Essays by Men on Pleasure, Power, and Change*. Ed. Michael Kaufman. Toronto: Oxford UP, 1987. 139–91.

Cass Timberlane. Dir. George Sidney. Perf. Spencer Tracy, Lana Turner. MGM, 1947.

Cogley, John. "Mysterious East." *Commonweal*, 22 June 1951: 254.

Cohan, Steven. *Masked Men: Masculinity and the Movies in the Fifties*.

Bloomington: Indiana UP, 1997.

———. "Masquerading as the American Male." *Male Trouble*. Eds. Constance Penley and Sharon Willis. Minneapolis: U of Minnesota P, 1993. 202–32.

———. "The Spy in the Gray Flannel Suit: Gender Performance and the Representation of Masculinity in *North by Northwest*." *The Masculine Masquerade: Masculinity and Representation*. Eds. Andrew Perchuk and Helaine Posner. Cambridge, MA: MIT Press, 1995. 43–62.

Come Back, Little Sheba. Dir. Daniel Mann. Perf. Burt Lancaster, Shirley Booth. Paramount, 1952.

"The Comic Spirit." *Time*, 30 March 1953: 40–46.

Connell, Robert W. *Gender and Power: Society, the Person and Sexual Politics*. Oxford: Polity Press, 1987.

———. *Masculinities*. Berkeley: U of California P, 1995.

Connery, Christopher L. "Pacific Rim Discourse: The U.S. Global Imaginary in the Late Cold War Years." *Boundary 2* 21.1 (spring 1994): 30–56.

"Consideration of U.S.-Japan Cultural Relations." *U.S. Department of State Bulletin*, 24 Sept. 1951: 493–94.

Cook, Page. "The Sound Track." *Films in Review*, May 1974: 294–96.

Corber, Robert J. *In the Name of National Security: Hitchcock, Homophobia, and the Political Construction of Gender in Postwar America*. Durham, NC: Duke UP, 1993.

Corrina, Corrina. Dir. Jessie Nelson. Perf. Ray Liotta, Whoopi Goldberg, Tina Majorino. Guild/New Line Pictures, 1994.

Cort, David. "The Book Clubs: Culture Once a Month." *Nation*, 16 Feb. 1957: 133–36.

Coughlin, Robert. "Modern Marriage." *Life*, 24 Dec. 1956: 109–16.

Cowley, Malcolm. *The Literary Situation*. New York: Viking Press, 1954.

The Crimson Pirate. Dir. Robert Siodmak. Perf. Burt Lancaster, Nick Cravat, Eva Bartok. Warner Bros.–Norma, 1952.

Crispell, Diane. "Myths of the 1950s." *American Demographics*, Aug. 1992: 38–44.

Davis, Kenneth. *The Paperbacking of America: Two-Bit Culture*. Boston: Houghton Mifflin, 1984.

Day, A. Grove. *James Michener*. Boston: Twayne Publishers, 1977.

d'Emilio, John, and Estelle B. Freedman. *Intimate Matters: A History of Sexuality in America*. New York: Harper and Row, 1988.

Dennis, Patrick. *Around the World with Auntie Mame*. New York: Harcourt, Brace and Co., 1958.

Désirée. Dir. Henry Koster. Perf. Marlon Brando, Jean Simmons, Merle Oberon. 20th Century–Fox, 1954.

Rev. of *Désirée*, dir. Henry Koster. *Newsweek*, 29 Nov. 1954: 97–98.

Rev. of *Désirée*, dir. Henry Koster. *Time*, 29 Nov. 1954: 76.

Desser, David. "The Cinematic Melting Pot: Ethnicity, Jews, and Psychoanalysis." *Unspeakable Images: Ethnicity and American Cinema*. Ed. Lester D. Friedman. Urbana: U of Illinois P, 1991. 379–403.

DeVoto, Bernard. "Dull Novels Make Dull Reading." *Harpers*, June 1951: 67–70.

Diane. Dir. David Miller. Perf. Lana Turner, Roger Moore. MGM, 1956.

Dobie, J. Frank. "Ranch Mexicans." *A Documentary History of the Mexican Americans*. Ed. Wayne Moquin. New York: Praeger Publishers, 1971. 289–93.

Dr. Jekyll and Mr. Hyde. Dir. Victor Fleming. Perf. Spencer Tracy, Ingrid Bergman, Lana Turner, Ian Hunter. MGM, 1941.

Dower, John W. *Embracing Defeat: Japan in the Wake of World War II*. New York: W. W. Norton & Co., 1999.

Dyer, Richard. "Don't Look Now: The Male Pin-Up." *The Sexual Subject: A Screen Reader in Sexuality*. London: Routledge, 1992. 265–76.

———. *Heavenly Bodies: Film Stars and Society*. New York: St. Martin's Press, 1986.

———. "Lana: Four Films of Lana Turner." *Imitations of Life: A Reader on Film and Television Melodrama*. Ed. Marcia Landy. Detroit: Wayne State UP, 1991. 409–28.

———. *The Matter of Images: Essays of Representations*. London: Routledge, 1993.

———. *Stars*. London: British Film Institute, 1979.

East of Eden. Dir. Elia Kazan. Perf. Raymond Massey, James Dean, Julie Harris. Warner Bros., 1955.

Ehrenreich, Barbara. *The Hearts of Men: American Dreams and the Flight from Commitment*. New York: Anchor Books/Doubleday, 1983.

———, and Deirdre English. *For Her Own Good: 150 Years of the Experts' Advice to Women*. New York: Anchor Books, 1978.

Eisler, Benita. *Private Lives: Men and Women of the Fifties*. New York:

Franklin Watts, 1986.

Ellis, Albert. "Sex—the Schizoid Best-Seller." *Saturday Review of Literature*, 17 Mar. 1951: 19, 42–44.

"The Emperor's New Girl." Rev. of *Désirée*, dir. Henry Koster. *Saturday Review of Literature*, 4 Dec. 1954: 38–39.

Feld, Rose. Rev. of *Peyton Place*. *New York Herald Tribune*, 23 Sept. 1956: 8.

Filene, Peter. *Him/Her/Self: Sex Roles in Modern America*. Baltimore: Johns Hopkins UP, 1986.

Finley, James F. Review of *Giant*, dir. George Stevens. *The Catholic World*, Dec. 1956: 221–22.

The Flame and the Arrow. Dir. Jacques Tourneur. Perf. Burt Lancaster, Virginia Mayo, Robert Douglas. Warner Bros.-Norma, 1950.

The Flame and the Flesh. Dir. Richard Brooks. Perf. Lana Turner, Carlos Thompson. MGM, 1954.

Forrest Gump. Dir. Robert Zemeckis. Perf. Tom Hanks, Robin Wright, Gary Sinise, Sally Field. Paramount, 1994.

Foster, C. "Rexalls for a Happy Marriage." *Parents Magazine*, June 1956: 32–33+.

Frank, Stanley. "Hollywood's New Dreamboat." *Saturday Evening Post*, 27 Aug. 1949: 30, 107–10.

French, Brandon. *On the Verge of Revolt: Women in American Films of the Fifties*. New York: Frederick Unger Publishing Co., 1978.

Freud, Sigmund. *Three Essays on Sexuality*. New York: Basic Books, 1962.

Friedan, Betty. *The Feminine Mystique*. New York: W. W. Norton & Co., 1963.

Friedwald, Will. *Sinatra! The Song Is You: A Singer's Art*. New York: Scribner, 1995.

Garber, Marjorie. *Vested Interests: Cross-Dressing and Cultural Anxiety*. New York: Harper Perennial, 1992.

Garcia, Mario T. *Mexican Americans: Leadership, Ideology, and Identity*. New Haven: Yale UP, 1989.

Rev. of *Giant*, dir. George Stevens. *Nation*, 20 Oct. 1956: 334.

Rev. of *Giant*, dir. George Stevens. *Time*, 22 Oct. 1956: 108–12.

Gilbert, Julie Goldsmith. *Ferber: A Biography*. Garden City, NY: Doubleday and Co., Inc., 1978.

"The Girl Who Walks Alone." *Look*, 13 May 1958: 91–95.

Gold, Herbert. "The New Upper-Middle Soap Opera." *Hudson Review* (spring 1957): 585–91.

Goldman, Eric. *The Crucial Decade and After: America, 1945–1960.* New York: Alfred A. Knopf, 1965.

Gosset, Pierre, and Renée Gosset. "Life in America—As Seen by Visiting Europeans." *U.S. News and World Report*, 1 Jan. 1954: 78–127.

Graham, Sheila. "Sense of Humor Is Best Asset for Star." *New Haven Register*, 18 Sept. 1955: n. pag.

The Great Garrick. Dir. James Whale. Perf. Brian Aherne, Olivia de Havilland. Warner Bros., 1937.

Green Dolphin Street. Dir. Victor Saville. Perf. Lana Turner, Richard Hart, Edmund Gwenn. MGM, 1947.

Greenberg, Clement. "Avant-Garde and Kitsch." *Mass Culture in America.* Eds. Bernard Rosenberg and David M. White. Glencoe, IL: The Free Press, 1957. 98–107.

Gubar, Susan. "This Is My Rifle, This Is My Gun: World War II and the Blitz on Women." *Behind the Lines: Gender and the Two World Wars.* Ed. Margaret R. Higonnet. New Haven: Yale UP, 1987. 227–59.

Guys and Dolls. Dir. Joseph L. Mankiewicz. Perf. Frank Sinatra, Marlon Brando, Jean Simmons. Samuel Goldwyn, 1955.

Hackett, Alice Payne. *Seventy Years of Best-Sellers, 1895–1965.* New York: R. R. Bowker Company, 1967.

"The Hairy Jape." *Time*, 15 July 1957: 106.

Halberstam, David. *The Fifties.* New York: Villard Books, 1993.

Haralovich, Mary Beth. "A Moral Crisis in Prime Time: *Peyton Place* and the Rise of the Single Girl." *Television, History, and American Culture: Feminist Critical Essays.* Eds. Mary Beth Haralovich and Lauren Rabinovitz. Durham, NC: Duke UP, 1999. 75–97.

Hark, Ina Rae. "Animals or Romans: Looking at Masculinity in *Spartacus*." *Screening the Male: Exploring Masculinities in Hollywood Cinema.* Eds. Steven Cohan and Ina Rae Hark. London: Routledge, 1993. 151–72.

Harrigan, Anthony. "The New Depravity in American Literature." *The Contemporary Review*, Feb. 1953: 106–8.

Hart, Elspeth. Rev. of *Peyton Place*, dir. Mark Robson. *Films in Review*, Jan. 1958: 26–27.

Harvey, Brett. *The Fifties: A Women's Oral History.* New York: Harper Collins, 1993.

Haskell, Molly. *From Reverence to Rape: The Treatment of Women in the Movies.* New York: Holt, Rinehart, and Winston, 1973.

Hatch, Robert. Rev. of *Sayonara*, dir. Joshua Logan. *Nation*, 21 Dec. 1957: 484.

His Girl Friday. Dir. Howard Hawks. Perf. Rosalind Russell, Cary Grant. Columbia, 1940.

His Majesty O'Keefe. Dir. Byron Haskin. Perf. Burt Lancaster, Joan Rice. Warner Bros.-Norma, 1954.

Hollway, Wendy. "Gender Difference and the Production of Subjectivity." *Feminism and Sexuality: A Reader*. Eds. Stevi Jackson and Sue Scott. New York: Columbia UP, 1996. 84–100.

Holmlund, Chris. "Masculinity as Multiple Masquerade." *Screening the Male: Exploring Masculinities in Hollywood Cinema*. Eds. Steven Cohan and Ina Rae Hark. London: Routledge, 1993. 213–29.

Howe, Irving. "Notes on Mass Culture." *Mass Culture in America*. Eds. Bernard Rosenberg and David M. White. Glencoe, IL: The Free Press, 1957. 496–503.

Hyams, Joe. "Rosalind Russell." *Theatre Arts*, June 1961: 20–23.

Jackson, Stevi. "The Social Construction of Female Sexuality." *Feminism and Sexuality: A Reader*. Eds. Stevi Jackson and Sue Scott. New York: Columbia UP, 1996. 62–73.

Jamison, Barbara Berch. "From Here to Maturity." *New York Times Magazine*, 23 Aug. 1953: 20, 31.

"Japan Set Up Brothels for American GIs." *Times Union* [Albany, NY], 27 Oct. 1995: A4.

Jim Thorpe—All American. Dir. Michael Curtiz. Perf. Burt Lancaster, Charles Bickford. Warner Bros., 1951.

Johnny Eager. Dir. Mervyn Le Roy. Perf. Robert Taylor, Van Heflin, Lana Turner. MGM, 1942.

Johnson, Hope. "Roz: No Longer Shy, 'All for Men.'" *N.Y. World Telegram*, 22 Sept. 1959: n. pag.

Johnson, Nora. "Sex and the College Girl." *Atlantic Monthly*, Nov. 1959: 56–60.

Jolly, Margaret, and Lenore Manderson, eds. *Sites of Desire/Economies of Pleasure: Sexualities in Asia and the Pacific*. Chicago: U of Chicago P, 1997.

Jordan, Richard Tyler. *But Darling, I'm Your Auntie Mame! The Amazing History of the World's Most Favorite Aunt*. Santa Barbara: Capra Press, 1998.

Julius Caesar. Dir. Joseph L. Mankiewicz. Perf. John Gielgud, James Mason, Marlon Brando. MGM, 1953.

Rev. of *Julius Caesar*, dir. Joseph L. Mankiewicz. *New Yorker*, 13 June

1953: 65.

Kael, Pauline. Rev. of *Mame*, dir. Gene Saks. *New Yorker*, 11 Mar. 1974: 122–24.

Kauffmann, Stanley. "New England Boiled Dinner." Rev. of *Peyton Place*, dir. Mark Robson. *New Republic*, 17 Mar. 1958: 21–22.

Kelley, Kitty. *His Way*. New York: Bantam Books, 1986.

The Killers. Dir. Robert Siodmak. Perf. Burt Lancaster, Edmond O'Brien, Ava Gardner. Universal, 1946.

Kinsey, Alfred C. *Sexual Behavior in the Human Female*. Philadelphia: W. B. Saunders Company, 1953.

Klein, Christina. "Cold War Orientalism: Musicals, Travel Narratives, and Middlebrow Culture in Postwar America." Diss. Yale University, 1997.

Klinger, Barbara. *Melodrama and Meaning: History, Culture and the Films of Douglas Sirk*. Bloomington: U of Indiana P, 1994.

LaGuardia, Robert. *Monty: A Biography of Montgomery Clift*. New York: Arbor House, 1977.

Laitin, Joseph. "Fawn on a Hot Tin Roof." *Coronet*, Dec. 1958: 139–44.

Latin Lovers. Dir. Mervyn Le Roy. Perf. Lana Turner, Ricardo Montalban. MGM, 1953.

Lears, T. J. Jackson. "A Matter of Taste: Corporate Cultural Hegemony in a Mass-Consumption Society." *Recasting America: Culture and Politics in the Age of Cold War*. Ed. Lary May. Chicago: U of Chicago P, 1989. 38–57.

Lee, Charles. *The Hidden Public: The Story of the Book of the Month Club*. Garden City, NY: Doubleday, 1958.

Leonard, George B. "The American Male: Why Is He Afraid to Be Different?" *Look*, 18 Feb. 1958: 95–104.

Lippe, Richard. "Montgomery Clift: A Critical Disturbance." *CineAction!* Sept. 1989: 36–42.

Lord Love a Duck. Dir. George Axelrod. Perf. Roddy McDowall, Tuesday Weld, Ruth Gordon. United Artists, 1966.

Lyndon, Louis. "Uncertain Hero: The Paradox of the American Male." *Woman's Home Companion*, Nov. 1956: 41–43, 107.

Lyons, Paul. "Pacific Scholarship, Literary Criticism, and Touristic Desire: The Specter of A. Grove Day." *Boundary 2* 24.2 (summer 1997): 47–78.

MacDonald, Dwight. *Against the American Grain*. New York: Random House, 1962.

————. "A Theory of Mass Culture." *Mass Culture in America*. Eds. Bernard Rosenberg and David M. White. Glencoe, IL: The Free Press, 1957. 59–73.

Machado, Manuel A. *Listen Chicano! An Informal History of the Mexican-American*. Chicago: Nelson Hall, 1978.

Magnificent Obsession. Dir. Douglas Sirk. Perf. Jane Wyman, Rock Hudson, Agnes Moorehead. Universal, 1954.

Mame. Dir. Gene Saks. Perf. Lucille Ball, Beatrice Arthur, Robert Preston. Warner Bros., 1974.

The Man in the Gray Flannel Suit. Dir. Nunnally Johnson. Perf. Gregory Peck, Fredric March, Jennifer Jones. 20th Century–Fox, 1956.

The Manchurian Candidate. Dir. John Frankenheimer. Perf. Frank Sinatra, Laurence Harvey, Janet Leigh. United Artists, 1962.

Marchetti, Gina. *Romance and the "Yellow Peril": Race, Sex, and Discursive Strategies in Hollywood Fiction*. Berkeley: U of California P, 1993.

Marcuse, Herbert. *One-Dimensional Man: Studies in the Ideology of Advanced Industrial Society*. London: Sphere, 1968.

Marling, Karal Ann. *As Seen on TV: The Visual Culture of Everyday Life in the 1950s*. Cambridge, MA: Harvard UP, 1994.

Martin, Pete. "The Star Who Sneers at Hollywood." *Saturday Evening Post*, 6 June 1953: 36–37+.

"The Master, the Challenger." *Movieland and TV Times*, Jan. 1957: 18–21.

May, Elaine Tyler. *Homeward Bound: American Families in the Cold War Era*. New York: Basic Books, 1988.

May, Lary. *Recasting America: Culture and Politics in the Age of Cold War*. Chicago: U of Chicago P, 1989.

McCann, Graham. *Rebel Males: Clift, Brando and Dean*. New Brunswick, NJ: Rutgers UP, 1993.

McCarten, John. Review of *Giant*, dir. George Stevens. *New Yorker*, 20 Oct. 1956: 178–79.

McCormick, Thomas J. *America's Half-Century: United States Foreign Policy in the Cold War and After*. Baltimore: Johns Hopkins UP, 1995.

Meet Danny Wilson. Dir. Joseph Pevney. Perf. Frank Sinatra, Shelley Winters. Universal, 1951.

Mellen, Joan. *Big Bad Wolves: Masculinity in the American Film*. New York: Pantheon Books, 1977.

Mellencamp, Patricia. "Situation Comedy, Feminism, and Freud: Discourses of Gracie and Lucy." *Studies in Entertainment: Critical Approaches to Mass Culture.* Bloomington: Indiana UP, 1986. 80–95.

Meyer, Richard. "Rock Hudson's Body." *Inside/Out: Lesbian Theories, Gay Theories.* Ed. Diana Fuss. New York: Routledge, 1991. 259–88.

Meyerowitz, Joanne. *Not June Cleaver: Women and Gender in Postwar America, 1945–1960.* Philadelphia: Temple UP, 1994.

Michener, James. *The Bridges of Toko-Ri.* New York: Random House, 1953.

———. "The Facts about the GI Babies." *Reader's Digest,* Mar. 1954: 5–10.

———. *The Floating World.* New York: Random House, 1954.

———. Rev. of *Homecoming. Saturday Review,* 22 Jan. 1955: 26.

———. "Japan." *Holiday,* Aug. 1952: 26–41+.

———. *Japanese Prints: From the Early Masters to the Moderns.* Rutland, VT: C. E. Tuttle and Co., 1959.

———. "Kabuki Is a Must for America." *Theatre Arts,* Mar. 1954: 74–75.

———. "Madame Butterfly in Bobby Sox." *Reader's Digest,* Oct. 1956: 21–27.

———. "One Must Respect Korean Culture." *Reader's Digest,* Apr. 1954: 15–19.

———. "Pursuit of Happiness by a G.I. and a Japanese." *Life,* 21 Feb. 1955: 124–41.

———. "The Sea of the Talented Traveler." *Saturday Review,* 23 Oct. 1954: 47–48.

———. "Thailand: Jewel of Asia." *Reader's Digest,* Dec. 1954: 57–66.

———. "The Way It Is in Korea." *Reader's Digest,* Jan. 1953: 1–6+.

———. "Why I Like Japan." *Reader's Digest,* Aug. 1956: 182–86.

Miller, Douglas T., and Marion Nowak. *The Fifties: The Way We Really Were.* Garden City, NY: Doubleday and Co., Inc., 1977.

Mister 880. Dir. Edmund Goulding. Perf. Edmund Gwenn, Burt Lancaster. 20th Century-Fox, 1950.

Mordden, Ethan. *The American Theatre.* New York: Oxford UP, 1981.

Morella, Joe, and Edward Z. Epstein. *Lana: The Public and Private Lives of Miss Turner.* New York: Dell Publishing Co., Inc., 1971.

Mortimer, Lee. "Gangsters in the Nights Clubs." *American Mercury,* Aug. 1951: 29–36.

Moskin, J. Robert. "The American Male: Why Do Women Dominate Him?" *Look,* 4 Feb. 1958: 77–80.

Mulvey, Laura. *Visual and Other Pleasures*. Bloomington: Indiana UP, 1989.

Munoz, Carlos Jr. *Youth, Identity, Power: The Chicano Movement*. London: Verso, 1989.

My Sister Eileen. Dir. Alexander Hall. Perf. Rosalind Russell, Janet Blair, Brian Aherne. Columbia, 1942.

Myers, Eric. *Uncle Mame: The Life of Patrick Dennis*. New York: St. Martin's Press, 2000.

"New Madame Butterfly." *Time*, 25 Jan. 1954: 114.

"New Plays in Manhattan." *Time*, 12 Nov. 1956: 71.

Nichols, Lewis. "Talk with Edna Ferber." *New York Times Book Review*, 5 Oct. 1952: 30.

"No Time for Subtlety." Rev. of *The Teahouse of the August Moon*, dir. Daniel Mann. *New Yorker*, 8 Dec. 1956: 144–45.

North by Northwest. Dir. Alfred Hitchcock. Perf. Cary Grant, Eva Marie Saint. MGM, 1959.

Oakley, J. Ronald. *God's Country: America in the Fifties*. New York: Dembner Books, 1990.

"Object Lesson." *Time*, 25 Dec. 1950: 10.

Oi, Atsushi. "Anti-Americanism in Japan." *The Reporter*, 16 Feb. 1954: 30–35.

On the Waterfront. Dir. Elia Kazan. Perf. Marlon Brando, Eva Marie Saint, Rod Steiger, Lee J. Cobb. Columbia, 1954.

Parker, John. *Five for Hollywood*. New York: First Carol Publishing Group, 1991.

Parsons, Talcott, and Robert F. Bales. *Family, Socialization and Interaction Process*. New York: The Free Press, 1955.

A Patch of Blue. Dir. Guy Green. Perf. Sidney Poitier, Shelley Winters, Elizabeth Hartman. MGM, 1965.

Rev. of *Peyton Place*. *Catholic World*, Nov. 1956: 152.

Rev. of *Peyton Place*. *Library Journal*, 15 Sept. 1956: 1993.

Rev. of *Peyton Place*, dir. Mark Robson. *Variety*, 18 Dec. 1957: 6.

Pietz, William. "The 'Post-Colonialism' of Cold War Discourse." *Social Text* 19–20 (fall 1988): 55–83.

Picnic. Dir. Joshua Logan. Perf. William Holden, Kim Novak, Rosalind Russell. Columbia, 1955.

A Place in the Sun. Dir. George Stevens. Perf. Montgomery Clift, Elizabeth Taylor, Shelley Winters. Paramount, 1951.

The Postman Always Rings Twice. Dir. Tay Garnett. Perf. Lana Turner, John Garfield. MGM, 1946.

The Prodigal. Dir. Richard Thorpe. Perf. Lana Turner, Edmund Purdom, Louis Calhern. MGM, 1955.

"The Quiet Young Lion." *Movieland and TV Times*, Oct. 1957: 17–19+.

Quiz Show. Dir. Robert Redford. Perf. John Turturro, Ralph Fiennes, Rob Morrow, Paul Scofield. Hollywood Pictures, 1994.

The Rains of Ranchipur. Dir. Jean Negulesco. Perf. Lana Turner, Fred MacMurray, Richard Burton. 20th Century-Fox, 1955.

Rebel without a Cause. Dir. Nicholas Ray. Perf. James Dean, Natalie Wood, Jim Backus, Sal Mineo. Warner Bros., 1955.

Rechy, John. "Jim Crow Wears a Sombrero." *Nation*, 10 Oct. 1959: 212.

Red River. Dir. Howard Hawks. Perf. John Wayne, Montgomery Clift, Joanne Dru, Walter Brennan. United Artists–Monterey, 1948.

Return to Peyton Place. Dir. José Ferrer. Perf. Jeff Chandler, Carol Lynley, Eleanor Parker. 20th Century-Fox, 1961.

Riesman, David, in collaboration with Reuel Denney and Nathan Glazer. *The Lonely Crowd: A Study of the Changing American Character*. New Haven: Yale UP, 1950.

Roe v. Wade. 410 US 113. U.S. Supreme Court. 1973.

Rogin, Michael. *Ronald Reagan: The Movie and Other Episodes in Political Demonology*. Berkeley: U of California P, 1987.

Rosen, Marjorie. *Popcorn Venus: Women, Movies, and the American Dream*. New York: Coward, McCann, and Geoghegan, 1973.

Rosenberg, Bernard, and David M. White, eds. *Mass Culture in America*. Glencoe, IL: The Free Press, 1957.

Ross, Andrew. *No Respect: Intellectuals and Popular Culture*. New York: Routledge, 1989.

Roth, Sanford H. "The Late James Dean." *Colliers*, 25 Nov. 1955: 62–65.

Russell, Rosalind. "I'm Glad I Didn't Marry Young." *Reader's Digest*, Nov. 1958: 75-77.

———, and Chris Chase. *Life Is a Banquet*. New York: Random House, 1977.

———. "What I've Learned about Men." *Reader's Digest*, Nov. 1953: 27-30.

Russo, Vito. *The Celluloid Closet: Homosexuality in the Movies*. New York: Harper and Row, 1981.

Said, Edward W. *Orientalism*. New York: Vintage Books, 1979.

Sarris, Andrew. "Tribute to Rosalind Russell." *The Village Voice*, 20 Dec. 1976: 57.

Rev. of *Sayonara*, dir. Joshua Logan. *Time*, 16 Dec. 1957: 94–95.

Schickel, Richard. "Accomplices: Brando and the Fifties, and Why Both Still Matter." *Film Comment*, July/Aug. 1991: 31–33 +.

Schlesinger, Arthur. *The Vital Center*. Boston: Houghton Mifflin, 1949.

Scullin, George. "James Dean: The Legend and the Facts." *Look*, 16 Oct. 1956: 120–24 +.

The Search. Dir. Fred Zinnemann. Perf. Montgomery Clift, Aline MacMahon, Ivan Jandl. MGM, 1948.

Sebald, William J. "Japan: Asset of the Free World." *U.S. Department of State Bulletin*, 31 March 1952: 490–94.

Sedgwick, Eve Kosofsky. *Between Men: English Literature and Male Homosocial Desire*. New York: Columbia UP, 1985.

Shane. Dir. George Stevens. Perf. Alan Ladd, Jean Arthur, Van Heflin, Jack Palance. Paramount, 1953.

Shelley, Joan Rubin. *The Making of Middlebrow Culture*. Chapel Hill: U of North Carolina P, 1992.

Sheppard, Dick. *Elizabeth: The Life and Career of Elizabeth Taylor*. Garden City, NY: Doubleday and Co., Inc., 1974.

Shipman, David. *Brando*. Garden City, NY: Doubleday and Co., Inc., 1974.

"The Simple Life of a Busy Bachelor." *Life*, 3 Oct. 1955: 128–32.

Simpson, Caroline Chung. "Out of an Obscure Place": Japanese War Brides and Cultural Pluralism in the 1950s." *Differences: A Journal of Feminist Cultural Studies* 10.3 (1998): 47–81.

Skinner, Cornelia Otis. "Women Are Misguided." *Life*, 24 Dec. 1956: 73–75.

Sklar, Robert, and Charles Musser. *Resisting Images: Essays on Cinema and History*. Philadelphia: Temple UP, 1990.

Smith, Harrison. "Sex and Literature." *The Saturday Review*, 12 April 1952: 26.

Smith, Janet Wentworth, and William L. Worden. "They're Bringing Home Japanese Wives." *Saturday Evening Post*, 19 Jan. 1952: 26–27 +.

"Soldier Versus System." *Life*, 31 Aug. 1953: 81–83.

Staiger, Janet. *Interpreting Films: Studies in the Historical Reception of American Cinema*. Princeton: Princeton UP, 1992.

Stalag 17. Dir. Billy Wilder. Perf. William Holden, Don Taylor, Robert Strauss. Paramount, 1953.

"Star with a Strange Horizon." *Coronet*, July 1958: 14.

"The Story of a Hard Man." *Look*, 20 Oct. 1953: 92–95.

Strauss, Harold. "The Illiterate American Writer." *Saturday Review*, 17 May 1952: 8–9+.

A Streetcar Named Desire. Dir. Elia Kazan. Perf. Marlon Brando, Vivian Leigh, Kim Hunter, Karl Malden. Charles K. Feldman/Elia Kazan, 1951.

Sunset Boulevard. Dir. Billy Wilder. Perf. William Holden, Gloria Swanson, Erich von Stroheim. Paramount, 1950.

Take a Letter, Darling. Dir. Mitchell Leisen. Perf. Rosalind Russell, Fred MacMurray. Paramount, 1942.

Taza, Son of Cochise. Dir. Douglas Sirk. Perf. Rock Hudson, Barbara Rush, Gregg Palmer. Universal, 1954.

The Teahouse of the August Moon. Dir. Daniel Mann. Perf. Marlon Brando, Glenn Ford, Eddie Albert, Paul Ford. MGM, 1956.

Tell It to the Judge. Dir. Norman Foster. Perf. Rosalind Russell, Robert Cummings, Gig Young. Columbia, 1949.

The Ten Commandments. Dir. Cecil B. de Mille. Perf. Charlton Heston, Yul Brynner, Anne Baxter, Edward G. Robinson. Paramount, 1956.

"Texas Tackles the Race Problem." *Saturday Evening Post*, 12 Jan. 1952: 23.

Theweleit, Klaus. *Male Fantasies*. Vol. 2. Trans. Stephen Conway in collaboration with Erica Carter and Chris Turner. Minneapolis: U of Minnesota P, 1989.

They Won't Forget. Dir. Mervyn Le Roy. Perf. Claude Rains, Gloria Dickson, Edward Norris. Warner Bros., 1937.

Thomas, Bob. *Marlon, Portrait of the Rebel as an Artist*. New York: Ballantine Books, 1975.

Thompson, Howard. "*Peyton Place* Finds a Home in New England." *New York Times*, 16 June 1957: sec. 2: 1.

The Three Musketeers. Dir. George Sidney. Perf. Gene Kelly, Lana Turner, June Allyson, Van Heflin. MGM, 1948.

"A Tiger in the Reeds." *Time*, 11 Oct. 1954: 58–66.

Tompkins, Jane. *West of Everything: The Inner Life of Westerns*. New York: Oxford UP, 1992.

Toth, Emily. *Inside Peyton Place: The Life of Grace Metalious*. Garden City, NY: Doubleday and Co., Inc., 1981.

Towne, Alfred. "Homosexuality in American Culture: The New Taste in Literature." *American Mercury*, Aug. 1951: 3–9.

Toynbee, Arnold. "The Impact of the West on Asia." *Commonweal*, 20 July 1951: 351–54.

Twitchell, James B. *Carnival Culture: The Trashing of Taste in America.* New York: Columbia UP, 1992.

Updike, John. "Legendary Lana." *The New Yorker*, 12 Feb. 1996: 68–75.

"Variation on the Puccini Caper." Rev. of *Sayonara*, dir. Joshua Logan. *New Yorker*, 14 Dec. 1957: 89–90.

Vengeance Valley. Dir. Richard Thorpe. Perf. Burt Lancaster, Robert Walker, Joanne Dru. MGM, 1951.

Viva Zapata! Dir. Elia Kazan. Perf. Marlon Brando, Anthony Quinn, Jean Peters. 20th Century–Fox, 1952.

Rev. of *Viva Zapata!*, dir. Elia Kazan. *Life*, 25 Feb. 1952: 59–61+.

Rev. of *Viva Zapata!*, dir. Elia Kazan. *New Republic*, 25 Feb. 1952: 21.

Rev. of *Viva Zapata!*, dir. Elia Kazan. *Saturday Review*, 9 Feb. 1952: 25.

Watney, Simon. *Policing Desire: Pornography, AIDS, and the Media.* Minneapolis: U of Minnesota P, 1987.

"We Have a Peace Treaty, But Peace Remains Coy." *Saturday Evening Post*, 6 Oct. 1951: 10, 12.

Weales, Gerald. "Movies: The Crazy, Mixed-Up Kids Take Over." *Reporter*, 13 Dec. 1956: 40–41.

Wenning, T. H. "This Is the Busiest Star at Her Busiest." *Newsweek*, 13 May 1957: 67–70.

Wexman, Virginia Wright. *Creating the Couple: Love, Marriage, and Hollywood Performance.* Princeton: Princeton UP, 1993.

What a Woman. Dir. Irving Cummings. Perf. Rosalind Russell, Brian Aherne, Willard Parker. Columbia, 1943.

Wheeler, Romney. "We Are Kidding Ourselves in Japan." *American Mercury*, Dec. 1950: 712–19.

"Whimpering in the Dark." *Time*, 31 July 1950: 47.

Whitcomb, Jon. "Auntie Roz." *Cosmopolitan*, 1 Dec. 1958: 16–19.

Whyte, William H. *The Organization Man.* New York: Simon and Schuster, 1956.

Wild in the Streets. Dir. Barry Shear. Perf. Shelley Winters, Chris Jones, Diane Varsi. American International Pictures, 1968.

The Wild One. Dir. Laslo Benedek. Perf. Marlon Brando, Lee Marvin, Mary Murphy. Columbia, 1954.

Wilson, Christopher P. *White Collar Fictions: Class and Social Representations in American Literature, 1885–1925.* Athens: U of Georgia P, 1992.

Wilson, Earl. "It Happened Last Night." *New York Post*, 1 Nov. 1956: n. pag.

Wittner, Lawrence S. "The Rulers and the Ruled: American Society, 1945–60." *A History of Our Time*. Eds. William H. Chafe and Harvard Sitkoff. New York: Oxford UP, 1983.

A Woman of Distinction. Dir. Edward Buzzell. Perf. Rosalind Russell, Ray Milland, Edmund Gwenn. Columbia, 1950.

The Women. Dir. George Cukor. Perf. Norma Shearer, Joan Crawford, Rosalind Russell, Paulette Goddard. MGM, 1939.

"The Wonderful Wizardry of Roz." *Look*, 28 May 1957: 68+.

Wong, Eugene. *On Visual Media Racism: Asians in the American Motion Pictures*. New York: Arno Press, 1978.

Worden, William L. "Where Are Those Japanese War Brides?" *Saturday Evening Post*, 20 Nov. 1954: 38–39+.

"Words and Music." *Time*, 21 Apr. 1947: 44.

Written on the Wind. Dir. Douglas Sirk. Perf. Rock Hudson, Lauren Bacall, Robert Stack, Dorothy Malone. Universal, 1956.

Wylie, Philip. *Generation of Vipers*. New York: Holt, Rinehart, and Winston, 1955.

Yergin, Daniel. *The Prize: The Epic Quest for Oil, Money, and Power*. New York: Simon and Schuster, 1991.

"Young Dean's Legacy." Rev. of *Giant*, dir. George Stevens. *Newsweek*, 22 Oct. 1956: 112, 114.

Ziegfeld Girl. Dir. Robert Z. Leonard. Perf. James Stewart, Judy Garland, Hedy Lamarr, Lana Turner. MGM, 1941.

Zolotow, Maurice. "How a Best-Seller Happens." *Cosmopolitan*, Aug. 1957: 36–41.

Index

MODERN AMERICAN LITERATURE
New Approaches

Yoshinobu Hakutani, General Editor

The books in this series deal with many of the major writers known as American realists, modernists, and post-modernists from 1880 to the present. This category of writers will also include less known ethnic and minority writers, a majority of whom are African American, some are Native American, Mexican American, Japanese American, Chinese American, and others. The series might also include studies on well-known contemporary writers, such as James Dickey, Allen Ginsberg, Gary Snyder, John Barth, John Updike, and Joyce Carol Oates. In general, the series will reflect new critical approaches such as deconstructionism, new historicism, psychoanalytical criticism, gender criticism/feminism, and cultural criticism.

For additional information about this series or for the submission of manuscripts, please contact:

Peter Lang Publishing
P.O. Box 1246
Bel Air, MD 21014-1246

To order other books in this series, please contact our Customer Service Department at:

800-770-LANG (within the U.S.)
(212) 647-7706 (outside the U.S.)
(212) 647-7707 FAX

Or browse online by series at:

www.peterlangusa.com